Al-Din

Al-Din

A Prolegomenon to the Study of the History of Religions

M. A. Draz

Translated and Edited by
Yahya Haidar

BLOOMSBURY ACADEMIC
Bloomsbury Publishing Plc
50 Bedford Square, London, WC1B 3DP, UK
1385 Broadway, New York, NY 10018, USA
29 Earlsfort Terrace, Dublin 2, Ireland

BLOOMSBURY, BLOOMSBURY ACADEMIC and the I.B. Tauris logo are trademarks of
Bloomsbury Publishing Plc

First published in Great Britain 2023
Paperback edition first published 2024

Copyright © Yahya Haidar, 2023

Yahya Haidar has asserted his right under the Copyright,
Designs and Patents Act, 1988, to be identified as Author of this work.

Series design by Adriana Brioso
Cover image © Eddie Gerald / Alamy Stock Photo

All rights reserved. No part of this publication may be reproduced or transmitted
in any form or by any means, electronic or mechanical, including photocopying,
recording or any information storage or retrieval system, without prior
permission in writing from the publishers.

Bloomsbury Publishing Plc does not have any control over, or responsibility for,
any third-party websites referred to or in this book. All internet addresses given
in this book were correct at the time of going to press. The author and publisher
regret any inconvenience caused if addresses have changed or sites have ceased
to exist but can accept no responsibility for any such changes.

A catalogue record for this book is available from the British Library.

A catalog record for this book is available from the Library of Congress.

ISBN: HB: 978-0-7556-4322-6
PB: 978-0-7556-4326-4
ePDF: 978-0-7556-4323-3
eBook: 978-0-7556-4324-0

Typeset by Newgen KnowledgeWorks Pvt. Ltd., Chennai, India

To find out more about our authors and books visit www.bloomsbury.com
and sign up for our newsletters.

Contents

Foreword	vii
Acknowledgements	viii
Editor's Introduction	ix
M. A. Draz	
Al-Din: Background, context and summary	xvi
Note on the translation	xxvii
Introduction: A brief overview of the history of the study of religions	1
The pharaonic age	1
The Hellenic age	3
The Roman age	7
The Christian age	8
The Islamic age	9
The European Renaissance	12
1 Determining the meaning of 'religion'	17
2 Religion, morality, philosophy and science	39
Religion and morality	39
Religion and philosophy	42
Religion and the sciences	55
3 Humanity's natural religious inclination	61
The antiquity of religions	61
The future of religion in the face of scientific progress	64
Sources of the religious sentiment in human nature	75
The social function of religions	78
4 On the origin of belief in God	83
Underlying factors in the human mind	83
Naturalism	93
Animism	104
Psychology	112

Morality	122
Sociology	127
Revelation	139
Conclusion	141
Editor's Bibliography	151
Author's Bibliography	155
Index	159

Foreword

In the Name of God, the most Gracious, the most Merciful

Three years ago, and for the first time in our modern higher education, Fu'ad I University introduced a course on the 'History of Religions' in the programme of Faculty of Letters, intended for students of Sociology at the School of Philosophical Studies. The teaching of this subject, as well as the design of the plan and curriculum, has been entrusted to me.

Rather than delving directly into a detailed study of the various religions – which may be done relatively easily based on one of the recognized primers available in Arabic or in other languages – I thought it beneficial to present by way of introduction general studies on 'Religion' – its essence, history and function in human life. These and other similar fundamental inquiries (never before grouped together in a single book) will offer students the chance to express their opinions and to sharpen their personal judgement skills.

Now that I have responded to the insistent requests by students to have at their disposal a published volume comprised of former studies and past opinions on these major questions, I hope to have succeeded in giving them and interested readers an opportunity for diligent reflection and calm and objective examination, so that if they find lacunae in the book or sections in need of further clarification it would be their right, indeed their duty, to share their valuable comments with me. May they accept my sincere gratitude in advance for their valuable contributions.

M. A. Draz
9 Sha'ban 1371 AH
4 April 1952 CE

Acknowledgements

I would like to express my foremost gratitude to Mohsen Draz and his family for entrusting me with the task of translating this valuable text into English and for graciously welcoming me into their home in Paris and sharing with me memories and photographs of the late M. A. Draz. I am grateful to the Oxford Centre for Islamic Studies (OCIS), especially its director Farhan Nizami, for hosting me as an academic visitor during the Spring of 2019 to work on this project. I would also like to acknowledge the generous grant I received from Rochester Institute of Technology in Dubai. Special thanks go to my editor Michel Pharand for his timely and careful work on this book, Adil Salahi for comments on parts of the translation and Ahmad Haqqi for introducing me to *al-Din* more than a decade ago. Lastly, I would like to thank my family for their love, faith and constant support. I thank my parents Raad and Suzan, my wife Arwa, my sons Alhasan and Salih, my daughter Salma and my siblings Mariam, Ibrahim, Yousif, Amina and Rahma.

Editor's Introduction

M. A. Draz[1]

On 6 January 1958, the proceedings of *The International Islamic Colloquium* held in Lahore, Pakistan, took an unexpected tragic turn when the representative of al-Azhar and member of Egypt's Assembly of Grand *Ulama* died of a sudden heart attack shortly before presenting his paper. The dramatic passing of Muhammad Abdullah Draz, in the company of the world's top Islamic scholars, might have seemed like a fitting finale to the remarkable life and career of one of the twentieth century's most eminent Arab Muslim intellectuals.

During his lifetime, Draz emerged as an exceptional *alem* who was as versed in traditional Islamic sciences as in modern European thought and scholarship; a man fully immersed in two intellectual worlds, not least as an accomplished student at prestigious Islamic seminaries and at Europe's highest seats of learning but also as an influential educator at Egyptian academies, including al-Azhar and its liberal counterpart Cairo University. Draz was also a proficient author, writing in Arabic and French seminal works in which his erudition in Islamic studies, philosophy, social science and history was infused with a reformist spirit that was mindful of the contemporary social, political and cultural challenges facing the Muslim world.

His last piece of scholarship – titled 'Islam's Attitude towards and Relations with Other Religions' – was read by someone else at the fateful *Colloquium* and concluded with the declaration that 'international cooperation for the

---

[1] This introduction is largely based on the primary sources published by A. Fadliyya in his *Awraq Muhammad Abdullah Draz*, which contains Draz's personal papers, letters and other documents, and the selected studies on Draz's thought and legacy in *Muhammad Abdullah Draz: dirasat wa buhuth*. Other sources include Mohsen Draz's biography of his father in his French translation of *Al-Din* (*Les hommes à la découverte de Dieu: Prologue à une histoire des religions: 'Ad-Din'*), pp. 9–16; Arabic translation in Fadliyya, *Dirasat*, pp. 13–18; Brodeur, 'Arabic Muslim Writings on Contemporary Religions Other Than Islam', pp. 244–5; Brodeur, 'Contemporary Muslim Approaches to the Study of Religion: A Comparative Analysis of Three Egyptian Authors', pp. 22–4; M. al-Shinqiti, *Failasuf al-Qur'an al-kareem*; and Waardenburg, *Muslim Perceptions*, p. 98 (fn. 50).

establishment of world peace is indeed among the teachings of the Prophet of Islam, the Messenger of peace'.

After his death in Lahore, Draz's body was taken to Cairo, where thousands of mourners marched out of the Azhar mosque to follow his funeral procession.[2] 'It was a gloomy day', remarked Ali Gomaa, Egypt's former grand mufti, recently on Egyptian television, 'a rainy day, in which the Heavens joined in weeping for the great scholar'.[3]

Six decades on, Draz continues to enjoy the kind of universal acclaim that few from his generation could hope to achieve. His intellectual output has retained its mesmerizing impact, and his written corpus has recently been invigorated in the Arabic publishing world. Politically, and despite his high stature and influence, he could well be among the least divisive figures of the period. Today, he is described as the philosopher of the Qur'an and a pioneer of the science of Qur'anic ethics[4]; he is also remembered as an ardent reformer, an intellectual activist who sought to preserve for Islam an authentic and dignified role in a rapidly changing society.

***

M. A. Draz was born on 8 November 1894 into a scholarly family based in Mahallat Diyai, a village on the banks of the Nile, in the northern Egyptian province of Kafr al-Shaykh. By then, the house of Draz had already produced a number of distinguished Azharites,[5] among them his father Shaykh Abdullah (1874–1932).[6] Draz lived his formative years in the shadow of his father. As

---

[2] An attendee of the colloquium reported the incident as follows: 'A number of the social events were cancelled because of the unexpected death of Shaikh Muhammad 'Abd-Allah Draz …. There was a short funeral service before the body was flown to Cairo for burial.' See D. Bayard, 'The International Islamic Colloquium', p. 173.

[3] *Misr ard al-mujaddidin* (2022), [TV programme] ON TV, 16 April. See also an eyewitness account of the funeral in Fadliyya, *Dirasat*, pp. 173–4.

[4] See Shinqiti, *Failasuf al-Qur'an al-kareem* ('Philosopher of the Holy Qur'an'); Anwar al-Jundi in Fadliyya, *Dirasat*, p. 160.

[5] The earliest known of them is his great grandfather Hasanayn Draz (died ca. 1900), who studied for eight years in Mecca before pursuing his education at al-Azhar. Other ulama from the Draz family of that period include Hasanayn's two sons, Ahmad and M. A. Draz's grandfather Muhammad. From the next generation, we have M. A. Draz's brother Abd-al-Majid (1896–1956) and his cousin Muhammad b. Abd al-Latif (1890–1977). For detailed biographies, see J. M. Hamada, *Tarajim a'yan al-usar al-'ilmiyya*, vol. 1, pp. 244–52.

[6] Draz wrote a detailed biography of his father (Fadliyya, *Awraq*, pp. 116–20). It was in response to a request by Abdullah al-Maraghi (brother of Shaykh al-Azhar Mustafa al-Maraghi, who would play a role in Draz's life in later years), who wanted to include it in his biographical dictionary of prominent jurists of the fourteenth century AH. It is worth noting that Abdullah Draz was among the Azhari teachers of Taha Hussein (1889–1973) before he abandoned Islamic learning to pursue literary studies at Cairo University.

a close associate of influential Islamic reformer Muhammad Abduh (1849–1905),[7] Abdullah was commissioned by Abduh months before his death to lay the foundation of the new Islamic Institute in Alexandria. Three years later he was selected by Khedive Abbas II to establish a similar institution at the Ahmadi mosque in Tanta, and it was from the latter that Draz earned his high school certificate in 1912.

We can discern two turning points in this early phase. The first is the transformation of Draz's life, while still in his teens, when his family relocated from the humble village of his birth to the bustling, cosmopolitan city of Alexandria. It was then, it seems, that he began to develop a keen interest in European culture. In 1916, Draz obtained the *'Alimiyyah*, al-Azhar's highest degree, from the Islamic institute in Alexandria, and despite taking up a teaching position there, he promptly enrolled in a three-year-long advanced evening programme in French language, which he would complete with distinction. The other critical moment in his early life came during the upheaval of the 1919 Egyptian revolution against British colonial rule, which marks the beginning of Draz's incessant activism against what he considered to be a European effort to marginalize Islam in Egypt and in other Muslim countries then under the yoke of colonialism. In this highly charged atmosphere, and due to his mastery of the French language, he soon became a kind of spokesman for al-Azhar on the international stage. Among the surviving documents from this period we have an open letter, signed by Draz, addressed to the League of Nations deploring the atrocities committed by the Italian occupying forces in Libya, declaring that, by its silence, 'it is conniving in the aggression, and working to revive memories of tragic historical encounters in al-Andalus and the Crusades'.[8] He goes on to affirm that the Azhar reserves the foremost right and duty to speak out against violations of the rights of Muslims all over the world. Draz also became an active participant in the mass protests of 1919 and concentrated his efforts on targeting European audiences by delivering rousing speeches outside foreign consulates in Alexandria, including one which the

---

[7] Abdullah Draz's high opinion of Abduh can be found in his impassionate elegy of him (in Fadliyya, *Awraq*, pp. 100–06), in which he describes Abduh as 'the only man in the entire world who could at once be an Azhari *alem*, a judge, a wise philosopher, a legal jurist as well as a competent and versatile administrator' (p. 104).

[8] Fadliyya, *Awraq*, p. 135.

French consul personally attended,[9] and by writing French leaflets expressing revolutionary demands and handing them to European delegates.[10] Some of Draz's writings even appeared in the French daily *Le Temps* as 'summaries of the political speeches made at al-Azhar'.[11]

In 1928, Draz was selected by the newly appointed Shaykh al-Azhar Mustafa al-Maraghi (1881–1945) to teach in the department of higher studies at al-Azhar in Cairo. Maraghi was another prominent disciple of Abduh and played a significant role in the restructuring of education at the ancient institution, which he sought to transform into a 'modern' global university.[12] He also recognized in Draz a great potential and would entrust him in later years with representing al-Azhar at various international events. Draz's rise to prominence in Cairo coincided with the waning career of his father, who resigned from all administrative duties in 1931, having established, for the third time, yet another reformed Islamic institute, this time in Damietta. The following year, Abdullah performed Hajj and died shortly thereafter. Meanwhile, his son Muhammad was taking up new teaching positions in al-Azhar – in the specialized studies department (in 1929) and then at the newly initiated colleges (in 1930). As an educator, Draz left a deep impression on his students, many of whom spoke fondly of his innovative approach during lectures and of his compassionate attitude at a personal level.[13] In a speech made in his honour in 1934 by a first-year student at the College of 'Usul al-Din, Draz was described as a paragon of scholarship, a renewer of Islamic learning in the twentieth century and the unrivalled 'master of language and the pen'.[14]

In 1936, Draz, by now in his early forties and a father of nine, was selected by King Fu'ad II on the recommendation of al-Azhar to study at the Sorbonne in Paris. This major milestone in his scholarly life appears to have been, like

---

[9] Fadliyya, *Awraq*, pp. 137–40. Draz's insistence on using the French language is considered by his son Mohsen as yet another form of resistance to British rule in Egypt (see Mohsen's biography of Draz in Fadliyya, *Dirasat*, p. 14.)

[10] Information provided by Draz's student al-Bayyumi in Fadliyya, *Dirasat*, p. 37.

[11] Ibid. According to al-Bayyumi this was suggested by Draz's cousin Abd al-Latif, who he describes as 'a prominent Cairene revolutionary'.

[12] For more on Maraghi, see A. Goldschmidt, *Biographical Dictionary of Modern Egypt*, p. 123.

[13] The list is long and includes illustrious figures such as Yusuf al-Qaradawi, Abd al-Azim al-Mat'ani and Abd al-Halim Mahmud, among others.

[14] Fadliyya, *Awraq*, pp. 333–5.

his move to Cairo eight years earlier, related to his association with Mustafa al-Maraghi, who had returned to the sheikhdom of al-Azhar in 1935, a position he would occupy until his death in 1945 (his first tenure lasted only one year). Draz would have no doubt seemed like an obvious candidate to Maraghi, who considered the immersion of distinguished Azharites in European systems of higher education integral to his reformist, modernizing vision.

During his twelve-year sojourn in France (from 1936 to 1948), Draz engaged in serious academic research and established a rapport with some of the country's leading scholars. We also get another glimpse of the activist intellectual that he was. On 22 August 1936, only three months after his arrival in Paris, Draz would deliver the welcome address, on behalf of al-Azhar's mission in France, to the delegation headed by prime minister Nahhas Pasha on their stopover in Paris before departing for London, via the port of Dover, to sign the historic Anglo-Egyptian treaty, which purportedly ended over half a century of British occupation of Egypt.[15] Draz described the delegation as a 'battalion' engaged in a form of political *jihad*, which was 'destined to write a new page of glory for modern Egypt'.[16] Around the same time, Draz reached out to Paris-based representatives of the Association of Algerian Muslim *Ulama* and corresponded with its founder, the influential Algerian reformer and outspoken critic of French authorities Abdelhamid Ben Badis (1889–1940), who specially thanked him in a letter dated 31 May 1938, for his efforts to facilitate the enrolment of Algerian students in al-Azhar.[17]

Draz, however, had the misfortune of living through the turbulent years of World War II in France, a country that would come under German occupation on 10 May 1940, coincidentally the same day Draz obtained his *licence* (Bachelor's degree) in literature from the Sorbonne. Draz soon found himself caught up in politics once again. When the German military *Kommandantur* ordered the arrest of a 'large number' of Egyptian students in France on suspicion of being British sympathizers, it was Draz who led a series

---

[15] An image of the delegation disembarking the 'Canterbury' steamer at Dover was published on the front page of the *al-Ahram* daily newspaper on 27 August 1936.
[16] A full transcript of the address is found in Fadliyya, *Awraq*, pp. 141–2.
[17] Shinqiti, *Failasuf al-Qur'an*, p. 29; 'Imarah in Draz, *Nazarat*, pp. 4–5.

of prolonged negotiations with the head of the German police force until all Egyptian detainees were released.[18]

Mohsen Draz provides a vivid account of the tribulations his father faced during these difficult times:

> Through his diary, which he kept daily from 1936 to 1958, the year of his death, we can clearly see the sort of resilience that Draz and his wife displayed in taking care of their ten children whose ages were between a few months and twenty-one years …. As the fighting intensified, he decided to take a small country house tucked amidst the fields of Seine-et-Oise in order to minimize the risk. Thus, the family was split into two parts: the youngest would settle in the countryside with their mother; the others (who were old enough to attend school) remained with their father who did not want to move away from the Parisian libraries or from his mentors at the Sorbonne and the Collège de France.[19]

But the worst was yet to come for the Draz family, especially during the battle of liberation. On 8 July 1944, in an unfortunate twist of fate, the family home in Seine-et-Oise was bombed by American warplanes, leaving his wife and some of his children with minor injuries.[20] Consequently, Draz and his entire family moved into another residence in the French countryside, one with an underground basement where they were forced, on one occasion, to take shelter for twelve long days.[21]

Nevertheless, and against all odds, Draz insisted on remaining in France. When informed by the Egyptian embassy of what was perhaps his last chance to repatriate to his country via Switzerland and Turkey, he replied that he was on a mission and that he would not return before finishing it. That mission was indeed his celebrated doctoral dissertation, *La morale du Coran*, which he could only begin working on in 1941.[22] Even when all studies were halted at the Sorbonne during the Nazi campaign to take over Paris, he briefly enrolled at the University of Bordeaux so that his education would not be interrupted. On 15 December 1947, Draz finally defended his dissertation at the Sorbonne.

---

[18] Mohsen Draz in Fadliyya, *Dirasat*, p. 16.
[19] Ibid., p. 15.
[20] Ibid.
[21] Fadliyya, *Dirasat*, pp. 356–7.
[22] Badawi in Draz and Abd al-Sabur Shahin, *Dustur al-akhlaq fi al-Qur'an*, p. viii. In other reports, he enrolled in the Sorbonne in 1942 (Fadliyya, *Dirasat*, p. 357).

There he sat, wearing the traditional Azhari turban and gown, before a committee of distinguished French academics[23] who, oddly enough, chose to challenge him on three general points that bear little relevance to his doctoral research: polygyny in Islamic law, the spread of Islam 'by the sword' and the cessation versus continuation of divine revelation.[24] After four hours of intense deliberations, his dissertation was approved with distinction. Draz's twelve-year mission in France had come to an end.

In March 1948, Draz returned to Cairo, where he would spend the closing years of his life. There, he enjoyed a high degree of recognition and quickly rose to prominence at various educational institutions: He taught Moral Philosophy at al-Azhar University, Qur'anic exegesis at Dar al-'Ulum – a teachers' college affiliated with al-Azhar – and History of Religions at King Fu'ad I University, in addition to delivering lectures at the police academy.[25] In 1949, he was elected to the Assembly of Grand *Ulama*, Egypt's highest religious body. He also became a member of higher committees of education, culture and broadcasting and regularly presented religious segments on Cairo radio.[26]

Meanwhile, Draz unfailingly participated in Egyptian political life, often in the capacity of his high-ranking Azhari affiliation. He became an advocate of al-Azhar's efforts to enlist students and teachers in vanguard resistance forces against the British.[27] In 1951, he publicly supported Nahhas Pasha's unilateral decision to annul the Anglo-Egyptian treaty of 1936,[28] which had become increasingly unpopular, sparking anti-British demonstrations. We also know of his attempts to maintain contact with King Farouk I (1920–65), to whom he gifted a copy of his doctoral dissertation on his return from Paris; and, only one month before the 1952 Free Officers coup d'état, he would send a memo to the head of the royal court warning the king of the deteriorating image of the Egyptian monarchy due to its failure to preserve the political autonomy of al-Azhar.[29]

---

[23] Draz's examination committee at the Sorbonne included Évariste Lévi-Provençal (1894–1956), Louis Massignon (1883–1962), René Le Senne (1882–1954) and Henri Wallon (1879–1962). See Fadliyya, *Dirasat*, p. 14, fn. 1.
[24] Fadliyya, *Dirasat*, p. 359.
[25] A. Salahi in Draz, *The Qur'an: An Eternal Challenge*, p. 6; M. 'Imarah in Draz, *Nazarat*, p. 5.
[26] Mohsen Draz in Fadliyya, *Dirasat*, p. 17.
[27] Ibid.
[28] Ibid.
[29] Draz, *Nazarat*, p. 5; Shinqiti, *Failasuf al-Qur'an*, p. 29.

Draz was immediately recognized as the country's foremost religious personality by the new military regime and was asked to assume the sheikhdom of the Azhar, an offer he indirectly turned down by demanding the absolute independence of the position.[30] Draz's last major political stance came during the fierce crackdown on the Muslim Brotherhood in the wake of the assassination attempt on then prime minister Gamal Abdel Nasser during a political rally at Manshiya, Alexandria, in October 1954. When asked to be among the signatories of a statement of condemnation (which denounced the Muslim Brotherhood as a group of unbelievers falling outside the pale of Islam[31]), he firmly declined, stating that it would lead to the indiscriminate suppression of many well-intentioned, devout Muslims.[32] He chose instead to join a group of *ulama* in writing a letter to the government, urging it to put a stop to the attempts 'by some deceitful individuals who turned the court's order against a few wayward Muslims[33] into an opportunity to propagate their subversive ideas' and to 'attack the foundations of Islamic belief and practice, even the very idea of 'religiosity'.[34]

Al-Din: Background, context and summary

Al-Din was M. A. Draz's last major work.[35] The book's contents, and the context of its publication, may be better understood in light of two vital aspects of Draz's intellectual biography: his deep association with the Azhar at a critical

---

[30] Mohsen Draz and al-Qaradawi in *Fadliyya, Dirasat*, pp. 17 and 23.
[31] Shinqiti, *Failasuf al-Qur'an*, p. 29.
[32] Ibid. M. 'Imarah in Draz, *Nazarat*, p. 5.
[33] While the statement above may indicate disapproval of the Muslim Brotherhood, other evidence shows that M. A. Draz had a generally sympathetic attitude towards the movement, at least at certain stages in his life. We know that he held, prior the Manshiya incident of 1954, numerous meetings and seminars at the Muslim Brotherhood's Hilmiyya headquarters in central Cairo (Shinqiti, *Failasuf al-Qur'an*, p. 24). Draz also enjoyed significant endorsement by prominent members of the Muslim Brotherhood, especially by the movement's influential ideologue Yusuf al-Qaradawi, who describes how Draz 'opened his heart as his home' to him and other 'brothers' after their release from the military prison in 1956 (Fadliyya, *Dirasat*, p. 24). Mohsen Draz confirms, however, that his father 'never joined any political party' (Fadliyya, *Dirasat*, p. 17).
[34] Fadliyya, *Dirasat*, p. 209.
[35] Much of Draz's thought is contained in his four major books: *Introduction to the Qur'an* and *The Moral World of the Qur'an*, both written in French as part of his doctorate at the Sorbonne (1947), *The Qur'an: An Eternal Challenge* (first published in 1933, then in 1957 in an expanded and updated edition) and *al-Din* (April 1952). Draz also wrote numerous articles, conference papers, radio

juncture in its history and his critique of European thought and its infiltration into Egyptian cultural life.

In his foreword to the book, Draz gives us two important hints as to the immediate context in which he wrote it. First, that it was intended as an introductory companion to students studying a course on the History of Religions for the first time in the history of Egyptian higher education. Second, that this course was offered at King Fu'ad I (Cairo) University,[36] which was designed to be a 'liberal idea' and which became an alternative, and no doubt a challenge, to its imposing rival al-Azhar: 'The establishment of Cairo University, which divorced knowledge from any religious matrix and compartmentalized learning into specialized departmental segments, with its respect for the methods of imported knowledge by infidel professors, was a reproach to al-Azhar, with its stress on memorization, recitation and received Islamic authority.'[37]

In some ways, *al-Din* is a response to the institutionalized 'westernization' of higher education at a university that became 'the prime indigenous model for state universities elsewhere in the Arab world'.[38] Although Draz taught at various institutions following his return from Paris, he nevertheless remained closely attached to the Azhar,[39] which became a vital part of his cultural and scholarly identity.[40] That he found it necessary to prepare Muslim novices through an Islamically informed account before delving into complex, erudite classical European theories on the world's religions (including Islam) is in fact consistent with the overall reformist paradigm of al-Azhar. It is worth noting here that Maraghi – the influential student of M. Abduh who embarked on

---

programmes and so on that have been made into at least 12 further titles bearing his name. For an up-to-date list of his works and their editions, see Shinqiti, *Failasuf al-Qur'an*, pp. 36–41.

[36] Previously named the Egyptian University and later, after Nasser's 1952 revolution, Cairo University. For an in-depth historical account, see Reid, *Cairo University and the Making of Modern Egypt*.
[37] Ibid., p. 139.
[38] Reid, *Cairo University*, p. 4. See also N. Reda, 'Holistic Approaches to the Qur'an: A Historical Background', pp. 495–506.
[39] On Draz's position on Azhari reforms, see his speech (Alexandria, 1922) on the reforms of M. Abduh and the detailed reform proposal that he presented to Shaykh al-Azhar (Fadliyya, *Awraq*, pp. 107–15 and 157–64). See also Fadliyya's study on the subject (*Dirasat*, pp. 334–41).
[40] To Draz, al-Azhar was 'the oldest religious university in the world' (Draz, *Dirasat*, p. 146) and the world's largest in terms of the number of enrolled students (Fadliyya, *Awraq*, p. 218). See also the report he presented to Shaykh al-Azhar on his participation at the first International Association of Universities conference which took place at Nice, France, in 1950 (Fadliyya, *Awraq*, pp. 212–26), where he describes his pride at being the embodiment of the Azhar and Egypt 'while wearing traditional Azhari clothes' (p. 217).

a rigorous reform campaign during his terms as Shaykh al-Azhar (1928–9, 1935–45) – espoused a particular philosophy on the position of Islam, and the Azhar (being the religion's foremost institution of learning), towards religious plurality and in the face of scientific progress. In his farewell address to Draz and other members of the Azhar's mission to Paris of 1936, Maraghi expressed the following views:

> I want you, as envoys of the Azhar, to live up to your duties towards our common humanity. Indeed, the advancement of modern science, and its integration into our university system, … has given us and the world great benefits. But those benefits have been submerged by many other concomitant evils. Because the progress of science was not matched by progress in the realms of religion and spirituality, all discoveries in the material world can find no resonance in desolate hearts already lacking in piety and fear of God. The modern mind has come to view religions as artifacts from the past, devoid of life, joy and inner peace. If the bearers of religion had proceeded in conformity with the upholders of (material) science, equipped by the power of certainty, to make religions more appealing, to invite people to true virtue, to promote the spiritual life in new attractive ways and to harmonize between scientific knowledge and religious virtue, the world would have indeed become a happier and more fulfilling place.[41]

Indeed, readers of *al-Din* will easily see that Draz was largely writing within the framework outlined by these words, one that seeks the harmony of tradition and modernity, 'Islamic spirituality' and 'Western science'.

Maraghi also sought to publicize a global image of the Azhar as promoter of *al-salam al-dini* (religious peace or harmony). To this effect, he commissioned eminent Azharites to speak at key international events, including the Congress of the International Association for the History of Religions (Brussels, 1935) and the World Congress of Faiths (London, 1936; Paris, 1939).[42] The last was held at the Sorbonne two months before the outbreak of the Second World War under the theme of 'Promoting the Spirit of World-Fellowship through Religion', and Maraghi appointed Draz, who was already in Paris, to deliver an address on behalf of the Azhar. In his paper, titled 'Islam and Global

---

[41] Fadliyya, *Awraq*, p. 229.
[42] Bayyumi, *al-Azhar bayna al-siyasah wa ḥurriyat al-fikr*, p. 142. See Braybrooke, *A Wider Vision: A History of the World Congress of Faiths, 1936–1996*.

Religious Harmony', Draz asserted – 'in the name of the Azhar, of Islam, and of humanity' – that the core message of all religions is to promote harmony and peaceful coexistence, and that 'the only solution to our current human malaise is to call upon all religious leaders to ... foster in their followers a genuine sense of human fraternity'.[43] Draz's speech was especially praised by the congress' founder Sir Francis Younghusband (1863–1942) for succinctly capturing the overall theme of the event.[44] This emphasis on the essential unity of all religions is clearly found in Draz's other writings on the subject, such as *al-Din* and the paper he wrote for the Islamic Colloquium of 1958.

Draz was also aware of the impact of compulsory civil education – spearheaded by prominent affiliates of Cairo University such as Taha Hussein, who became the education minister (1950-2) – on the centrality of Qur'anic studies in the intellectual formation of Egyptian students. Among Draz's personal papers is a series of letters (between 1948 and 1950) from an *imam* in Damietta named Muhammad Tawfiq Siyam which describe the predicament as follows: 'The Qur'an has long been uprooted from the villages of the Egyptian countryside, since the introduction of compulsory primary education twenty years ago .... The Azhar must know that ... this will eventually lead to the uprooting of the Azhar itself and the suppression of religion.'[45] This was certainly a source of great concern to Draz, who had memorized the entire Qur'an before the age of ten at a traditional school in his home village, and who had made the Qur'an the cornerstone of his intellectual project. In response, Draz wrote to Shaykh al-Azhar in 1948 urging him to take measures against 'the limited attention paid to the memorization of the Qur'an in school curricula'.[46]

Al-Din also represents the culmination of Draz's lifelong critique of Western thought, particularly of matters related to Islam. His interest in European culture, and its subsequent influence on him, may be traced to his early years in Alexandria, when he immersed himself in advanced studies of French language and literature. An early example of this is found in the predominantly European sources that he used for his lecture notes

---

[43] Draz, *Dirasat Islamiyya fil al-'alaqat al-'jtima'iyya wa al-duwaliyya*, pp. 147, 155.
[44] Draz's student M. Bayyumi also states that a summary of the speech was published in the French press. See Fadliyya, *Dirasat*, p. 39.
[45] Fadliyya, *Awraq*, pp. 231–5.
[46] Ibid., pp. 195–6.

in geography (a subject he briefly taught in 1921 at the Islamic Institute in Alexandria).[47] On 10 August 1921, Draz published a fierce rejoinder against a sarcastic piece that had appeared in the French daily *Le Temps* under the title '*Éclairage profane*' (Secular Lighting), which reflects on the irony whereby the Kaʿba at Mecca is illuminated by 'modern European technology' while Muslims 'keep to the archaic rituals of their ancestors'.[48] In this long article, Draz wanted to 'remind the French people' of their indebtedness to the Islamic civilization for their modern material progress and charts a long list of scientific and technological fields in which Muslims were early pioneers.[49] In 1946, Draz wrote a personal review of Malek Bennabi's *Le phénomène coranique* (The Qurʾanic Phenomenon) in which he explicitly admonished the francophone Algerian intellectual's nonchalant and uncritical use of orientalist writings on the Prophet.[50] Another critique of orientalism is found in his report (requested by the Azhar) on the 'accuracy and reliability' of Claude-Étienne Savary's (1750–88) French translation of the Qurʾan. He confirmed that 'scientific dishonesty' is commonplace in orientalist translations of the Qurʾan, and that it is found in Savary's work as in later ones by such figures as Albert Kazimirski (1808–87) and Édouard Montet (1856–1934), among others.[51]

An example of Draz's cultural criticism in the wider public sphere is found in his letter of support to the director of Egypt's State Information Service for banning the broadcasting of 'some songs' that contain heretical statements, in which he tries to turn his attention to yet another song, which 'calls for the worship of the land of Egypt alongside the worship of God' and attempts to 'revive paganism in the name of nationalism'.[52] In 1949, he petitioned Shaykh al-Azhar to use his powers to challenge the 'screening of foreign films

---

[47] Ibid., pp. 61–82.
[48] The piece was originally published in *Le Temps* on 2 July 1921. Draz's response came following an Arabic translation which appeared in the *Wadi al-Nil* newspaper on 4 August of that year. The article also suggests that lack of adequate sanitary measures (due to the nature of the Islamic pilgrimage) contributed to the spread of cholera. See the Arabic translation in Fadliyya, *Awraq*, pp. 46–7.
[49] Fadliyya, *Awraq*, pp. 48–54 (contains various references to French sources). In 1957, Draz began writing a similar article on 'The Civilization of Islam and its Influence on the Modern World', left unfinished at his death (Fadliyya, *Dirasat*, pp. 342–6).
[50] Fadliyya, *Awraq*, pp. 300–6. It was originally written in French. A translation appeared in later Arabic editions of Bennabi's popular book.
[51] Fadliyya, *Awraq*, pp. 193–4.
[52] Fadliyya dates the letter to 1928 (*Awraq*, pp. 289–92). However, Draz's description seems to correspond to a line in a song by Umm Kulthum titled *Bi ʿAbi wa Ruhi*, written by Ahmad Shawqi (1870–1932) and released following the signing of the Anglo-Egyptian treaty of 1954.

in Egyptian cinemas that depict the rise of Christianity in clear violation of Muslim beliefs'.[53] Six months before his death Draz joined a public forum, to discuss Julian Huxley's *Man in the Modern World*, which was held in response to a letter by a concerned reader from Damanhur exclaiming that 'the book contains statements advocating disbelief, atheism and denial of the existence of God; would it then be justifiable for the Directorate of Culture, or any other body [in Egypt], to publish this book and to promote it among the youth in educational institutions?' Draz not only endorsed these words but also used the forum to attack the editorial boards of major publications, such as the magazine of the Egyptian Military Forces (for disseminating unfounded religious opinion) and *Al Gomhuria* (for printing books promoting sexual freedom and atheism).[54]

***

Writings on religion, its history and religiosity as a universal phenomenon have been and remain relatively limited in modern Arabic scholarship.[55] It is noteworthy, however, that the decade leading up to the appearance of Draz's *al-Din* in April 1952 saw a particular surge in Arabic publications that investigate similar problems, most notably *Religion, Revelation and Islam* (1945) by M. Abd al-Raziq, *Allah: On the Origin of Belief in God* (1947) by A. al-'Aqqad, *Religion and Science* (1948) by al-Musheer 'Izzat Pasha, *Emotional Life and Religious Belief* (1948) by M. Hubb Allah and *The Rise of Religion: Evolutionary and Theistic Theories* (1949) by A. al-Nashshar. All these works appear in *al-Din*'s bibliography, and they certainly left their mark on its overall purpose and structure. Draz's disapproval of some of the methods and conclusions of these studies was perhaps an additional trigger for writing *al-Din*, especially al-'Aqqad's *Allah*, which he criticizes twice in the text and makes the book's subtitle (*fi nash'at al-'aqida al-'ilahiyyah*, 'On the Origin of Belief in God') the name of *al-Din*'s fourth and longest chapter. In 1951, the essay on 'Religion and Philosophy' in Chapter 3 of *al-Din* appeared

---

[53] Ibid., pp. 199–200.
[54] Ibid., pp. 307–9.
[55] See Waardenburg (1999b), 'The Contemporary Period: 1950-1995', pp. 90–2, 99 (fn. 52); Brodeur, 'Contemporary Muslim approaches to the Study of Religion', pp. 2–8; Gul, 'Current Trends of Muslim Academia in Comparative Religions', pp. 53–70, 105; Yousif, 'Studying the "Other": Challenges and Prospects of Muslim Scholarship on World Religions', pp. 77–94.

as a two-part article in the Egyptian Islamic journal *al-Hady al-Nabawi* (Prophetic Guidance). Concerned by its unconventional claims, the editors published it with footnote commentaries by renowned *hadith* scholar Ahmad M. Shakir (1892–1958), who objected in particular to Draz's assertion that 'many philosophies have reached – through independent reasoning – the same overall conclusions decreed by religions'. Shakir insinuates that Draz was influenced by 'the scientific heritage of pagan, atheistic Europe' and compares him to the likes of al-'Aqqad, who 'shamelessly used the divine name *Allah* as the title of his book'.[56]

Nevertheless, *al-Din* remains unique in its erudition, approach and scope. Most importantly, Draz goes beyond the confines of religious affiliation and intends his book to be an introductory *summa* on universal intellectual problems concerning 'Religion' – its definition, rationality, psychology, role in society, earliest historical expressions and future under an increasingly secular world order. He is aware that while many such questions have not generated much interest in modern Islamic scholarship, they have in fact been a major concern for thinkers and academics in post-Enlightenment Europe. Thus, the book ultimately brings together two perspectives on the study of religion: one represented by classical European theories and another inspired by the author's understanding of the inner logic of the Qur'an. This is typical of Draz's entire scholarly corpus – that a deep reading of the Qur'an, as God's eternal and final message to humanity, will of necessity provide answers to all questions. While this perspective is consistent with a long line of Islamic writings that ground all knowledge in the Qur'an, *al-Din* steers it into the uncharted territory of comparative religion. Another feature of the book is the near-complete absence of traditional Islamic authorities such as al-Bukhari, Ibn Hazm, al-Ghazali and others (frequently cited in the author's other major work, *The Moral World of the Qur'an*). This is interesting, especially in light of the rather surprisingly vicious attack on the Arabic lexicographical tradition outlined in Chapter 1 of the book.

---

[56] The article was published in *al-Hady al-Nabawi* (vol. 15, nos. 4 and 5) in Rabi' al-Thani-Jumada al-'Awwal 1370 AH [Jan–Feb, 1951]. For more on this exchange and Draz's response to Shakir, see Fadliyya, *Awraq*, pp. 29–41.

Al-Din is a critical examination of classical Western scholarship on religion based on a variety of primary European (mostly French) sources, ranging from Kant's 1794 *Critique of Practical Reason* through to Bastide's 1947 *Éléments de sociologie religieuse*. It articulates a lively discussion aimed at exposing fallacies, contradictions and methodological problems in prominent European narratives of religious studies and the history of religions, attempting to revive from the wreckage a renewed unifying vision inspired by Qur'anic revelation and 'sound reason'. Draz is also mindful of his intended audience and of the introductory nature of the book, and endeavours to refute, but also to explain and simplify, complex theories and philosophies.

On the whole, the book offers a rare insight into the mind of an Arab Muslim scholar who confronts and engages with a branch of knowledge under-represented in modern Islamic scholarship. Indeed, many of the book's themes continue to resonate in contemporary debates on the historicity and the presumed neutrality of the Western study of other religions and cultures.[57]

***

Al-Din comprises four chapters, in addition to an introduction and a conclusion.[58] The author opens the book with a brief survey of the history of studying religion as an independent field of inquiry, covering the ancient civilizations of Egypt, Greece and Rome, followed by the rise of Christianity and Islam, and concludes with the European Renaissance. The author traces the development of scholarship on religion in these historical phases, highlighting intellectual exchange and cultural fraternization, and the factors that led to, or prevented, a more objective assessment of the phenomenon of religion; the latter would be pioneered by Arab Muslim scholars and taken to new and unprecedented heights by later European authors, especially from the eighteenth century onwards.

---

[57] See Asad, *Formations of the Secular: Christianity, Islam, Modernity*, pp. 1–17; Ugurlu, Book Review of Talal Asad's *Secular Translations: Nation-State, Modern Self, and Calculative Reason*, pp. 197–201; Platvoet and Molendijk, *The Pragmatics of Defining Religion Contexts, Concepts and Contests*, pp. 23–40, 338–78 and so on.

[58] For useful summaries and analyses of the book in Arabic, see articles by Othman, Saleh and al-Mat'ani in Fadliyya, *Dirasat*, pp. 242–73; 'Imarah in Draz, *al-Din*, pp. 10–40]). See also Brodeur, 'Contemporary Muslim approaches to the Study of Religion', pp. 42–5 and 110–17.

Chapter 1 is concerned with the question 'What is Religion?' It begins with a critical study of what classical Arabic lexicons have to say about the word *din* and argues that, due to their deficiencies and faulty authorship, the word has assumed multiple, even contradictory, meanings. This chapter furnishes a list of standard definitions of religion, beginning with the common one found in Islamic literature, followed by fourteen definitions propagated by prominent Western scholars, starting with Cicero, then Kant through to Reinach and Durkheim (all of them also quoted in French in footnotes). In scrutinizing these definitions, the author develops the following series of arguments: (i) the thing to which the 'religious person' submits is an independent self-sufficient *essence*, (ii) this essence is metaphysical and *unseen*, (iii) it is an *active* and *effective* power, (iv) this power is not an abstract mental concept but an *extrinsic reality*, and (v) this reality is *higher* and *exalted*, overpowering and undefeated. Draz is particularly interested in the difficulty of distinguishing the religious from the non-religious domain and concludes by providing his own universal definition of religion based on the foregoing arguments.

Chapter 2 deals with the overlap and divergence of religion and other 'modes of cultural refinement' – namely, morality, philosophy and practical science. The first section ('Religion and Morality') is built on two approaches to the study of the relation between religion and morality: theoretical-abstractive and practical-historical. While the former might vindicate an opposition between religion (as knowledge and veneration of Truth) and virtue (as propensity to do good), the author argues that a complete ethical law should of necessity appease man's conduct in himself, with other beings and with his relationship with God. Likewise, an all-inclusive religious law ought to satisfy both sides. Nevertheless, no unity as such has been observed in history. Draz declares at the outset of the next section ('Religion and Philosophy') that no form of human knowledge bears as strong an affinity to religion as does philosophy in its theoretical and practical aspects. But this unity of aims and intentions does not echo unity of outcomes. Thus, he devotes this lengthy chapter to the causes of separation between the two camps, beginning with spiritual philosophy, which – unlike its opposite, materialism – is far more entangled with the subject matter of religion. The seeming unity of religion and spiritual philosophy, insofar as they share the belief that the world emanates from a Higher Being, is challenged by two factors: (i) the creation of the world *ex nihilo* and (ii) the idea of lordship or continued care. Next, the author delineates a series of quoted treatments on the relationship between philosophy and religion, starting with the arguments by the Muslim philosophers al-Farabi and Ibn Sina, followed by a summary of six points representing the Western view of the relationship between them. After lengthy discussions of these views, Draz presents his own final judgement: that philosophy's end goal is knowledge and religion's ultimate aim is faith. The third section ('Religion and the Sciences') of this chapter argues that because there is a substantive dissociation between the goals of religions as means of divine knowledge, on the one hand, and the practical aims of material sciences, on the other, any conflict between them is 'rationally impossible'. Draz then attempts to explain the undeniable historical antagonism between religion and science by proposing that it occurs in two situations. The first is fear of the unknown, which breeds arrogance and bigotry; this occurs when religions and sciences venture into each other's territory. The second is when they provide conflicting answers to some questions of science and phenomenology and when religions make their own positions (on scientific matters) obligatory and part of religious belief. Religion and science are indeed two facets of the same truth. However, if they do not seek to coexist in harmony, they will inevitably view each other as false and deviant.

Chapter 3 deals with the following key questions: When did religion first appear on earth? What will be the fate of religion in the face of scientific progress? What is the psychological and sociological function of religion? It begins with a criticism of eighteenth-century French intellectuals who saw religions as (quoting Voltaire) accidental schemes invented by cunning and deceitful churchmen or (according to Jean-Jacques Rousseau) as simply fulfilling the purpose of practical governance by deceiving the masses and misleading the poor. Arguing that these views are renewed forms of ancient Greek sophistry, Draz goes on to suggest that two reasons led to their popularity: the moral corruption of the institutionalized religion of the time and the inherent injustice of the common laws, in tandem with prevailing social inequality. Nevertheless, these opinions were short-lived and were challenged later in the same century by the new European writings on foreign religions. The author contends that religiosity is as old as humanity itself and goes on to maintain that the great advances in science during the nineteenth century have in fact shaken the foundations of the old view that religions are 'merely accidental' in human evolution, or that they will eventually 'wither away'. Because the widening of the scope of knowledge is also a widening of the scope of mystery; scientific progress has in fact sharpened the religious instinct of modern man in his quest for the unknown.

The next section investigates religious mentality and psychology. One source of the religious sentiment in human nature is drawn from the human mind's instinctive yearning for eternity and its insistent quest for infinite universals. This deeply intimates that the seeker moves towards the sought after voluntarily and not by compulsion, and that there is in man a noble, heavenly essence made for eternal existence and immortality – even if man is sometimes oblivious to it. Another is human conscience: the noble emotions of love, yearning, gratitude, humility and so on find in religion an 'unbounded expanse' and an 'inexhaustible fountain'. Human willpower is also empowered by religion, as it equips it with supreme impetuses and motivations, and shields it against hopelessness and despair. Draz then turns to the social function of religion, arguing that no power in the world could parallel, or even approach, the power of religiosity to guarantee respect for and abidance with laws, which are necessary for maintaining peaceful coexistence among members of any society. Religions provide what the author terms an 'incentivizing and deterring' authority to guarantee conformity to these laws. Compared with religion, science acts as a double-edged sword in society – as much as it is capable of improving the human condition, it could also bring about total destruction and annihilation; therefore, science must be subordinated to ethical standards. The chapter concludes by vindicating that religions occupy a place within human communities similar to the place of the heart in the human body, and that spirituality is the strongest possible social bond.

In his fourth and longest chapter, Draz turns to the question of the origin of religious belief. Chapter 4 begins with a critical examination of the shortcomings of the points of departure and methods employed by Western thinkers in their search for origins. The author then proposes 'to present a survey of some of the theories that have dealt with the first triggers of the belief in God in the minds of men' and offers a detailed explanation and evaluation of 'arguments' and 'historical references' in Western schools of Naturalism, Animism, Psychology, Morality and Sociology. Here, Draz is especially hostile to Durkheim and Kant but more favourably inclined towards Tylor and

Descartes. According to the author, the serious error of these theories stems not only from their internal contradictions, eurocentrism and unscientific methodologies but also from their very point of departure, which supposes that man 'arrived at the idea of God by himself'. The chapter ends with a brief note on what the author calls 'the theory of Revelation', which 'maintains that man did not go to religions but that religions came to him, that he did not ascend to them but that they descended to him, that people did not discover God by the light of reason, but by the light of revelation'.

Based on this premise, the book's conclusion attempts to locate traces and echoes of all the modern theories discussed in Chapter 4 in the Qur'an, 'humanity's open book and the spring to which all men are led to quench their thirst'.

Note on the translation

This translation is based on the Arabic edition of *al-Din: Buhuth mumahhida li dirasat tarikh al-'adyan* published by Dar al-Qalam (Kuwait, 1970).[59] It also draws on two earlier translations: Mohsen Draz's French edition *Les hommes à la découverte de Dieu: Prologue à une histoire des religions: 'Ad-Din'* (1999)[60] and, to a lesser extent, the Turkish translation *Din ve Allah İnancı* (1987) by Bekir Karlığa.[61] When available, I have tried to use English translations of the European sources used in the text, all of which are cited in the footnotes. All Qur'anic references are derived from Muhammad A. S. Abdel Haleem's *The Qur'an: A New Translation* (2004).[62] I distinguish between two uses of Qur'anic statements. The first are direct quotations by the author, which are followed by chapter and verse numbers within the body of the text. The second relates to the author's style, which is strongly influenced by the language of the Qur'an, as we find throughout the book numerous Qur'anic expressions, idioms and allusions, all of them referenced in footnotes.[63] I have retained words such

---

[59] Draz, *al-Din: Buhuth mumahhida li dirasat tarikh al-'adyan*.
[60] Draz and Mohsen Draz, *Les hommes à la découverte de Dieu*.
[61] Draz and Karlığa, *Din ve Allah İnancı*.
[62] Abdel Haleem, *The Qur'an: A New Translation*.
[63] For the influence of the Qur'an on Draz's language and style, see Shinqiti, *Failasuf al-Qur'an*, pp. 33–6.

as 'primitive', 'savage', 'man', 'mankind' and so on as intended in the original text and corresponding to the European sources used by the author, which reflect the style and diction of the time. Lastly, this English translation has two omissions. The first is Draz's posthumous article 'Islam's Attitude towards and Relations with Other Religions', which was not included in the edition Draz published during his lifetime but has since been included in most later printings of *al-Din*, including the French edition (but not the Turkish one). The second is the removal of a rather superfluous footnote on types of magic (also excised from the French and Turkish editions).

Introduction: A brief overview of the history of the study of religions

The expression 'History of Religions' came into the Arabic lexicon from European languages. It is a latecomer, remaining unknown in Europe well until the dawn of the nineteenth century. Yet discussing matters related to belief is, and has always been, an unwavering human concern, born of humanity's perpetual tendency to segregate into diverse religions and sects. The scope of this interest has widened at times, narrowed at others, depending on the degree of mutual understanding reached by adherents of different religions and on their acquaintance with each other's beliefs. In a similar vein, the nature and trajectory of this interest has also varied according to the dispositions of concerned researchers and their respective goals.

By tracking the evolutionary path of views and theories on religion, from the era of the ancient civilizations of Egypt, Greece and Rome, through the religions of Christianity and Islam and into to the European Renaissance, we will be able to discern the various forms they took across the ages, even between two periods within the same historical era.

The pharaonic age

No compendium has reached us wherein the ancient Egyptians have registered the details of their own religions or the religions of neighbouring peoples. However, recent research has proven, and quite conclusively, that Egyptians had in fact begun to record, albeit sparingly, their beliefs, customs, chronicles and ways of life thousands of years before Christ (peace be upon him). They inscribed them on papyrus scrolls and engraved them on the walls of tombs and temples, not to mention the surviving abundance of sculptures, mummified bodies of their kings and leaders and objects representing sacred animals, birds, human beings and so on. We also know that they behaved similarly in the regions they conquered (Nubia, Syria, Mesopotamia and others).

Their wide-reaching conquests were matched by an openness to different beliefs, as they gave the people they encountered the freedom to sanctify what they saw fit to sanctify and to retain their desired sacred symbols. Their spirit of tolerance was such that it extended to their spiritual philosophies, which sought to achieve harmony among all divinities and objects of worship by supposing that all gods were part of the same family, connected by marriage or birth, and consisted of groups of three (triad), nine (ennead) and so on.

Tolerance and understanding were the prevailing norm except at a few historical junctures when efforts were made to impose certain beliefs while opposing others. Attempts by the School of Heliopolis to prohibit any worship other than of the sun god are one instance; the reign of Amenhotep IV (Akhenaton) is another. This king campaigned against all forms of idolatry, leading him to purge icons, remove statues from temples and decree the worship of a single divine being who was at once 'Sun' in the heavens and 'Lord' on earth.

The effects of these religious reforms were short-lived, however, because the primary concern of kings and priests had always been to maintain peace between their protected or vassalized peoples by granting them the freedom to fill their temples with their own religious designations and symbols.[1]

---

[1] The papyri preserved in Berlin and Leiden corroborate the claim that the ancient Egyptians, from olden times, recognized the existence of a unique, mysterious and eternal God, indeterminate in form and description and defying definition (see *Histoire Générale des Religions* by a group of French authors, vol. 1, pp. 251–2). But this mystical monotheism was marred in the popular imagination by the idea that this single deity is manifested or represented, or has its 'secrets' instilled in some higher forms of creatures (humans, animals or inanimate objects). People were persuaded that the 'divine' capacity for direction and administration (*tadbir*), for example, was found in kings, vegetative fertility in the Nile and animal fecundity in the Apis bull. Moreover, insofar as all these powers were ultimately drawn from heaven (through the rays of the sun, e.g.), these privileged creatures were deemed worthy of veneration and worship because of their 'secret' or mysterious communion with the higher God.

The Hellenic age

No one doubts today that the scholars and philosophers of ancient Greece were, so to speak, graduates of earlier Eastern civilizations,[2] of ancient Egypt in particular. This is certainly not to imply that the Greeks were merely indifferent vessels passing on eastern concepts and science in a literal manner – a claim that defies reason and lacks textual evidence – or that they did not fashion their sciences out of past precedent, as some have speculated. Rather, having discovered original material in the East, they adapted it and it became of invaluable assistance to them.

The ancient Greeks themselves, when confessing this studentship, go as far as to assert that great pioneers like Pythagoras and Plato owed their foremost theories to Egyptian thinkers. Even recent critics, while rejecting the literal replication of theories, could not but concede the dependence of these philosophers – at least in the realms of religion and ethics – upon earlier Egyptian theories.[3]

The oldest surviving Greek writings date to the tenth century BCE. Most famous among them are, without question, the two works attributed to Homer:[4] the *Iliad* and *Odyssey*. These ancient epics recount travel adventures, the pains of war, brawls over bounties and the curious tragedies that befell the Greeks collectively and individually.

However, almost none of these events and occurrences, whether of minor or major importance, take place without references to the gods of the Greeks or of their enemies, and without elucidations of the sacrifices and pleas offered to personal deities by the mistreated and the wretched. These authors furnish us, moreover, with deliberations they suppose took place among the Olympian gods and their quarrels in support of one hero over another and so on.

Writings belonging to this period were characterized by (i) a narrow territorial and demographical scope, (ii) a treatment of religious affairs that appears only

---

[2] See Bréhier's *Histoire de la Philosophie*, pp. 3–5 and Masson-Oursel's *La Philosophie en Orient*, p. 7 (of the French edition), translated into Arabic by Dr Muhammad Yusuf Musa.
[3] See Boulaye's comparative study of religions, *Étude comparée des religions*, vol. 1, pp. 8, 11, and 14 fn.6).
[4] Historians have differed over Homer's precise birthdate (estimates range between the ninth and eleventh centuries BCE) and over the authorship of the two works.

fortuitously,[5] rather in the shadow of more vital affairs, and (iii) a mythical and allegorical character, as authors drew on their own imagination and personal beliefs in elucidating chronicles and occurrences.

Descriptive travelogues by historians such as Herodotus would emerge in the next period (fifth century BCE). Although this era, like the preceding one, produced no monographic treatment of religious themes – which continued to be melded into other geographic descriptions – at least we must recognize that the authors now relied on first-hand observations and not on their imagination alone. They also tended to compare Greek deities with their counterparts in other cultures, often showing a preference for Egyptian religious conceptions. Lastly, we note their reproach of misnomers found in lay beliefs, whereby a designation (like Heraclius, e.g.) would assume the contradictory meanings of an eternal god or a mortal human hero.

The conquests of Alexander of Macedon (Alexander the Great, who died in the last quarter of the fourth century BCE), whose armies reached as far as India – as reported by Megasthenes (third century BCE) – widened the scope of knowledge of other religions. And along with descriptive accounts of extant religions, there arose new critical investigations concerned with scrutinizing the general concept of religion, albeit carried out in the shadow of greater philosophical researches into the nature of reality.

In this type of scholarship, the influence of the two great philosophers, Plato (late fifth to early fourth centuries BCE) and his disciple Aristotle[6] (fourth century BCE), cannot be overstated. They maintained the notion that the primary eternal cause and principle of all change and motion is not matter but a rational governing soul who has mastery[7] over all substances. They further

---

[5] More detailed accounts of ancient Greek objects of worship appeared at a later date. These may date back to the eighth century BCE in the treatise on the genealogy of the gods – *La Théogonie* – attributed to Hesiod or one of his disciples.

[6] Aristotle recognizes Anaxagoras (fifth century BCE) as a predecessor in this approach.

[7] Plato declares in *The Laws* (bk X) that 'the soul is the first origin and moving power ['*le point de départ*'] of all that is, or has become, or will be', and that it 'controls heaven and earth, and the whole world'; 'soul is the cause of good and evil, base and honourable, just and unjust, and of all other opposites' (§. 896 of bk X; §. 899 for the soul as the origin of all things, *à l'orgine de la génération de toutes choses*). He asks the following question: What then is the nature of this eternal soul? Is it a soul endowed with wisdom and virtue, or is it bereft of these qualities? He replies that the minute precision prevalent in the stable ordering and organization of the universe demonstrates that it is endowed with ideal virtues (§. 897). Aristotle, for his part, declares in *Metaphysics* (bk XII, ch. 6) that there exists, of necessity, an eternal, unmovable spirit capable of bringing about change, that this spirit can only be immaterial and that unless it exists in actuality (and not mere power and potentiality) nothing else would exist: 'Wood will surely not move itself – the carpenter's art must act on it' (§. 1074b).

asserted that beliefs and philosophies were in their beginnings pure and noble, then degenerated[8] over time. They also understood virtue to be the middle course between the extremes of excess and negligence.[9]

It is to these two philosophers and to their master Socrates (flourished at the end of the fifth century BCE) that we owe the laying of the foundations of positive constructive philosophy, which recognizes the existence of realities and the possibility of knowledge. We also owe to these thinkers the refutation of theories premised on denial and stubbornness that reject the existence of fixed eternal truths, presumed by them impossible to know or – if they exist at all – impossible to teach.

The latter refers to the ideas propagated by the Sophists, a group of individuals who indulge in disputes,[10] falsification and deception, utilizing philosophy as a rhetorical device to support either side of a debate and to bring to ruin all knowledge and common sense. The Sophists sought, through rhetorical dexterity and manipulation, to turn meanings around and to attain high social standing, wealth and authority.

Next came generations of thinkers who claimed affiliation with Plato and his Academy, a school whose fame would live on until the first century BCE. These newcomers, however, were not worthy of such filiation, as they departed from the original teachings of their master and, moreover, were increasingly inclined[11] to doubt the existence of reality. Such was their tepidness that they would soon pave the way for the emergence of Scepticism, whose teachings of systematic doubt were advanced by Pyrrho in the era of Alexander of Macedon.

Initially a Sophist, Pyrrho grew weary of disputation and futile polemics and adopted an indecisive attitude that wavered between constructive thought – which affirms the existence of a definite and eternal truth – and negative philosophy – which radically rejects this existence in the first place.

---

[8] Aristotle, *Métaphysique*, Part 8, bk XII. The opposite is the doctrine of the Sophists who claim that the principle of all things is non-conformity to religion and laws, and that these are false innovations and political tricks to control the public.
[9] Aristotle, *Ethique á Nicomaque*.
[10] The expression '*qaumun utu al-jadal*' (people who indulge in disputes) is found in *hadith* literature. See al-Tirmidhi, *al-Jami' al-sahih*, vol. 5, p. 377. (Ed.)
[11] They proposed that Truths exist. However, their existence is not certain; it is only probable.

Faced with a multiplicity of contradictory arguments, he found no other way out except in suspending[12] judgement altogether.

Leaving aside the doctrines of denial (Sophistry) and doubt (Scepticism), and returning to tracing the route of positive philosophy in ancient Greece, we find that its glorious page had been fatefully turned by the end of Aristotle's time and following the division of Alexander the Great's kingdom. Thereafter, anomalous doctrines of theoretical and practical extremes emerged.

On the practical side (i.e. the principles of ethics), the doctrine of Epicurus (mid-fourth to early third centuries BCE) represented a low point. He deemed bodily, mental and spiritual sensations of pleasure and pain to be the sole criterion of good and evil, as well as the unrivalled measure of virtue and vice. In contrast, the 'Portico' School (Stoicism), better known as the school of Determination and Endurance, represented a high point. Its founder, Zeno of Citium[13] (third century BCE), opposed the Epicureans. He believed that virtue consisted in freeing oneself from pleasure and pain by combatting human emotions and natural sentiments to such an implacable degree that a human being might readily kill himself or be indifferent to the consumption of human flesh.

On the theoretical side (i.e. metaphysics and physics), however, although Stoicism had indeed turned away from pure materialistic atheism towards upholding contrasting positions, such as affirming the existence of an intelligent soul that maintains and directs the universe, this soul was only *part* of the universe. It resides in matter, like sap in a tree or fire in embers, oblivious to its own existence, unable to exert any effect on matter of its own volition. Rather, it would itself be subject to the laws of nature – vegetal growth, for

---

[12] According to historians of philosophy, Pyrrho would not have doubted sense-perception (*hissiyyat*) or emotions (*wijdaniyyat*) albeit ephemeral in nature and fast-disappearing momentary accidents; nor would he have doubted that he doubts because he was no longer a self-conceited sophist (see Adolphe Franck, *Dictionnaire des sciences philosophiques*). On the whole, he believed in an essence independent of matter, a sort of stable reality around which these ephemeral elements visible to man would be renewed. It may be true that he sided with the Sophists on the relativity of sensory knowledge insofar as it varies with the state of the observer, the observed object and the instruments of observation and so on, and that each person's judgement of reality is a reflection of his own consciousness which remains a particular and not universal 'truth'. However, he did not agree with them when they declared that no stable and eternal truth exists beyond ephemeral phenomena, or when they concluded that knowledge of it is impossible. His position was neither to affirm nor negate the existence of this reality.

[13] Not to be confused with his predecessor Zeno of Elea (fifth century BCE), who argued against motion, or with his successor Zeno the Epicurean (Zeno of Sidon), a contemporary of Cicero.

example. The Stoics ultimately held that matter and spirit are not independent of each other, for they form a uniform whole, an existing reality that is simultaneously active and passive, creator and created, God and universe. This counter-intuitive and inherently contradictory theory – both internally and in its practical implications[14] – is what the Stoics called 'Unity of Existence' (Pantheism). Yet despite the nominal unity provided by its pantheon, Stoicism would still succumb to paganism and polytheism by yoking a personalized god to each of nature's elements. Thus, Zeus became the god of life, Athena (Aether) the god of ether, Hera the god of wind and so on.

The Roman age

During the second century BCE, the Romans politically dominated the Greek State, which became one of their provinces, having hitherto been subservient to it. If anything can amaze you, then you should surely be amazed[15] at how centuries of cohabitation between these two peoples did not succeed in making them a single nation sharing a common language, religion, art, legislation or any other facet of social life, the way in which Islam succeeded in achieving unity in the regions that came under its dominion.

It may be argued that desiring such unity is idealistic. Still, one cannot help but expect that the intellectual and scholarly circles of Rome would benefit from the vast scientific and literary heritage deposited in the Hellenic capital. However, nothing of the kind happened! The only thing that the Roman intelligentsia brought back from Athens following its conquest were a few ideas that were popular among the masses and which they reproduced superficially and without thorough examination – as if they were ideas about the latest trends in fashion, food or drink.

Testifying to this is the fact that the dominant doctrine in Athens during the third and second centuries BCE, which was Stoicism, would be the only one

---

[14] The internal contradiction lies in the fact that it determined that one thing and its opposite are one. The contradiction in practical outcomes is revealed when it calls upon men to free themselves from the shackles of nature, while claiming at the same time that the universe, as well as its creator, are also subject to external forces and constraints.
[15] Qur'an 13:5. (Ed.)

brought back into Rome. Even then, it was not introduced in its entirety, but only through what required the least effort by scribes and what most appeased the conquerors' pride – namely, the practical side of Stoicism: a vain and conceited call to warp human nature by expunging the meaning of pleasure and pain from its core elements. On the other hand, we find no traces of the theoretical share of Stoicism in the writings of Latin authors such as Seneca and Epictetus (first century CE). Be that as it may, Stoicism would not long survive, and its last advocate in Rome was Marcus Aurelius (second century CE).

Just as the Roman conquest of Greece prompted the transfer of the latter's popular beliefs, likewise the invasions of Asia and Africa enabled the Latins to bring back new religious ideas. Hence, such deities as Mithra, Baal and Isis (among others) were commonplace.

In addition to their accounts of local cults, certain works composed by Latin authors in the first century BCE contained descriptions of religions originating in distant lands. Cicero, for example, wrote philosophical reflections on the nature of divinity, while Varro dealt with the religious rites and observances of Rome. Their writings, however, lacked critical erudition and comparative examination. Rather, they sought to speculate about and reconcile – sometimes eclectically – disparate beliefs. This attitude denotes hesitation, perplexity and apathy towards serious research, more than it points to the supposed spirit of religious tolerance often attributed to the Roman era. In fact, ascribing 'tolerance' to a given historical period because certain communities felt no attachment to a particular religion and participated in heterogeneous rites, deeming them all as equal and indifferently representing the same truth, is an ill-fated, unverified and misguided inference. This attitude does not imply mutual respect among adherents of different religions – this being the true meaning of tolerance and forbearance – but rather self-indulgence and lack of trust in a given religious canon.

The Christian age

It was around the middle of the first century CE that Christianity arrived in Europe as a new, divinely inspired religion, resisting established paganisms and seeking to dominate and replace them. Long and arduous were the struggles and confrontations, exchanges and fraternizations, between Christianity and, initially, local cults, then with contemporary rivals, such as Manichaeism and Neo-Platonism, both of which arose during the third century CE.

Long and arduous, too, were the persecutions and deep resentment of missionaries and practitioners of the new faith by Roman emperors, which lasted until the arrival of emperor Constantine (early fourth century CE), who, following a decree of religious amnesty, declared Christianity the official religion of the State insofar as it remained within the terms defined by the Council of Nicaea in the year 325.

Among the most ardent defenders of Christianity who opposed emerging rival sects, the name Saint Augustine (mid-fourth to the first third of the fifth century) shines brightest. Having adopted Manichaeism in early life, he would later convert to Christianity and became a bishop. Of his many works, the most celebrated are *Confessions*, a book on grace, and *The City of God*. This last is especially noteworthy, as it engages with religious as well as secular philosophy.

The polemical spirit of the age would persist, unfolding as attack and defence – destructive at times, constructive at others – not only between Christians and their adversaries but also amid the varied factions of Christianity itself. The real concern of authors was not so much to objectively explicate different creedal points of view as to detect weaknesses in the arguments of their opponents to better destroy them while also empowering the spread of their own beliefs by highlighting their strengths.

The Islamic age

Then, at the beginning of the seventh century CE, Islam emerged. However, the call to Islam could only breathe free after leaving Mecca in the year 622, and the faith would soon spread at lightning speed north and south, east and west. In less than a century, Islam would pervade Western Europe, bringing with it Muslim science, literature and law, and Greek knowledge and philosophy, as well as the vast scientific and literary heritage accumulated by Muslims through their conquests of the East, in addition to their own novel research and contributions.

That the West is indebted to the Arabs for its knowledge of Asian sciences is a case in point. What is entirely dazzling and extraordinary, however, is that they are also indebted to the Arabs for discovering the scientific heritage of Europe itself and for remaining thus enlightened through a prolonged period of history. As noted above, the Romans were indifferent towards the Greek literary heritage, with the exception of superficial views and distorted ideas on popular display in the marketplace. Meanwhile, the Christian era, occupied by internal and external religious strife, had bypassed Greek sciences, histories and ways of thinking. Thus, Western Europe languished in virtual isolation from the scholarly culture of the East, with which it otherwise had the strongest material-cultural bonds. When the Europeans opened their eyes and realized the value of these intellectual treasures, they found them in the hands of the Muslim Arabs, whose conquests had reached Europe from across the seas at the beginning of the eighth century, in the name of knowledge and peace, justice and tolerance. These conquests were not carried out with arrogance or tyranny, or with the aim of satisfying bloodthirst, greed and unrestrained instincts.

Therefore, people rushed from every direction to absorb Arab knowledge. The Jews were the first to make the most of this studentship, as they took it upon themselves to translate these scientific texts from Arabic into Hebrew and then from Hebrew into Latin. If Rome had been the true heir of Greek thought, it would have transcribed those texts from the early days of the Roman conquest, and future generations would have read them in Latin or Greek without having to discover them through a fourth layer of translation.

What the Greeks and Romans had been unable to fulfil was undertaken by Muslims who, via Arabic, became the sole custodians of these scientific texts for centuries (from the eighth to the thirteenth centuries and beyond). Today, Western scholars, without exception, agree that Aristotelian philosophy and science were only disseminated in the West thanks to the works of twelfth-century Muslim philosopher Ibn Rushd (known as Averroes) and his disciples, the Jewish philosopher Maimonides being one notable example. Moreover, no one denies the extent of the influence of their teachings on European thought in the thirteenth century through the writings of St. Thomas Aquinas.

As for what Westerners gleaned from Arab sciences in particular, whether in literature, poetics and jurisprudence, or in the fields of medicine, astronomy, history, natural science, chemistry, algebra, time measurement and numbering (among various arts and industries), one would have to venture far beyond the scope of this brief prologue. Western scholars have produced a great many works, both wide-ranging and compact, on this topic.[16] After all, our purpose here is limited to delineating the contribution of the Arabs and Muslims to the science of religion. And indeed this contribution is most impressive in view of two novel characteristics that are, to our knowledge, absent in all preceding scholarship.

The first is the transformation of the study of religions – erstwhile submerged in the clamour of worldly affairs, or forced into distant currents of research, whether psychological, philosophical or polemical, or at best confined within fixed local dogmas and so on – into a descriptive and practical inquiry, separated from other sciences and disciplines yet including the extant religions of the world. For the first time, the study of religions became, in Arab scholarship, an independent science – ten centuries before it was so in Modern Europe!

The second characteristic, no less crucial than the first, lies in the fact that the Arabs, in describing religions, paid no heed to the fantasies and speculations, dubious reports, legends and other hocus-pocus prevalent among the less educated, who tend to deviate from the original orthodoxy of their beliefs. Instead, Arab scholars gleaned their information on any given religion from its own reliable primary sources. Hence the study of religions became an autonomous discipline, sustained through a robust scientific methodology.

Here is a brief chronological list of some of the better-known Arabic works in this field:

- *Jumal al-Maqalat*[17] by Abu al-Hassan al-Ash'ari (d. 330 AH; tenth century CE)
- *Al-Maqalat fi 'Usul al-Diyanat* by al-Mas'udi (d. 346 AH; tenth century CE)
- *Al-Fisal fi al-Milal wa al-Nihal* by Ibn Hazm al-Zahiri (d. 456 AH; eleventh century CE)
- *Al-Milal wa al-Nihal* by al-Shahrastani (d. 548 AH; twelfth century CE)

---

[16] For an extensive encyclopedic treatment, see Le Bon, *La Civilisation des Arabes*. A shorter survey is found in Gautier, *Moeurs et coutumes des Musulmans*, bk IV.

[17] In this book, the author gathers the reflections he had included in two previous works: *The Doctrines of Muslims* and *The Doctrines of Non-Muslims*.

- *I'tiqadat al-Muslimin wa al-Mushrikin* by Fakhr al-Din al-Razi (d. 606 AH; thirteenth century CE)

Would it then be fair to claim that Islam made no contribution to the history of comparative religions?[18]

The European Renaissance

Western Europe began to gradually awaken during the thirteenth and fourteenth centuries, turning its gaze towards the East, the original impulse of its enlightenment. Franciscan and Dominican clergy were dispatched on missions to regions as far away as India and China, thus becoming acquainted with their religious traditions.

During the fifteenth and sixteenth centuries, in what came to be known as the European Renaissance or Revival, enthusiasm for the study of the Greek language was revitalized in order to read ancient texts in the original language. The chief focus in this early stage was to study mythologies and to understand their religious and historical contexts.

The Christian reform movement known as Protestantism would soon emerge in the sixteenth century, enhancing this crucial aspect of the scientific revival in Europe through instating the study of Hebrew[19] and other Semitic languages. This was done in order to better understand the texts of the Torah and the Gospel, since the Reformers strictly insisted on returning to the literal meaning of scriptures. On the other hand, however, the Reformation plunged Europe in a mire of dissonance and religious conflicts that delayed the exploration of distant lands and the further dissemination of Christianity. Hindered as they were from actively participating in missions, the Protestants gave way to the Catholics (Spanish, Portuguese and French) who, for two centuries, bore the burden alone.

Missionaries of both camps resumed their travels in earnest, increasingly taking an interest in the unexplored regions of Asia, Oceania, America and

---

[18] Schmidt, *Origine et évolution de la religion*, p. 34.
[19] It has been argued that this interest in Hebrew stemmed from the fact that both Protestants and Catholics shared the belief that it was the first language spoken by human beings.

'darkest' Africa. It was towards the end of the eighteenth century, a time of unprecedented scholarship in describing the beliefs and rituals of 'exotic' cultures, that inquisitive minds began to ponder the nature of the religion of the first humans, trying to describe it in correlation with the religions of newly discovered 'primitive' peoples. Attempts were also made to envision the possible evolutionary path of religions from the dawn of humanity to the present day, and the manner in which one religion could have engendered another. Since that time, the science of religions has been divided into two branches: one modernist and innovative, the other traditionalist and only partially modernized.

The traditionalist branch comprises descriptive and analytical studies of a specific, well-defined religion, probing into its origins, the life of its founder, the basis of its beliefs and rituals, the causes of its diffusion and the modes of its evolution, with more of the same kinds of questions that were and remain the object of humanity's concern ever since their confessions began to diverge. This branch is usually called the History of Religions – although to describe it more precisely it should be called *Histories* of Religions.

The recent renewal of this old branch has affected both its substance and methods of investigation. While in early times its geographical research scope hardly stretched beyond the Mediterranean and Red Sea basins – in other words, the meeting point of three continents - that scope quickly extended to the five continents. Moreover, while it had been more or less confined itself to studying civilized peoples, their recorded histories and ancient relics, it began to encompass 'savage' tribes and extinct ethnic groups, even venturing into prehistoric timelines.

There is no doubt that by thus broadening the fields of inquiry, contemporary scholars have moved away from the strict, orderly methods adopted by Arab authors. However, this has nonetheless opened up new horizons that past scholars never glimpsed. In particular, this affected contemporary research means and tools, which are now diversified to such an extent that they incorporate comparative linguistics, geology and semiotics, not to mention psychology, sociology, ethnology and everything that bears some relation to the phenomenon of religion.

It goes without saying that the primary means of research of this branch must continue to be the investigation of beliefs and rituals of each religious denomination on the basis of direct testimonies and concrete observations, and that the function of the new auxiliary disciplines must be no more than to guarantee that the course of research is correct and that the outcomes do not contravene the dictates of these sciences. This is the role of scientific criticism,[20] which entails calling upon historiography, for instance, in order to verify the reliability of documents and historical authorities, or consulting philology and terminology to ascertain the meanings of certain expressions and so on.

The new, innovative branch of religious studies, on the other hand, takes the form of theoretical and deductive studies of universals. It aims to quench an intellectual thirst which tends to transcend the multiple divisions and ramifications of beliefs in order to attain a knowledge of their common origin.

Let us explain it in terms of the topic at hand. If one undertook to interpret and compare the manifold beliefs of the world, isolating their differences and anomalies, one would invariably find common ground where all religions meet. An overpowering impulse would then compel one to extract the essence of these common principles and to group them together in a kind of universal whole that aims to explain the nature of 'religion' *per se*. Likewise, by observing the pervasiveness of the phenomenon of religiosity in all societies – whether past or present, civilized or nomadic – one cannot but wonder about the origin of this global reality and seek its causes. Are religions innate in human nature or in the nature of human societies? Are they born of chance or are they the product of human invention? Or are they something else altogether? Do their myriad manifestations throughout history indicate a process of regeneration among them in a kind of logical sequence? Is there a consistent, be it progressive or digressive, evolutionary course among them, or do they evolve in a disorganized and haphazard manner, moving forward at times, backwards at others, standing still then starting all over again?

The researcher of different religions, having confronted all these questions and many more, will eventually encapsulate them into seemingly clear and precise formulations. But the mystery and ambiguity will again murmur in the minds of concerned scholars, particularly those who seek genuine

---

[20] This is different from moral criticism, which scrutinizes the moral value of beliefs and rituals, judging them on an established criterion of rights and wrongs. This could be regarded as a third branch in the study of religion, which we could call 'Comparative criticism of religious morals'.

understanding and who are not acquainted with religions other than their own. Contemporary European scholars and authors have devoted themselves to these questions, each offering a personal point of view. But their studies remain dispersed and sporadic: some induce a subsidiary discussion in the middle of a literary work or in the development of general philosophical theories; some add a third-rank problem in the introduction to a work devoted to the study of a particular religion, or develop one or more of these questions in the foreword to a book on the history of religions; and some treat the problem only in passing, as one reports an anecdote, while others overindulge in perusing superficial phenomena and ignore their deep roots and substance.

It will have become clear by now that these questions are neither literary nor artistic, but belong to the realm of religious studies, that they deserve, by virtue of their thematic unity, to be grouped and studied in one place and to form an independent branch of scholarship whose object of study is the religious phenomenon as a whole. Such a branch would explicate different points of view and generate balanced assessments without bias or prejudice.

Thus, studying the general history of religion should always take precedence over traditional histories of specific religions. On the merits of its instructive nature, this type of scholarship deserves to be made the essential introduction to all other types of religious studies, since it defines general principles and lays the necessary groundwork before engaging in observing the particularities of each religion separately. It seems appropriate, therefore, to turn our attention now to this field of research and to begin our study with a critical review of what scholars have said on the subject.

1

Determining the meaning of 'religion'

Proper logical reasoning demands that when we seek to define a particular concept, we must begin by knowing its most general and definitive elements before undertaking to examine its particulars. If one wishes to learn about the essence of Islam or Christianity, Judaism, Mazdeism, Buddhism, Paganism or any other world religion, the point of departure should be to know their shared meanings and common elements. Religions may appear divergent – in their origins, aims or moral values – yet are all grouped under the name of 'religion', a term that should resonate with some kind of meaningful unity underlying the basic core of all religions.

What is this unity? In other words, what is *din* (religion)? As we enter into the study of the history of religions, this is the first question we should turn to. To answer it, we must first have recourse to Arabic dictionaries in order to form an impression of the meanings that linguists have associated with the word *din*. We say 'an impression' so as not to pretend that we will find satisfactory answers to our proposed searches in Arabic lexicons. We have all come to know, and very well at that, the pains and frustrations that await the users of these works, and the virtual impossibility of extracting precise definitions from related entries therein.

If despair is indeed, as the Arabs say, one of the two comforts of life,[1] then we will find solace when we lower our expectations of these books, and when we stop seeking in them what is beyond their intended design and purpose. People who consult these lexicons will be reassured if they embrace the fact that they were created more for word adjustment than to enjoin precise definitions, that they sharpen the tongue but not the mind. Indeed, these books divulge the meanings of words, but in the form of synonyms and antonyms, and only

---

[1] The other being death. (Ed.)

in the assumption that the reader is already familiar with the unique meaning of each word.

Try, for instance, looking up the attributes and descriptions of a bird, an animal, a plant or the location of a certain city. Consider, then, what you see: 'a known bird', 'a known animal', 'a known plant' or 'a famous city' – in short, nothing but confirmations for those who already know the meanings of these words. As for those who do not know them, they will not find that the required information here.

Often the closest one gets in these volumes to a complete definition of an object is when the object is, rather brazenly, defined either by itself or its opposite. A word like *balagh* (proclamation), for example, may be defined as that by which a thing is proclaimed (*yutaballaghu bihi*), *dawa'* (remedy) as that which heals (*yutadawa bihi*) or *din* (religion) as that to which one adheres (*yudanu bihi*). But *din* could also refer to a religious community (*milla*), and when you look up the meaning of the latter, you will find that it will be defined again as *din* (religion). Likewise with a word like *halal* (religiously permitted), which may be defined as the opposite of *haram* (religiously forbidden), and vice versa. Not to mention the clumsy arrangement, confusions and vain repetitions, or the dispersion rather than grouping, of words despite their identical etymology. Indeed, the latter is a lesser evil and one that is easy to unravel.

Therefore, we must brace ourselves for the same kind of disorderly, unbounded thronging and accumulation of meanings when we turn to the dictionary entry under scrutiny here. Consulting traditional Arabic lexicons – such as *al-Qamus al-Muhit* or *Lisan al-Arab* – one will quickly become lost in a wilderness where the simple word *din* designates many far-fetched, even contradictory, concepts. We will learn that religion (*din*) is defined at the same time as supremacy (*mulk*) and service (*khidma*), as might (*'izz*) and humility (*dhul*), compulsion (*ikrah*) and benevolence (*ihsan*), habit (*'adah*) and ritual devotion (*'ibadah*), subjugation (*qahr*) and mastery (*sultan*), humiliation (*tadhallul*) and surrender (*khudhu'*), and obedience (*ta'a*) and disobedience (*ma'siya*). It is also the religion of Islam and monotheism, or indeed the proper name for any form of religious belief or practice, and so on.

All this calls for relentless efforts on our part to penetrate the façade of these tangled proliferations and to uncover a sense of semantic unity and order. In fact, if we take the trouble to analyse the various meanings and conjugations of this term, we will see that, despite these apparent divergences, there is great convergence, even exact affinity, among them. We will also find that all this multiplicity of apparently incoherent and contradictory meanings is in fact traceable to three concomitant meanings that are ultimately signified by the Arabic word *din*. In other words, the concept we are trying to define is not represented by one but rather three words, which correspond to three verbal forms.

In actual fact, the word *din* (religion) is sometimes derived from the transitive verb *danahu/yadinuhu*, and sometimes from a verb that is transitive through the preposition *li-* (for): *dana lahu*, or the preposition *bi-* (by): *dana bihi*. Thus, the formal meaning of the word will depend on the different conjugations of these verbal forms.

1. With the transitive form (i.e. someone *dana* another), we express the ideas of authority, governance, rulership, power, judgement, reward and punishment. *Din* in this usage signifies mastery and all that befits the conduct of kings. The Qur'an says of God that he is the 'Master of the Day of *Din*'[2] (i.e. the day of reckoning and recompense). In prophetic tradition, we read that a wise man is the one who 'calls himself to account' (*dana nafsahu*). Moreover, one of the holy names of God is *al-Dayyan*, which means the arbiter and ruler.
2. The transitive form through the preposition *li-* (i.e. someone *dana for* another) signifies obedience and submission, humility and adoration. But while *din* here means submission to authority, it can also refer to the authority itself. An expression like *al-dinu li-llah* (religion belongs to God) comprises both meanings – that power belongs to God and that God is the only being deserving of others' submission.

    Clearly, then, the second form complements the first: A *dana* B (*-hu*), and B *dana* for A (*la-hu*) – that is, A compelled B to obedience, and B (in return) obeyed and submitted.
3. As for the transitive form through the preposition – *bi-* (i.e. someone *dana by* something), this implies accepting certain beliefs, customs and morals, and making them one's own religion. Religion, in this view, is a path or way that one follows at the theoretical or practical level. As far as

---

[2] Qur'an 1:4. (Ed.)

the practical rules are concerned, they are a person's habits and customs; hence, the expression *hadha dini wa daydani* can be literally translated as 'this is my way and my habit'. Beliefs and faith, on the other hand, are theoretical. For example, the statement *dayyantu ar-rajul* refers to when someone grants another person religious freedom, raising no objection to what he deems justified belief.

The third form of the concept of *din*, while in some way different from the preceding ones, still relates to them, because the custom or belief one adopts as one's own assumes authority and ascendancy over the one who adopts it. It becomes a power to which one owes obedience and submission.

In summary, these linguistic deliberations elucidate rather clearly that the meaning of *din* – the Arabic word for religion – involves a relationship between two entities, one of which glorifies the other and surrenders to it. On the one hand, the word *din* means submission and abidance, while on the other, it implies authority and obligation. As for the bond of union between the two sides, its meaning relates to the code or charter through which this relationship is conducted and manifested.

It is reasonable, then, to propose that all of this word's lexical entries in fact revolve around the idea of obligation of obedience. It is either obliging (*ilzam*) obedience, keeping to (*iltizam*) obedience or the observed principles that enable the expression of this obedience.

It should also be noted that the idea of obligation is also present in the meaning of the word *dayn* (= debt, vocalized with a short 'a'), which has the same etymology as *din* (= religion, vocalized with a short 'e').[3] The former implies financial obligation and the latter moral obligation. In Arabic, the distinction between corporeal and incorporeal things of the same genus can be achieved by a slight modification of word form while retaining the same linguistic root. We find this in words such as *'awaj* (morally twisted) and *'iwaj* (physically bent), *khalq* (shape) and *khuluq* (moral character), *ru'ya* (eyesight) and *ru'yah* (dream), *kibar* (bigness) and *kibr* (arrogance), among others.

---

[3] In the commentary on the *Qamus* it is reported by al-Iraqi that al-Asma'i heard from some Arabs of a curious linguistic distinction. He said, When the 'd' in the word *dayn* (debt) is vocalized with the short vowel 'a', it is because the debtor is above the one in debt. But when the short vowel 'e' is used in the word *din* (religion), it signifies submission. As for the short vowel 'o' in the word *dunya* (earthly life), it is because this life is premised on hardship. (See al-Zabidi, *Taj al-'arus*, vol. 35, p. 50. [Ed.])

This goes to prove that the word *din*, with all its varied meanings, is, and has always been, native to the Arabic language. Indeed, some Orientalists[4] have claimed that it was introduced into Arabic from Hebrew or Persian. However, these unfounded claims are largely motivated by deep anti-Arab sentiments, which endeavour to deprive Arabs of all merit, even in eloquence, one of the most celebrated aspects of their civilization.

Let us return to the topic at hand. Of the meanings mentioned above, we are especially interested in the second and, even more so, the third. In discourses of the history of religions, the term 'religion' has two referents: the psychological state (*état subjectif*, or the subjective state), which we will call 'religiosity', and the objective fact (*fait objectif*), which consists of outward customs, legendary narratives and vestiges of the past. These are the beliefs and rituals that comprise the 'religious doctrine' of nations. Obviously, the latter is more common.

While linguistic analyses may reveal roots and etymologies of the word 'religion', they fall short of providing a clear and satisfactory understanding of its place in the minds of people and in the conventions of everyday language. There is indeed a gap between the linguistic meaning of this word, on the one hand, and conventional usage, on the other. For example, not every form of submission or obedience can always be described as religiously motivated. The surrender of the defeated to the victor, the obedience of a son to his father or the deference of an individual towards his superiors, all have a nature other than religious. Similarly, not every opinion or ideology, way of life or moral behaviour, can rightly be classified as religious.

So, then, what are the specific elements that characterize the religious idea, behaviour and sentiment? Evidently, we can only hope to achieve an accurate and complete understanding of these elements when we reach the end of our research – that is to say, when our comparative studies of the various world beliefs can finally give us a sense of the common ground they share. But since a full examination of religions to establish their minimum common denominator would be hasty and impractical, we shall instead outline some of the definitions that Muslim and Western experts have given for the word *din*

---

[4] See '*Din*' in Gibb, *Encyclopaedia of Islam*.

or its equivalent, 'religion'. This will enable us to determine, through critical analysis, to what extent these definitions apply to the known religions of the world.

In the Islamic tradition, past scholars have commonly given the following definition: '*al-Din* (religion) is a divine setting that guides rational beings, by their free choice, to wellbeing in this life and salvation in the hereafter.' Put differently, 'Religion is a divine setting that guides to Truth in matters of faith and to the Good in human conduct and interaction.' Westerners, on the other hand, have given many definitions for the word 'religion', of which the following are but selected examples:

> Marcus Tullius Cicero (106–43 BCE) says in his *On the Laws*: 'Religion is the bond connecting humans with God.'[5]
>
> Immanuel Kant (1724–1804) says in his *Religion within the Boundaries of Mere Reason*: 'Religion is (subjectively regarded) the recognition of all our duties as divine commands.'[6]
>
> Friedrich Schleiermacher (1768–1834) says in his *On Religion: Speeches to Its Cultured Despisers*: 'Religion is the feeling of absolute dependence.'[7]
>
> Ferdinand François Châtel (1795–1857) says in his *The Code of Humanity*: 'Religion is the sum of duties of the created towards the creator: man's duties towards God, society, and himself.'[8]
>
> Herbert Spencer (1820–1903) says at the end of his *First Principles*: 'Indefinite consciousness of existence transcending relations … forms the essence of Religion.'[9]
>
> Edward Burnett Tylor (1832–1917) says in his *Primitive Culture*: '[Religion is] the belief in Spiritual Beings.'[10]

---

[5] 'La religion est le lien qui unit l'homme à Dieu' (Ciceron, *de Legibus*, I, XV). (This definition appears at the end of St. Augustine's (354–430 CE) De vera religione [of true religion]. In Latin: Religet ergo nos religio uni omnipotenti deo (see Burleigh, Augustine: Earlier writings, p. 282. [Ed.]).

[6] 'La religion est le sentiment de nos devoirs en tant que fondés sur des commandements divins' (Kant, *La Religion dans les limites de la raison*, 4ème partie, 1ère section).

[7] 'L'essence de la-religion consiste dans le sentiment de notre dépendance absolue' (Schleiermacher, *Discours sur la religion*, second Discours).

[8] 'La religion est la collection des devoirs de la créature envers le créateur: devoirs de l'homme envers Dieu, envers la société et envers soi-même' (Abbé Châtel, *Code de l'humanité*, ch. 5).

[9] 'La croyance en un pouvoir dont on ne peut concevoir les limites dans le temps ni dans l'espace est l'élément fondamental de la religion' (Spencer, *Premiers principes*).

[10] 'La religion est la croyance en des êtres spirituels' (Tylor, *Primitive culture*, ch. 11).

Friedrich Max Müller (1823–1900) says in his *Lectures on the Origin and Growth of Religion*: '[Religion is] a struggle to conceive the inconceivable, to utter the unutterable, a longing after the Infinite, a love of God.'[11]

Émile-Louis Burnouf (1821–1907) says in his *The Science of Religions*: 'Religion is an act of adoration, and adoration is at once an intellectual act, by which man acknowledges a superpower, and an act of love, by which he craves protection.'[12]

Albert Réville (1826–1906) says in his *Prolegomenon to the History of Religions*: 'Religion is the determination of human life by the sentiment of a bond uniting the human mind to that mysterious Mind whose domination of the world and of itself it recognizes, and to whom it delights in feeling itself united.'[13]

Jean-Marie Guyau (1854–88) says in his book *The Non-Religion of the Future*: 'Religion is universal socio-morphism. The religious sentiment is primarily, no doubt, our feeling of dependence on volitions placed in the universe by primitive man.'[14]

Michel Mayer (1823–1905) says in his *Religious and Moral Instructions*: 'Religion is the set of beliefs and precepts that should guide us in our conduct with God, humans, and ourselves.'[15]

Sylvain Périssé says in his book *The Science of Religion*: 'Religion is the ideal side of humanity.'[16]

Salomon Reinach (1858–1932) says in *A General History of Religions*: 'I propose to define Religion as a sum of scruples which impede the free exercise of our faculties.'[17]

---

[11] 'La religion est un effort pour concevoir l'inconcevable, pour exprimer l'inexprimable, une aspiration vers l'infini, un amour de Dieu' (Müller, *Origine et développement de la religion*, Leçon I, ch. 4).

[12] 'La religion est un acte d'adoration et l'adoration est à la fois un acte intellectuel par lequel l'homme reconnait une puissance supérieure et un acte d'amour par lequel il s'adresse à sa bonté' (*Science des religions*, ch. 12).

[13] 'La religion est la détermination de la vie humaine par le sentiment d'un lien unissant l'esprit humain à un esprit mystérieux, dont il reconnait la domination sur le monde et sur lui-même, et auquel il aime à se sentir uni' (Réville, *Prolégomène à l'histoire des religions*).

[14] 'La religion est un sociomorphisme universel. Le sentiment religieux est le sentiment de dépendance par rapport à des volontés que l'homme primitif place dans l'univers' (Guyau, *Irreligion de l'avenir*, pp. 1–3).

[15] 'La religion, c'est l'ensemble des croyances et des préceptes qui doivent nous guider dans notre conduite envers Dieu, envers notre prochain et envers nous-mêmes' (Mayer, *Instructions morales et religieuses*, 1ère leçon).

[16] 'La religion, ... c'est la part de l'idéal dans la vie humaine' (Périssé, *Science et religions*, ch. 1).

[17] 'La religion: Un ensemble de scrupules qui font obstacle au libre exercice de nos facultés' (Reinach, *Orpheus*, p. 4).

Émile Durkheim (1858–1917) says in his *The Elementary Forms of the Religious Life*: 'A religion is a unified system of beliefs and practices relative to sacred things, that is to say, things set apart and forbidden – beliefs and practices which unite into one single moral community called a Church.'[18]

Thus, it appears that the ideas of absolute belief and submission do not suffice, by themselves, to define the notion of religion, and that other restrictions must be added to bring out its basic elements. This is evinced by all the sample definitions we have just provided.

At the same time, we can easily see that the great majority of definitions, whether by Muslims or non-Muslims, in fact break the rules of logic when they confine the term to proper religions based on divine revelation and which admit of only one God who is the creator and master of all things. In so doing, natural religions based on pure reason, superstitions based on myths and illusions, and all religious forms based, if only in part, on the worship of manmade idols or the worship of animals, stars, demons or angels, all of these will, by virtue of these reductive definitions, be excluded from the domain of religion. And yet the Qur'an defines them as religions when it states,

If anyone seeks a religion other than [Islam] complete devotion to God. 3:85

And (addressing the unbelievers),

You have your religion and I have mine. 109:4

It should also be noted that certain scholars, in their accounts of the idea of religion, have gone so far as to elaborate highly philosophized descriptions of religion which turn out to be alien to the minds of common religious folk. In this connection, we think of Herbert Spencer, for example, who declares that 'the essential element in religion is belief in a power whose infinity in time and space is inconceivable'. While this notion of the infinite may have been conceived and adopted by eminent philosophers and scholars, it cannot in any way apply to the beliefs of those who attribute human or spatial qualities to God, or who declare that God is resident in the sky above. Our task here,

---

[18] 'La religion est un système solidaire des croyances et des pratiques relatives à des choses sacrées, c'est-à-dire séparées et interdites – croyances et pratiques qui unissent en une même communauté morale appelée Eglise tous ceux qui y adhèrent' (Durkheim, *Formes élémentaires de la vie religieuse*, p. 65).

however, is not only to seek out the definitions of proper revealed religions but also to encompass 'religion' in its totality with all its varying forms and expressions.

We also saw how Max Müller went further than Spencer in narrowing his definition by declaring that religion is 'the attempt to conceive the inconceivable'. This formulation can only strictly apply to religions which establish an absolute separation between faith and reason, and which demand their adherents to blindly believe in what their minds can neither imagine nor conceive.[19]

We see in the list of definitions above that excessively reductionist accounts of religion are matched by equally unwarranted attempts to expand the boundaries of definition. The latter is represented by sociologists and anthropologists such as Émile Durkheim and Salomon Reinach who not only eliminated from their universal definitions of religion the idea of an 'infinite, inconceivable, creating deity' but also went so far as to dispense with the very idea of divinity with all its manifold expressions. To justify their position, they argued that there are religions in the East, such as Buddhism, Jainism and Confucianism, which are exclusively founded on moral standards and devoid of any deification. Those among the followers of these religions, so they reasoned, who may later come to deify the Buddha or Jina, for example, have in reality moved away from the original teachings of these faiths.

Let us consider the soundness of these arguments more closely. They seem to suggest that these Eastern religions contain no element of theoretical or abstract belief. Yet it is a well-known fact that historians of religions unanimously agree that no human community, even a great nation, ever appeared on earth without having reflected, in one way or another, on the origin and destiny of man, and on the explanation of the universe and its phenomena, and without having adopted on these questions an opinion – justified or erroneous, assured or speculative – positing the existence of a higher power on which depends all phenomena, their origins and the fate of creation after its disappearance.

---

[19] If the idea of 'conception' here indicates apprehending God as a substantial entity, and not as a purely mental and abstract representation, then this formulation would apply well to the higher idealistic religions and our objection would no longer stand.

The religions referred to here are no exception, for they have never denied the existence of Indian deities such as Indra, Agni, Varuna and so on. As for the destiny of man, they adhere steadfastly to the ancient Hindu theory of life as suffering – that the desire for the pleasures and delights of life is what keeps man in the cycle of death and rebirth, where he is ceaselessly transferred from one suffering to another; that, to reach perfect bliss, man must lead a life of complete austerity until he dies a final death and escapes the cycle of suffering.

Historians of Eastern religions may argue, however, that these Hindu gods, who found their way into ancient Buddhism, have no power except over the material world, which is precisely what the Buddhist wants to rid himself of. This is why a Buddhist does not worship these deities or seek their favours. On the contrary, he wants to escape their reign by taking refuge in eternal death. Neither does he turn to these gods to learn the moral code of his 'religion' because he relies exclusively on his own mental and spiritual efforts. Whether we say that Buddhism does not recognize deities, or admits of deities without having to worship them, the outcome is the same – that there are religions devoid of the idea of worship. This is either because they reject all abstract notions concerning the origin of creation or because they are sharply dualistic, consisting of two spheres that have no relation to each other. These religions could admit, in the realm of theory, the existence of an all-powerful force that reigns supreme over creation, but it is a force that does not, in any practical sense, interfere in human affairs or actions. In a similar vein, they might lay out the practical means to achieve salvation from the sufferings of worldly life but without assuming any need to establish a relationship with that otherwise powerful force.

But can we apply the term 'religion' to these types of beliefs? Perhaps we can. But we must also admit that it would be an unusual application of the term, and one which goes against linguistic norms, particularly the Arabic language, which for the word *din* admits of no meaning other than a relation with a power to which man submits and to which he turns with affection, awe and reverence. In fact, we suggest, with some confidence, that any doctrine lacking this kind of religious submission would be more rightly labelled an 'arid philosophy' rather than a religion. We contend that these confessions (Buddhism, Confucianism etc.) were only admitted into the fold of religions because, at some stage in their evolution, the idea of divinity was integrated into them and then assumed to be in their very nature.

Above all, we object to the removal of the principle of divinity from the definition of religion, and we find ourselves in agreement with the German philosopher Friedrich Schleiermacher when he declares that it is indeed this feeling of absolute dependence and subservience to a creative force that constitutes the backbone of religion per se. There is no doubt, then, that this feeling should be made the essential element in any inclusive definition of religion.

But it is not the only one. For if any feeling of dependence and submission to an overpowering force, whatever form it takes, were considered a 'religion', then we should of necessity class among the religions our need to breathe or to nourish ourselves, or our surrender to the physical laws of motion and gravity, and, obviously, no one would endorse these positions. Thus, we must continue our search for other differences and characteristics that could enable us to tell which type of submission rightly belongs to the category of religion.

A close analysis of the mentality of the believer will reveal two other specific characteristics. The first relates to that which the believer sanctifies and considers the object of his submission. The second deals with the very nature of this submission. Let us begin with a crucial distinction, made by the believer himself, between the character and the extent of his religious submission vis-à-vis the sacred, on the one hand, and those of what he reveres and surrenders to in any other domain, on the other.

Integrity, honour, freedom and dignity are all noble principles that we revere. Likewise, we conform and surrender to the fixed ordinances of nature, which we cannot change or ignore. But what the believer sanctifies is not of the same nature as these abstract mental principles, nor is it among such vague social precepts. His religious veneration is addressed to an extrinsic reality, an entity outside the realm of reason. If he tries to represent this entity to himself, he will conceive of it as an independent, self-sufficient entity, not a mere contingent or nominal existence. Religious faith is distinguished by the fact that the relation between the believer and the entity to which he submits is above all a relation between two beings, and not between a being and an abstract idea, as intimated in the foregoing definitions.

Furthermore, this veneration is not addressed to just any being, but to an entity endowed with special attributes, chief among them that it lies outside the sphere of cognition and is beyond the reach of our senses. It is mysterious, transcendent, and fathomable only through our mind and conscience. All religious beliefs thus presuppose a faith in the unseen, or, in other words, in the realm of metaphysics. And in this lies the second criterion of distinction between religious and non-religious submission.

This hidden mystery on which believers base their faith is nothing like the passive nature of the physical world. It is an active and effective power. In contrast to the way matter exerts an effect on its surroundings, whereby it is unconscious of its own power and has no control over it, the power to which the believer submits is felt by him as a rational, conscious power which acts freely and of its own volition.

The believer does not perceive this intelligent governing power as withdrawn into itself, isolated from him and the world. On the contrary, he sees it as being intimately connected with him and with other people, attentive to their confidences and grievances, concerned by their sufferings and their hopes and with the capacity, if it so decides, to answer their prayers.

With all this in mind, we are already in a better position to determine the overall meaning of sanctity and deification found in religions. It can be summed up as follows: Religious submission is deification and veneration, and its object is a divine being worthy of worship. This definition, however, could call into question our very approach, because when what is worthy of deification is restricted to hidden mysterious entities, we are in fact oblivious to all those peoples who worship rocks, trees, rivers, birds, animals – even human beings.

But it is important to remember that the great majority of researchers who study the mentality and psychology of believers agree that there has never been a religion, no matter how debased and irrational, which stopped at the boundaries of the senses and deemed a visible substance to be sacred in itself. Neither has there been any worshipper of images and idols who could be said to genuinely venerate the tangible material forms or to see in them anything that could merit such glorification on his part. To the worshipper, they are nothing other than receptacles of a mysterious force or the symbolic representations of a hidden secret power, and only then could they warrant such profound veneration.

In the eyes of believers, these representations do the work of amulets and talismans – they attract blessings and grace, ward off magic spells and the evil eye. This is not because they are seen to have certain innate properties like fire in the ashes, or actual physical powers like magnetic bodies, but because there lies, around and beyond these objects, an intelligent governing spirit[20] with an independent will and with the capacity to change, if it so wishes, the natural order and course of things. It is a spirit that gives and takes, harms and helps and often when one least expects it. Therefore, consecrated material forms are deemed nothing other than a visage through which this mysterious spirit is projected, and any shrine erected in honour of this or that deity is frequented and venerated by virtue of its connection with that spirit.

---

[20] This idea of an invisible spirit is so pervasive that it is even found in the most primitive pagan beliefs. This point is clearly illustrated in the example of the human god venerated by the blacks of the Nuba Mountains. The story of this cult is reported by Azzam Pasha, who even met the 'human god' in person during one of his expeditions to South Kordofan. The members of the tribe, having noticed in this man a strange predisposition to predict future events and an ability to perform extraordinary acts, adopted the habit of turning to him when needing protection from calamity and disease, to solicit advice on the best season for hunting or war and to send down rain for their plantations and animals. In return, they offer him oblations and gifts; men and women gather in his presence, they sing and dance to win his favour. If it so happens that he refuses their requests, they implore him and go out of their way to appease him, until, faced with his repeated refusals, they lose hope in him. He is then locked up or even killed, and a new individual, in whom they recognize extraordinary gifts similar to his, is appointed in his place (see *The Eternal Message* by Azzam Pasha, pp. 6–7). We can clearly see from this example that it is not this man in flesh and blood – whom they dare to imprison, torture and kill – that the members of the tribe worship. Rather, they address themselves, through him, to a hidden mystery, which is above and beyond everyone.

The author goes on to say that he could not ascertain 'whether this man is in their view an absolute deity or an idol, like the idols of the ancient Arabs, worshipped only to connect them to what they believe to be a greater and more elevated being'. We are inclined to the opinion that though his followers greatly admired his knowledge of secrets and the ability to deliver on their requests, this admiration is much like the faith that people have in saints and holy men – it is not absolute and does not rule out the belief in a Higher God. The same is observed in other primitive religions known to experts and is further attested by the Nubians themselves in their attitude towards their 'human god'. They do not ask him to turn mountains into gold or change the water of the seas into nectar, nor to reverse the cycle of the stars or to grant them eternal life. Neither do they suspect him of having created himself, nor of having created heaven and earth, nor of being able to control their movements. Rather, the 'miracles' they ask him to perform are within his reach and the likes of which had already been witnessed by them. When they reach out to him, they seek to improve their living conditions through his knowledge and powers, in the manner that a sick man implores his doctors with generous gifts in the hope of recovery. In their view, the steady rejection of lavish offerings and the ongoing indifference to their threats and intimidations do not mean that the 'human god' is vile and avaricious; they simply confirm his incompetence and the limits of his knowledge and powers. Therefore, faced with the failures and defeats of gods and the desperate hopelessness of believers, people instinctively recognize the existence of a higher force, a force next to which all forms of knowledge and power are in vain. In other words, they may sometimes seek the help of lower powers, but only when such help is believed to be tenable and within reach.

Let us recapitulate the four elements of the definition we have identified thus far: that what the believer venerates is not a simple abstract or mental concept, but *an extrinsic reality*. This reality is *mysterious* and imperceptible by the senses. This mysterious force is also *intelligent*, acts on its own will and is freed from the kind of compulsion observed in magnetic or electric forces. Lastly, this force is constantly *attentive* to the affairs of the world that it governs and maintains a reciprocal spiritual relation with its inhabitants.

Thus, we find ourselves agreeing with the erudite Tylor that religion necessarily includes 'the belief in spiritual beings', but on condition that we take the term 'spirit' in its broadest meaning, without trying to limit its nature, power or behaviour. Insofar as we can describe it as an invisible, rational and governing force whose will provokes and directs action, and which hears the appeals of those who invoke it without being compelled to accede or decline them, we must therefore allow the term 'spirit' to admit of all these meanings and attributes.

These four elements – extrinsic reality, mystery, intelligence and spiritual relation – offer the minimum criteria which distinguish the religious from the non-religious.

Whereas theories based on logic or psychology lock themselves inside the narrow space of reason or the psyche, study meanings they discover in these domains and ignore what is outside their limits, and whereas materialist theories turn to external reality and refuse to be interested in anything beyond and outside direct sensory experience and observation,[21] the religious attitude goes beyond all these contingencies and is projected towards another truth, a truth not identifiable in the depths of the human psyche nor in its physical environment. It is a mysterious truth that transcends nature. The believer needs to find meaning in sensory experience, an inner reality aside from

---

[21] It would be wrong to assume that the materialists 'surrender' to the laws of nature because they recognize in them rational souls or hidden mysteries. When they go beyond their immediate observations, it is only to decree laws that ultimately remain within the same paradigm. In the end, a scientific law is nothing other than the distillation of observations that are repeated in the course of successive experiments, and according to a pre-arranged plan. They are condemned to studying a reality while having no rational knowledge of its origin, and whose first cause is of no concern to them. Religious attitudes, on the other hand, even if they sometimes incline to fallacy and superstition, aspire to wider and more distant horizons. They make the believer submit in awe to a principle initiator, the master and director of the universe, regardless of what form the believer chooses to give it.

appearances. He wants to assume an active agent behind every phenomenon – that at the origin of any important or minor event, the will and providence of one (or more) gods are expressed. Certainly, spiritual philosophy shares with religion the idea of the metaphysical existence of an intelligent and active force (or forces). However, the difference between them lies in the fact that the philosopher has no moral relation with this force. Between them there is no relation of rights or duties, no spiritual bond that allows one to formulate a wish or a prayer. The believer, on the contrary, is intimately attached to this bond, to the extent of making it a vital part of his being. This is why we see him, in times of affliction and desperation, turn to this dominant force to entrust in it his requests and wishes.

However, not every belief in a mysterious and invisible force, nor any invocation addressed to it, can be attributed to religiosity. The spiritualist, who invokes spirits, is no less religious than his fellow materialist, who admits the existence of a phantom world. Even if some resemblance is suspected between the attitude of the spiritualist and that of the believer, since they both enter into a relation with an invisible force which they invoke and from which they seek help, these two attitudes are in fact totally different. The nature of the relationship between these forces can vary between religious and non-religious settings to the point that they become the exact opposite of each other. Indeed, the mysterious forces which the magician[22] or the sorcerer or the spiritualist calls upon are not perceived by him as higher powers which he must reach out to, but either as rivals to fight with or as equals to win over and pacify. He may even feel himself superior and more powerful than these intangible forces, feel that he could succeed in dominating them, make them bend to his will and work them to his advantage. In this he is similar to the chemist who utilizes, or exploits, the elements of nature to achieve his own private ends. The believer's

---

[22] Magic is a craft that creates supernatural events by means of secret practices. It branches into different schools. It also varies according to its objectives (some are beneficial, such as healing the sick or finding criminals, while others are evil, such as causing illness or sowing discord between spouses or friends) and according to the methods and means it employs (which could be natural means, also called white magic, or supernatural and satanic – i.e., black magic).

Our discussion is limited to this last group, which invokes the intervention of the spirits to allow the magician to achieve his ends. It is to the latter type of magic that the term particularly applies, and its practices happen to bear the most resemblance to those of religion. These practices, nevertheless, differ from religious attitudes in that the spiritualist's invocation of the spirit is an attempt to subjugate and control it. He does not turn to it in supplication as a superior, sanctified being worthy of veneration.

attitude is quite different. He seeks his Master's pleasure and fears his wrath, standing before his object of veneration in submission and humility.

We arrive now at the final criterion of distinction that defines the power to which the believer submits – it is *higher* and *exalted*, overpowering and undefeated. It is he, the believer, who submits to it, and not vice versa.

To give a concrete illustration of these points, let us think of the focus of the materialist as being at his feet. He is dealing with elements that are blind and unresponsive; he sees and feels them, but they do not. The focus of the spiritualist is in some way on par with his level, because even if he believes that the spirits with which he deals are more powerful than him, they remain in his view no more active or intelligent than he is. In reality, they are subject to him, for they are at his mercy, act on his orders and are exposed to the effects of his amulets and talismans. As for the believer, his goal is higher because he addresses himself to an absolute power. If the others are forced to lower their eyes, the believer looks up to the heavens.

Having analysed the five objective elements comprising the definition of religious belief, we must now address the subjective dimension – that is, the psychological state of the believer that characterizes his submission to the object of his faith.

Let us explain. Everyone can see that the cosmos stands under the dominion of destiny. It is subject – whether in its motions, proportions, dispositions and so on – to restrictive laws it cannot break and cycles it cannot bypass. This is also the case with our terrestrial world, where everything seems to us to be governed by rules and measured according to precise proportions which determine, for example, the distance between our earth and the sun or other stars, the quantity of light and heat it receives, its atmospheric pressure and so on. The same applies to the creatures that live in it. We see that all are subject to the natural cycle of aging, decrepitude and, finally, death.[23]

---

[23] Modern developments in natural sciences and medicine have been extraordinary indeed, so that people are wondering whether a day will come when, with the help of science, they will live for eternity, or whether the phenomenon of death will become a thing of the past.
This aspiration is not new. Man has always entertained the wish for eternal life, a wish that echoes a deeply rooted survival instinct. Man has a sense, ingrained in his psyche, that he is destined for eternal existence. But humans go astray when they expect this wish to be fulfilled by mental concepts, or 'idols', of their own making which they call 'science'. Science is innocent of this delirium, for it knows its limits and weaknesses better than the deceived ones who cling to it. Let us suppose that we are, one day, able to provide men with the glands, hormones, devices and technical means of all kinds that allow the physical configuration of the human being to function

All these are types of submission to the laws of nature. Some of them are unconscious and involuntary, while others are conscious but inevitable. The man who falls from a high floor can only surrender, against his wish, to the forced motion brought about by his descent into open space. The believer's submission, however, is both conscious and voluntary. When he prostrates himself before the omnipotence of the Being he adores, he does so out of his own free will and with a contended heart. His submission is driven by inner impulses of glorification and veneration, which are, by nature, antithetical to coercion. These spontaneous impulses are addressed, freely and passionately, to a being who deserves them, but only when the believer is convinced that this being truly deserves veneration. There are indeed means of coercion, such as threats of punishment, which produce a formal appearance of reverence, but never reverence itself or its inmost place in the heart.

The following line from the Quran indicates another difference that distinguishes the service of God from general servitude.

> *All that are in heaven and earth submit to God alone, willingly or unwillingly.* 13:15

---

eternally and without a hitch. How far would humans have progressed at that stage on the path to eternal life? All that science would have succeeded in doing would be to safeguard people against one of the many causes of death – that is, the physiological causes. These are the symptoms of old age resulting from the gradual deterioration of bodily organs, and they are, in fact, the least common causes of death in men. As for the myriad other causes that fight their battles tirelessly both inside the human body and outside of it, anticipating the opportunity to attempt to destroy our lives, whether in the safety of our homes or during travels in distant lands, in wakefulness and in sleep, motionless or in motion or unconsciously and in conscious experience, they are everywhere – in what we see and what we do not see, in the higher and lower elements of nature and in all that defies description and eludes analysis. In order to be able to control the innumerable other causes, science should also be able to foresee any event, of universal or particular dimension, likely to occur at such a precise moment. It should also be ready to act when it occurs, be informed of all the stages of its development once it occurs, be able to predict its occurrence, and be able to erase its aftermath afterwards. And since the only way to prevent an incident is to uproot its causes, all the foregoing precautions to ward off danger are obsolete without the need to return to the causes of evil, then to the causes of these causes, right up to the original moment of life's creation, or the very inception of matter, to try to weed out the roots of evil.

We can see the impossibility, the absurdity and the contradiction that such a loose hypothesis leads to – that the human being, born only yesterday compared with the rest of creation, should have to exist before existing, should have witnessed the creation of the worlds and of himself; that man, a creature endowed with limited power and means, could have unlimited powers and means which would enable him to encompass all knowledge and be the master of everything. This logic speaks of the human being as a creature other than the one we know. Truly, the one who possesses the keys to eternity is the one who created life in the first place, not the one to whom life is a gift, not knowing how and when he received it and how long it will last.

Here is another observation. The believer's submission to his object of worship, even if sometimes defined as total surrender to a dominant force, remains very different from other forms of imposed submission which induce hopelessness and frustration, curtail human effort and action and leave no room for hope. The believer's submission, on the contrary, revives the heart by opening new horizons of possibility and by freeing the self from its shackles. The word 'impossible' does not figure in the believer's vocabulary. When adversity intensifies before him and its noose tightens, he senses that there may nevertheless be openings and solutions that he can only avail himself of by the grace of God. That is why when he addresses God, his soul oscillates between hope and fear, and his aspirations are beset, paradoxically, by certainty and doubt. He knows that the powerful being whom he invokes in his prayers is too honourable and sovereign to depend on a will other than his own. The believer is ever so bewildered by the divine will, whose mysterious ways he cannot learn or predict. Torn between hope and caution, the believer observes the wheel of time with careful anticipation of the future. This attitude is not found except in those who believe in a will that prevails over the natural order. When naturalist thinkers perceive the regular chain of things and their uninterrupted succession, their gaze is fixed on this regularity, and reassured of its stability and continuity, they become despondent of any interruption or disunity. This is why we see them at one end of two extremes – oblivious bliss or terminal despair. Religious faith, and spiritual philosophies in general, does not succumb to limiting dictates of observed reality. It projects its thought towards the inmost depths of things; while it applies the laws of reason to the created world, it does so by taking into account an infinite range of possibilities. In this way, the true nature of the universe will be unveiled where its ostensibly orderly schemes need not be perpetually fixed and unchanging. The universe will simply be seen as the work of artistry and the outcome of a premeditated plan. The continuity and progression of the universe is, in its view, contingent on the will of the power that created it in the first instance and which ensured its perpetuation. For he who strung the chain together can also break it; he is able to turn the wheel to the left while it turns to the right; he can, by his own choosing, initiate in the order of the universe unsuspected wonders and occurrences that unravel all considerations. Thus, the incurably ill is healed, the incarcerated prisoner is freed, rain will fall in the midst of drought, a few troops will prevail over a great army and so on.

For this reason, we see that religions, in all their forms and whatever their modes of expression, stand resolutely on the side of hope, possibility and freedom. By admitting to alternative conceptualizations in the course of things, they provide invaluable help for the proper sciences and pave the way for their advancement. They open up a horizon of new possibilities, wider than anyone could ever conceive. Stated plainly, sciences, locked into various forms of determinism, tend to operate in an atmosphere of despondency.

Indeed, each time the sciences discover a new law, we see them languish in idleness and rebuild the world on the basis of their latest findings. But when they move to the next stage in their research, they find themselves having to abandon the chains of laws they had once imposed on themselves for new ones that shackle them just as much. They live one day at a time, believing only what they see, scarcely looking past the observed reality of the moment. But in their relentless quest for new discoveries, the material scientists, as a matter of fact, are unwittingly driven by a hidden impulse that tells them that the world offers infinite possibilities. They observe, in their daily experiences, that each new adjustment of their view of the role and place of things in the world invariably confirms the notion that they are the work of an active will and an intelligent force. For since the dawn of man's observation of the universe, there has never been an instance where changes and upheavals in the created scheme of things have occurred without the interference of a rational force independent of matter and prevailing over it. This observation can only reveal to us that all of the schemes of things and the progression of events in the universe did not spring into existence by virtue of themselves or under the effect of an unconscious and blind force. This idea is predominant in all religions and spiritualties – that by tracing the chain of causes of each phenomenon, we inevitably end up with the existence of a free choosing power, a power capable of creation, initiation and invention, and all these partial causes must of necessity be consolidated into a first cause.

When materialist sciences inspect the meticulous mechanics of the universe to study its components and understand their functions, in effect they only aim at a better organization of human activities according to the same laws they had discovered. From this perspective, we cannot reproach the sciences themselves for neglecting the question of knowing who is the inventor and organizer of this machinery, since this question falls beyond the scope of their mission. However, all the blame goes to man, precisely because he is a man. When he places his reason into shackles of his own making, when he amputates himself of an essential element of his being by banishing this question from his reflections, hiding inside the present moment without taking into account either the immemorial past or the distant future, he simply abdicates his quality of being human. He imposes silence on the heavenly voice that urges him, from the depths of his soul, to let his nature flourish, and reproaches himself for wanting to fix his gaze only on the here and now of himself and of things at the expense of contemplating their first origin and ultimate destiny.

***

Let us now attempt to formulate a complete definition of religion by integrating the core principles realized from the foregoing examinations. As a subjective fact, religion is

> the belief in the existence of a being (or beings) that is mysterious and transcendent, conscious and free choosing, a being who prevails over and manages the affairs of the universe and all that affects the human condition in general. This belief is such that it prompts the believer to turn to that exalted essence in an outburst of longing and fear, submission and veneration.

Simply put, 'Religion (or rather, religiosity) is faith in a divine being to whom we owe obedience and adoration.' As an objective fact, religion is 'the set of theoretical laws which specify the attributes of this divine being, as well as the set of practical rules which delineate the precise manner for the believer to express his adoration to him'.

It will now be easy for readers to realize to what extent the definitions of religion cited at the beginning of the chapter faithfully represent the phenomenon, without excess or deficiency. At the outset, we can raise two important objections to the definitions of Durkheim, Reinach and their supporters.

The first is that these scholars seem to have understood 'religious sanctity' only in practical and negative terms. That is to say, they exclusively ascribed it to what is forbidden to undertake or to approach; in other words, what is 'taboo'. It seems to have escaped them, however, that the prohibition to touch or approach one thing or another is not necessarily proof of the purity or holiness of that thing. Prohibition can also indicate impurity and malevolence. It has also escaped them that the practical rites found in any congregation tend to be symbolic expressions of their belief as a whole.

Now, if sanctification is, in one respect, the prohibition of approaching impurities and vices, it also designates what is beautiful and perfect, and implies respect for ideal qualities and noble virtues. The sacred then appears to signify, in its negative aspect, prohibition to transgress taboos and, in its positive one, the appeal to draw upon virtuousness and noble qualities, to delight in their beauty and to assimilate their intrinsic values. Therefore, this definition is inadequate, since it does not take into account all the aspects of the phenomenon it claims to define.

***

The second objection is more critical and pertinent. By eliminating from the religious fact the two notions of spirituality and divinity, these scholars strip it of its two essential characteristics and cast out the pivot around which all its elements revolve. These two notions are in fact the measure of all religious expression, for they distinguish, better than anything else, what belongs to religion and what does not.

The definition of religious phenomena, deprived of these two notions as proposed by these sociologists, could equally well apply to any social activity – whether moralistic, artistic, economic or other – especially if an activity emerges over time as a form of traditional practice which people would be expected to respect. Hoisting flags to celebrate festivals, standing for national anthems, dressing in black to express mourning, wearing a wedding ring on a given finger, holding welcome receptions, bestowing honourific titles, wearing national and regional costumes or indulging in conduct associated with certain political ideologies – all these are customary practices the violation of which is deemed improper and offensive to public sensibility. Yet, according to the French school of sociology, these 'etiquettes' and 'protocols' could legitimately be admitted as religious and devotional practices.

***

To remove this ambiguity, it does not suffice to say that the religious idea thrives on 'the conviction that not everything in existence is of the same nature, or of equal rank, but that some beings are more noble and elevated than others'.[24] While this qualitative disparity of beings may be present in the realm of religion, it is also observed elsewhere – for example, when some nation is persuaded that it is of purer extraction, or of nobler stock, and therefore more worthy of world leadership. With this approach, things go haywire, and to distinguish between the religious fact and other fields becomes very difficult indeed. This is why we wanted, from the outset, to fix the meaning of concepts and to delimit the exact field of application so that no one meaning infringes on another.

---

[24] See Abd al-Raziq (Shaykh), *Revelation, Religion and Islam*, pp. 28–9. This distinction is also found among Western authors, see Laland, *Vocabulaire Technique et critique de la philosophie*, p. 705.

2

Religion, morality, philosophy and science

Religion and morality

The relationship between religion and morality can be studied from two angles: either from an abstract theoretical angle, which considers these relations as they *could* or as they *should* be, or from an empirical and historical angle, which studies *how* these relations were, and are, maintained in reality.

At a theoretical level, we could, in some sense, consider religion and morality either as two totally independent facts or as two closely related notions.

That is to say, if we regard religion as the knowledge and veneration of a higher truth, and morality as the propensity to do good and to restrain one's instincts, we will end up with two independent concepts, each of them perfectly conceivable without the other. The first pertains to theoretical virtue, the second to practical virtue. Now, if practical virtue is concerned with man's relation with himself, with the rest of creation, and with God, a complete moral law must therefore dictate man's attitude towards the divine as much as it must define man's attitude towards his fellow human beings.

Likewise, if we accept that a developed religious idea cannot be satisfied with conceiving divinity only as an active governing principle, but also as a source of authority and legislation, it will appear that a complete religious law cannot limit itself to describing higher abstract truths, calling people to revere and worship them, without extending to the realm of practical life and instating the moral path that the individual and society have a duty to follow.

Thus, religious law, if it means to be complete, will have to include not only the established principles of morality but also the laws governing relations among humans and among nations. These laws, now endowed with a sense of sanctity, become an integral part of its reality. Respect for moral precepts, both individual and social, will then be experienced as a form of obedience to religious commandments, a pious action and ritual devotion, thereby warranting social justice and attending to humanity's natural instinct for virtue and righteousness.

Religion and morality, which first appeared to us as two entities with differentiated vocations and contents, would now seem to be ultimately interconnected, each, in its own way, advancing into the territory of the other, like two neighbouring trees growing in the shade of their extending and interweaving branches. It must be recognized, however, that in everyday life we seldom see morality and religion reach such a degree of harmony and mutual accolade. This is neither the case when they first appear in the minds of individuals, nor when they are applied in the form of laws and rules established in society. At the individual level, this is clearly manifested in children and adolescents in whom the moral sense precedes, and is more instinctive than, religious consciousness. We see how children approve certain behaviours and condemn others, out of modesty and aversion, and without sensing the need to rationalize natural phenomena or sanctify the mystery of creation. Both the latter tend to emerge at a later phase of intellectual development, when young minds are more mature, serene, attentive and observant. At the societal level, too, we find that the harmony between moral and religious laws is far from being achieved universally or across epochs and milieus. Indeed, many moral laws have appeared in history without referring to any divine revelation or religious inspiration. They are based, instead, on rational thought, on the dictates of conscience, on social conventions, according to a specific interest or benefit and so on. Conversely, we see certain religious groups which, oblivious to the practical and social aspect of morality, turn their followers into individuals withdrawn into themselves, plunged into solitude, silence and deep meditation.

Certainly, recognizing the truth and glorifying it cannot, for the most part, do without an external appearance that expresses it. This is why religious sentiment often feels the need for a concrete element that acts as a focal point between religion and morality. This is realized, at the very least, in the realm of divinity and in the duties and practices we call worship. However, sometimes the meaning of these outward manifestations can fade, even disappear, causing feelings of emptiness and casting doubt in the hearts of believers who have lost sight of how to approach the unfathomable mystery. The faith of the Hanifs of pre-Islamic Arabia is a good example. Ibn Hisham reports that one of these pious men, named Zayd ibn Amr ibn Nufayl, while leaning his back against the Ka'ba, was heard to say, 'O God, if I knew how you wished to be worshipped, I would so worship you; but I do not know how.'[1]

It remains now for us to inquire into what is really meant by the terms 'religion' and 'morality' in contemporary discourse. Here, too, we will notice that these two signifiers are used sometimes with such flexibility that they seem to overlap, and sometimes with a rigidity that separates them from each other, thus making the precise definition of their respective referents all the more difficult. It does seem, nevertheless, that these words still follow the common rules of the Arabic language regarding words of the same family, such as *ra'fa* (clemency) and *rahma* (mercy), *birr* (good doing) and *taqwa* (piety), *iman* (faith) and *islam* (submission) and so on. When these twin terms are used in the same expression, their meanings tend to diverge, whereas if they are used separately, they are more likely to become synonymous. If we say, *'fulan dhou din wa khuluq'* (so-and-so is a man of faith and good morals), each of the two terms will necessarily refer to a different meaning, distinct from that of its next of kin; otherwise, we fall into redundancy and wordiness. In this expression, the word *din* (religion) refers to the divine, and the word *khuluq* (good morals) refers to the domain of human relations. The word *din* will therefore signify faith and private piety – that is to say, fulfilling the duties of worship – and the word *khuluq* the respect for virtues and social niceties.

But if we limit ourselves to saying, 'So-and-so is a man of religion', and if the religion we are referring to supposes a moral standard, then the word 'religion' will also encompass the meaning of its, albeit absent, next of kin – social morality. Only then will the term 'religion' be broad enough to include the full meaning of absolute piety – that is to say, the fulfilment of all duties and obligations, whether divinely prescribed or socially constructed.

The same applies if we are satisfied in saying, 'So-and-so is a man of morals', and if 'morality' here is understood as a catchall term for all the duties one owes to God and to other humans. It must be pointed out, however, that even if the term 'moral' encompassed a very wide spectrum of meanings,

---

[1] Ibn Hisham, *al-Sira al-nabawiyya*, vol. 1, p. 144.

it would not be a synonym for the word 'religion'. The latter will always be distinguished by an essential theoretical element that cannot be ignored, even if other religious concepts can be. It is the recognition of God and of the faith that is placed in him. These abstract elements are extraneous to the concept of morality because it tends to be, for the most part, practical by nature. And even if morality sometimes draws on faith and religious influence, it does so to gain additional support and credence and not to make them essential components of its true nature. Morality could very well, as already mentioned, dispense with this 'religious support' and replace it with other influences – for example, the voice of conscience. Then, as both differ in their tendencies and respective goals, morality retains no more than a superficial resemblance to religion.

Religion and philosophy

If there is a form of human knowledge that parallels religion more than any other, and which forms a privileged and unrivalled part of its immediate family, it is what scholars commonly call general philosophy, or knowledge in the absolute.

Is not the domain of philosophy the same as that of religion? Is not the problem posed by philosophy the one that religions are tasked with solving? Their common goals are the understanding of the origin and destiny of existence as well as the quest for human happiness in this life and in the hereafter. Furthermore, these two goals are represented not only by the two main subdivisions of philosophy – the theoretical and the practical – but also in the full sense of religion, which comprises fundamental principles and practical applications.

At any rate, even if related fields of inquiry share similar objectives, this does not mean that they will necessarily reach the same conclusions. Just as different religions[2] have diverged in their formulated solutions to the big questions,

---

[2] Clearly, this discussion concerns all religions in general and not specifically 'revealed' religions, whose differences did not extend to general principles or fundamental laws. When disagreements occurred in the latter, albeit infrequently, they were born of erroneous understandings and anomalous interpretations.

philosophical systems have often found themselves in disagreement, and their differences have in fact been more profound than those among religions.

Obviously, our objective is not to inspect the causes of the internal conflicts within philosophy or religion. Rather, it is only to study the factors that set the two camps apart, to the point that they have become distinctly named and impossible to confuse.

In order to probe into the causes of separation between religion and philosophy, we must shift our focus from studying their similar goals and shared substance and limit ourselves to examining the conclusions which each of them has reached on its own.

Let us clarify that we could not possibly come up with a final recipe that attempts to determine, once and for all, either their communion or their sharp separation. Many philosophical schools have been led by their independent reflection to confirming the principles proclaimed by religions, while others, on the contrary, tend to break away from them either at the start of their reflection or shortly thereafter.

The fiercest and most relentless distancing from religion came from materialist philosophies for which what exists is only that which is met by sense and perception, thus rejecting the fundamental (spiritual) principle on which all religions are based, and which is admitted by other philosophical schools as well.

Moreover, certain spiritual philosophies, while sharing with religions the belief in the existence of an all-powerful creator, could only admit to the relation between this creator and the world in a restrictive way that makes them fall behind all religions. And in doing so, they forego two essential elements of religion:

1. The origin of creation – that is, the generation of matter *ex nihilo*: While all religions agree on this principle, some philosophers in ancient Greece argued that the spirit that made the universe did not initiate its substance, but, having found the elements of nature chaotically scattered, only rearranged them into the perfect designs that we know. God was not, in their view, the creator, but only the master maker, the demiurge.[3]

---

[3] This is the name given to the creator by Plato and the Platonists.

2. Divine lordship – that is, the creator's continued care towards his creation: Religions are founded on the veneration of a higher power that controls everyday life, constantly attentive and unceasingly sustaining all beings. This vital principle is at the root of the idea of worship, and without it the word 'religion' would have no meaning. However, not all philosophies that believe in the divine admit of this aspect of 'lordship'. Some of them maintain that the creator of the world is nothing more than a distant first cause who cares nothing for his creation past the point of completion. The first cause relates to our universe, they conclude, like an architect who, after drawing up the plans and building the structure, needs no longer interfere in its internal organization or in its maintenance.[4]

Let us leave aside this brand of philosophy, which lags behind the march of religion, and try instead to examine philosophies that share with religions their focus and fundamental elements. Will their points of convergence lead to complete unity? Can we say that they are in fact identical disciplines bearing only different names?

Alas, we are far from that, and the points of divergence between religion and philosophy remain numerous. Some scholars have argued that these discrepancies arise from simple differences in approach and methods of reflection, others from their heterogeneous sources and references and still others from their dissimilar historical experiences and circumstances. For our part, we see much deeper causes that stem from significant disparities in their basic constitutive elements.

Let us begin with the opinions of early scholars on the matter and conclude with our personal point of view on this debate.

Al-Farabi declares that, for the ancient Greeks, the word 'philosophy' denotes the science that tries to know the reality of things in themselves without recourse to allegory. This science seeks to establish the existence of

---

[4] Epicurus famously claimed that the gods lived an idyllic life of pleasure and bliss, and that they had no relation with earthly life. This is why, he said, it is useless to seek their favours or fear their wrath. Conversely, Plato argued that there were two kinds of heresies: that which consists in denying the existence of the gods, and that which, admitting their existence, claims that the gods are indifferent to human affairs. He then applied himself to rationally demonstrating the invalidity and corruption of these opinions (Platon, *Les Lois*, bk 10, p. 900.

things by rational proofs and not by persuasion, unlike religions, which use conviction and allegorical representations.

This description, while it holds true for some religions, does not apply to all of them. Islam, for instance, integrates in its teachings the methods of rational demonstration and verification with persuasion and allegory. Ibn Rushd (Averroes) confirms this fact when he practically applies these methods and ways to many problems and debates in his *Decisive Treatise on the Harmony of Religion and Philosophy*. After establishing that the dispositions to assent to the truths of faith are indeed manifold (while some humans are persuaded by definite proofs, others are inclined to give as much credence to legends as they do to irrefutable facts, while others still will only be convinced through the power of rhetoric), Ibn Rushd adds,

> Thus since this divine religion of ours has summoned people by these three methods, assent to it has extended to everyone, except him who stubbornly denies it with his tongue or him for whom no method of summons to God the Exalted has been appointed in religion owing to his own neglect of such matters. It was for this purpose that the Prophet, peace on him, was sent with a special mission to 'the white man and the black man' alike; I mean because his religion embraces all the methods of summons to God the Exalted. This is clearly expressed in the saying of God the Exalted, 'Summon to the way of your Lord by wisdom and by good preaching, and debate with them in the most effective manner.'[5]

He goes on to say in the same work, 'For if the precious Book is inspected, there will be found in it the three methods that are available for all the people, namely the common methods for the instruction of the majority of the people and the special method.'[6]

It cannot be claimed, therefore, that *all* religions have recourse only to allegory and oratorical style and never to demonstration or reasoning. On the other hand, it is also wrong to suggest that philosophical teachings are invariably based on the light of reason and irrefutable evidence. If this were the case, all their internal contradictions and disputes would have been impossible

---

[5] Ibn Rushd, *Facl al-Maqal*, p. 8 [See Hourani, 1976. Ed.].
[6] Ibid., p. 30.

because truth cannot contradict or impede another truth; on the contrary, it can only support and endorse it.

These disagreements and contradictions will only prove that no single philosophical school should have the final word on absolute truth. At most, they either imply that each one of these philosophies contains one part of a compound truth, or that one philosophy leads to truth and all the others are wayward and invalid, or simply that absolute truth lies elsewhere, beyond them all. To know which of these the case is, we would have to engage in a close analysis of each doctrine and cross-examine all arguments presented therein.

Now, we already know, through careful inference and by experience, that most of these philosophical opinions are in reality hypotheses and conjunctures that operate in the unruly space of the possible and the contingent. Differences among them stem from varying degrees of the quality of presentation, internal coherence, richness of imagination and eloquence of style. Above all, they do not (necessarily) reside in the rational bases of their arguments, nor in the solidity of the proofs they put forward. These theories, by and large, do not go beyond the artifice employed by poets – appealing to emotion, enchanting the heart, without having to satisfy our need for certainty or to resolve a debate through complete proofs.

This alleged criterion of distinction between religion and philosophy is therefore irrelevant. Let us consider another. According to Ibn Sina (Avicenna), although philosophy and religion share a common definition of the True and the Good, they diverge over the amount of attention each of them gives to these two principles. 'Divine Law', he says, 'delivers the basics of practical virtue in the complete, ultimate sense, while it only provides a few rudiments of theoretical wisdom, as if to attract our attention to it. It leaves the attainment of the complete and perfect understanding of wisdom to our own rational thought.'[7]

This observation, unlike that reported by al-Farabi, applies perfectly to the Islamic *sharia*, which, while exhaustively delineating practical morality, only tackles theoretical principles in a subtle and partial manner. But does this hold true in all revealed canons, let alone the rest of the religions of the world? It is quite clear that the importance given by religions to the practical side exceeds

---

[7] Ibn Sina, 'Book of natural philosophy', in *al-Shifa*, pp. 2–3.

that accorded to theoretical principles. Nevertheless, some philosophical schools remain almost completely dominated by practical concerns.[8] As such, this criterion is unsustainable and cannot be taken as an adequate distinction between the teachings of religion, on the one hand, and philosophy, on the other.

Contemporary Western thinkers point out other differences between religion and philosophy:

1. The problems of philosophy are exclusively pursued by unique individuals with superior intellects, while religious matters may be openly pondered by the popular masses. This is why the origins of religions, the lives of their founders and the circumstances of the appearance of their books remain shrouded in mystery, buried in the darkness of the past – contrary to the historical facts of philosophy.
2. People receive religion as an inheritance, while the philosopher derives his theories from his own thought and personal observation, without caring whether they adhere to, or indeed contradict, the inherited beliefs of the ancestors.
3. Philosophical thought evolves, while religion tends to permanence and therefore to immobility because people abhor change and refuse to reconsider their convictions, especially if they are assured that the texts of their religions are words of divine origin.
4. In societies, religion always takes precedence over philosophy, not least because it is imbued with a sense of antiquity, which carves out a special place for religion in the popular imagination, and because it tends to appeal to anyone, no matter what their mental calibre, and is therefore embraced by the masses.
5. Religion cannot dispense with collective, social expressions of faith and seasonal festivals, which serve to solidify the sympathetic bond between individuals and their co-religionists. It also requires representative images and recognizable symbols that allow the believer to renew his allegiance to faith – since they are often threatened by neglect and oblivion due to the materialistic nature of everyday life. Philosophy, on the other hand, does not need these symbolic expressions and assemblages because the conviction of the philosopher mostly resides in his heart. This conviction

---

[8] This is evident, for example, in Socratic philosophy.

cannot be represented by signs or forms of ritualized worship because these have no referent in the demonstrative schemes of reason. If, by any chance, a philosopher enacted similar formalities and made them symbolic expressions of his thought, he would surely devolve into eccentricity and buffoonery and justly expose himself to ridicule.
6. Religion can only survive protected by authority, like that of the State, while philosophy can only live in an atmosphere of total freedom.

Let us reflect on these statements. It is already evident that these differences between religion and philosophy only retrace the historical evolution with an incomplete vision of the past. More precisely, they tend to describe the prevailing condition in Christian Europe. They speak about religions inherited from the past, but only at the moment of their maturation and stability, when people had adopted them, made them a glorious part of their history and had ensured the protection of powerful churches, having forgotten the tragic time of their birth. Philosophy, on the other hand, is portrayed as emerging from the mind of the philosopher, marked by the seals of his own intelligence, dispositions, and feelings, free from all shackles and capable, at any moment, of appearing in a new guise.

It stands to reason that by thus making a sharp comparison, one can only end up with contrasting images: Religion appears as a stable social fact and philosophy as self-assured and dynamic individualism. In this view, it would be reasonable to say that 'religion is the philosophy of the popular masses' and that 'philosophy is the religion of exceptional and superior individuals'. Yet if we go back to the time when these same religions first saw the light or when they went through their reforms, will we not see the mark of strong individualism in figures such as Moses, Buddha, Jesus, Mani, Mohammad, Luther, Abdul-Wahhab and others? The pagan religions themselves were not bereft of leaders who laid new foundations and who elaborated their schemes either by trickery or fabrication or, as historians teach us, by appropriating new images of deities from foreign lands.

The fact that some people are ignorant of the life and times of the founder of their religion does not necessarily indicate that this religion was an invention of their own, or of a former generation. All we can say is that these people simply do not know whence this heritage came. Of course, over time, this spiritual legacy could well be more or less altered or reworked, thus becoming a sort of amorphous vestige of the past, a patchwork attributed to different individuals which people eventually endorse for better or for worse. But if we go back in time, we will not fail to arrive at a single originator who can neither be the whole population nor even a select group from it. If not, let us have one historical instance where a single people, wholly or represented by their notables, decided to come together to decree the creation of a new religious system, with all its beliefs and rituals, starting from nothing and without the slightest reference to an ancestor or to any instructive text that serves as the genesis of their studies and reflections.

As for the assertion that the biographies of the founders of religions are always obscure and imprecise, as well as the dates and circumstances in which their books were produced, this is certainly contradicted by the example of Islam, its book and its prophet. There they are, luscious and green as if born yesterday. Western scholars themselves readily recognize this with honest impartiality, even if they might consider Islam at this point to be an exception among religions. In reality, what Islam should be considered an exception to is the unparalleled historical transparency and reliability of the detailed references and connected authorities through which its book has been transmitted. As regards the general historicity of the founders of religions, as well as the entirety of their teachings, Islam is by no means the only religion to preserve such detailed accounts. And even if it were, this exception alone would be insufficient to demonstrate that the difference between the allegedly ambiguous origin of religion and the clear-cut birth of philosophy is false and irrelevant. Just as religions, once established, are said to stand still until the coming of revivers or reformers, we can say that the same applies to philosophical theories. Physical and natural sciences themselves have known periods of stagnation, and their revival was often met with fierce resistance. How many inventors and discoverers have been accused of madness by political establishments or by the scientific circles themselves!

As concerns the point about social expressions of faith through rituals, it would seem to rightly apply to religions, but only once they have reached the stage of complete development. It certainly cannot be extended to individual religious feelings, which murmur mysteriously in the intimacy of hearts and whose bearers do not know how to express them. We have seen this in the case of the Hanifs, those believers before Islam. Similar individuals have always existed in communities yet to receive the teachings of revealed religion. Some people, discontented with the aberrant beliefs and deviant customs that prevail around them, find themselves helplessly searching for a fixed framework that would allow their faith to be expressed. They are strangers among their own people. Nothing inspires them to be out in public, and nothing moves them to agree on a common hymn or a unified gesture that would become the outward manifestation of their faith in gestation. Furthermore, the argument concerning rituals and other social phenomena does not apply to all popular religions. Early Buddhism, for example, knew nothing other than solitary retreat and spiritual concentration and was far removed from any kind of outward and collective display of faith. On the other hand, we can see certain philosophers (like Auguste Comte, e.g.) adorning their theories with a kind of ritual symbolism observed in the prevailing religions of their time. Here, yet again, is another distinction between philosophy and religion that fails at both ends.

It remains to examine the last point, which affirms that philosophy can only live in an atmosphere of freedom, while religion can only take root under the protection of powerful authority. This statement is true only in a general sense and not in an absolute one. Yet it is precisely by extracting this very assertion that we will succeed in identifying the real difference between philosophy and religion: If the assertion implies that religion only survives thanks to the support of the State and its power, it would surely be a false claim. We know of many religions that have been able to live and prosper thanks to the tolerance of indifferent authorities that kept them away from power. Buddhism is an example, but also Christianity and Islam, at least at the beginning of their preaching. These religions spread because they endorsed freedom of conscience and of belief. However, we also know of philosophies which, having assumed the reins of power, were up in arms to pursue and track down their adversaries and subject them to their yoke.

This formula could suggest that religion depends on collective moral authority, whereby, under its hegemony, social life is inevitably cast in the same mold, condemned to a uniform mindset, to a single idea and to identical beliefs and customs, and that any nonconformity would bring about rebuke and dishonour. If we accept this, then we must also be prepared to admit that this description can only faintly apply to the social life of certain 'primitive' peoples living in isolation and not to all societies at large. We can indeed see around us, and in every age, nations and communities that shelter under their wings different beliefs and canons. This, however, in no way prevented people from cooperating in the service of the common good, or from joining forces towards the fulfilment of national duty.

But if this formula wants to express the idea that the hold of religion is so strong that it imposes itself on the souls of those who embrace it, then there is no doubt that this is, in fact, the exclusive monopoly of religion, a monopoly which philosophy cannot hope to achieve, because it would then overstep its bounds and contradict its own principles. Philosophy, inasmuch as it is 'love of wisdom' and 'the desire for knowledge alone', thus has as its role the search for truth, to the best of human ability, and the presentation of the outcomes of this search. Now, philosophers are the first to recognize the limits of human reason and the fact that all things human fall short of perfection. That is why tolerance and humility have always been among their primary virtues. The best example of this modesty comes from Socrates, who declared, 'I know one thing, that I know nothing.' In contrast, any religious idea, because founded on mystery, presupposes that all its prescribed instructions emanate from the transcendent secret of the universe and therefore represent the true reality of things. Religion is binding by nature. It demands from the one who embraces it an attitude of submission and surrender. It accepts neither controversy nor opposition about its judgement, nor indeed uncertainty or hesitation as to its entity. If someone were to allow himself such questioning, his attitude would cease to be that of a believer, but be that of a philosopher, until he settled on a perspective whose validity he accepts as a matter of belief. He embraces it in extraordinary faith, accepts no compromise and is willing to sacrifice his own life for its sake. Thus, it seems impossible to find in the world another power, whether political, scientific or so on, which can have a hold on people similar to that of religion.

If we want to refine our analysis and find an explanation for this curious phenomenon, we will find it, on the one hand, in the difference between scientific knowledge and faith and, on the other, in the varying limits of the human role in the quest for both.

Each of us can have an idea about hunger and thirst without needing to feel their pangs, can know the meanings of love and passion without ever falling in love or can ponder a beautiful work of art and understand its masterly techniques without being touched by its beauty or even truly admiring it. You can recognize in a person forms of wisdom and prudence, refinement and finesse or all of these at the same time, without feeling towards him or her loyalty or a bond of love. You could, on the contrary, be permeated by spite and envy and even deny the virtues that your eyes clearly see. All of these are types of knowledge provided to us by the senses, by reflection, by surmise or by intuition. Our mind can see the facts, but they remain foreign, or like fleeting moments, unable to penetrate into the depths of our feelings. We can observe them without having to assimilate them or make them our own. Every psychology that ignores these ideas and principles beyond the thin façade of observation does so because it is driven by an attitude that has no relation to faith. This is a form of knowledge whose echo resonates within conscience and in the intimacy of hearts, without feeling any embarrassment or distress, but rather a kind of tranquillity and peace. Faith is at the same time knowledge and sensitivity. It transmits its object from the heights of reason to the depths of souls. It turns it into a source of nourishment that permeates the inner self and makes it an integral element of its existence.

And since the object of faith is directed towards transcendent Truth and ideal virtue, this idea will then transform into a powerful drive, a dynamic and creative force which tends towards its goal, unimpeded by every obstacle that might stand in its way.

This is one of the real differences that distinguishes religion from philosophy. Knowledge is the real goal of philosophy, and faith is the real goal of religion. Philosophy seeks a dry idea represented by fixed formulations, whereas religion seeks an exuberant spirit and a mobilizing force.

However, we will not follow those who say that philosophy appeals to reason while religion appeals only to the heart and emotions without taking into account the principles of logic and the laws of science. Neither do we agree with St. Augustine when he says, 'I believe because it is absurd' (*credo quia absurdum*). This statement simply does not apply to all religions. Let us rather say that religion only surrenders to the proofs of reason when these are ratified by a confiding heart.

Philosophy, therefore, acts only on a part of human nature, whereas religion takes hold of it entirely. Philosophy is observation, analysis and synthesis; it is a technique that dismembers the body of truth and attempts to fashion from the lifeless parts a new artificial design to be contemplated by human acumen, and which ends up covering the mind with a dry layer. Religion is a traveller's chant, a hymn that carries with it the whole truth. It crosses the superficial layers of being and plunges into the depths of the soul, which offers itself entirely and surrenders its reins of power.

From this we can deduce another subtle difference between religion and philosophy. The objective of philosophy is theoretical, even in its practical part, while religion maintains a practical objective, even in its theoretical considerations. The ultimate pursuit of philosophy is to teach us what the True and the Good are, and where they can be found. What we do with these theoretical truths and virtues is of no concern to philosophy. Religion, on the other hand, not only claims to make us recognize them but also, above all, to make us love and glorify them. It instructs our obligations and urges us to practice them totally and faithfully so that our souls may advance on the path to perfection.

The first of the practical effects of the religious idea is that it draws the attention of the believer to the existence of a relation between himself and the transcendent Truth in which he places his faith. This relationship is based on moral obligation and obedience. Philosophy, precisely because it is 'philosophy' (I mean because it relies on human reason alone, without any appeal to mysticism or emotions), can live without recognizing this relation. The objective of the philosopher, by relating effects to their causes, is to understand things in a logical and rational way so that each element in existence occupies its rightful place. The higher power, which the philosopher posits at the top of the cosmic chain of cause and effect, can adequately assume the role of an artisan with respect to the object he makes, as a captain steers his ship. It is a mechanical, external relation which leaves no room for communication or for supplication, and in which we will never see a philosopher, as in the case of religion, addressing his Unmoved Mover with love and deference or with fear and anticipation. All these are elements without which the concept of religion would lose all its meaning. Religion, in fact, is not only faith and knowledge. It is a reciprocal spiritual consideration, a bond made of obedience and loyalty, of sympathy and care, between the believer and the higher entity in which he believes.

We now understand, in view of the above, why scholars of religion invariably refuse to apply the term 'religion' to the cult which appeared in the eighteenth century under the name of 'natural religion', and which can be summed up in three principles: the existence of a creator God, the immortality of the soul and the supremacy of moral duty. However, as long as it lacks the spiritual bond between man and his creator, its declared principles of faith lose the necessary condition to warrant the name of religion, and remain, at most, a form of dry philosophy.

Another practical aspect of religion is its tendency towards social engagement. Faith is by nature a generous and overflowing feeling which tends to spread, to call for participation and which prompts the faithful to make their faith known through missions and preaching. By contrast, scientific or philosophical ideas, like all human riches, favour retention, avarice and monopoly. Philosophy, at the very least, lacks a natural propensity to spread, nor does it care whether or not it is understood by the masses. Perhaps we would not be wrong to say that the difference between these two ideas is similar to that which separates democracy and aristocracy. Thus, if you ever see a philosopher proselytizing and zealously recruiting adherents to his theories, rest assured that his idea has turned into faith. He will have renounced the habit of philosophers and assumed the burden of prophets and messengers. Conversely, if you see a believer withdrawn into himself, indifferent to the deviations and social corruption that surround him, you can conclude that the flame of his faith is buried under heaps of ash, or that it has itself been reduced to ashes.

All these considerations have helped us differentiate between philosophy and religion in general. But if we wish to ascertain the distinction between philosophy and revealed religion in particular, we will discover an additional element with which we will close our deliberation on the differences between the two facts.

Philosophy is, above all, a human effort subject to all the limits and constrains inherent in human nature – an arduous progress towards the unknown, beset by the prospects of change and degeneration, wavering between certainty and perplexity, nearness and distance from the desired goal. Revealed religion, on the other hand, is a heavenly handiwork that possesses all the attributes of the divine – a truth whose words do not change[9] and whose rigorous authenticity falsehood cannot touch from any angle.[10] It is, above all, a 'free gift' offered to its recipients and emissaries without effort or toil, quickly engulfing them in light, like the blink of an eye, or even quicker.[11]

If philosophy decided to work alone, it could not be safeguarded against error. But if reason accorded with revelation, the torches of the night would join in the brightness of day.

Light upon light, God guides whoever He will to his Light. 24:35

Religion and the sciences

Thus far, we have seen the degrees of affinity with which religion, philosophy and morality are united, and how they remain united through undeniable bonds of kinship. Now, if the value of human effort is measured by the nobility of its objectives, to what nobler end could the seeker be devoted than the quest after the supreme Truth which outlasts the vanishing creation, or the absolute Good which, immeasurable in itself, is the measure of everything?

These are indeed the great values and the superior virtues towards which the mind cannot imagine a more noble effort than one devoted to their study. Most human activities, whether intellectual, physical or spiritual, pursue relative objectives whose value and nobility vary according to how close they draw to those higher ideals. The scientist who spends a lifetime developing new varieties of animal feed, for example, will be readily recognized as having a certain role in the preservation of human society, even if in a roundabout way. By preserving the quality of livestock, on which the physical fitness of people depends, he indirectly determines their thoughts and attitudes towards faith, which ultimately dictates their perfect spiritual happiness. Likewise, the objectives pursued by the manifold sciences could be classified according to a scale that begins with sciences whose sole objective is one of utility, through to objectives that serve and are served by other sciences to varying degrees,

---

[9] Qur'an 10:64. (Ed.)
[10] Qur'an 41:42. (Ed.)
[11] Qur'an 16:77. (Ed.)

until it reaches the science which devotes itself to the transcendent ideal, an objective which is served by all.

Now, if we cease to classify the sciences according to the 'nobility' of the ends they pursue but rather according to the progressive complexity of their programs and the widening extent of the scope of their inquiry, we will again end up with a gradual scale that takes us from the lowest to the highest. Each stage, while retaining the conclusions of the previous one, adds others that are specific to it. Vegetative growth, for example, supposes the existence of material substances, their elements, their molecules, their atoms, their energies and includes others of its own. The animal life cycle contains all the structures of vegetation and enriches them with others. Likewise, the human being takes up the rudiments of the preceding domains and adds others which themselves comprise gradations that overlap one another, and of which the highest is, without a doubt, the spiritual activity aspiring towards transcendent Truth.

This preamble will allow us to ascertain the kind of relation that knowledge of the divine maintains with the sciences. Certainly, we cannot claim that it is thematic unity of contents that brings together religion and the sciences, be they physical, mathematical, astronomical, psychological, economic, logical, sociological, historical, linguistic and so on. Neither can it be claimed that it is an identity of goals, since no science sets out to deal with the major problem that religion vows to undertake. In fact, all that the sciences inquire into are the created beings, without worrying about either their primary source or their final destiny. All, however, can serve this higher purpose in one way or another. It must be pointed out that religion can do without the sciences as the end could do without the means leading to it, or that the assertions might forgo the arguments supporting them. Just as the unknown can only be conceived of through the known, and the invisible can only be imagined in relation to the visible, we can only attain higher truths by climbing the ladder of those truths that concern our lower physical world.

Certain sciences may appear to have only a distant relation with religion, unable to help religious contemplation in any tangible way. It is, however, indisputable that by their struggle against ignorance and illusions, and because of their shining light that enlightens our mind, the sciences enable a process of mental purification and catharsis much needed for religious beliefs to be rooted in solid intellectual grounds. For even if faith wins our conviction, it must be able to do so on the basis of a clear vision and sound evidence, away from fierce ignorance and naive imitation.

How can those who know be equal to those who do not know? 39:9

Even if we accept that full cooperation between religion and the sciences is more or less untenable, one could at least hope that they maintain between them a semblance of tolerance and good-neighbourliness of the kind that exists, for example, among the craftsmen of various guilds. Indeed, as long as they exclusively pursue different objectives, they cannot be said to be competitors, and therefore any opposition or animosity among them is rather inconceivable.

And yet everyone is aware of the violent quarrels between religion and science that have occurred time and again throughout recorded history. We do not speak here of those superficial conflicts whereby fortune, influence, power and other material objectives or ulterior motives were sought under disingenuous banners of religion and science. Nor do we wish to recall those persistent clashes that have always set defenders of noble spiritual principles – which encourage the sacrifice of oneself, the control of one's inclinations and the search for one's equilibrium – against their materialist opponents who aim to establish laxity, anarchy and greed. Rather, what we wish to discuss here, and seek an understanding of, are the intellectual debates in which each of the two parties applied itself in good faith to criticizing the position of the other.

To better answer this, we argue that these clashes occur in two ways.

In the first, we observe that each party takes to systematically invalidating everything that the other puts forward. This is often done readily and arbitrarily, without recourse to convincing arguments, and without pointing to logical flaws – as if anything which does not enter within the framework of its own knowledge does not exist. To deny that which we do not understand – or whose explanation has yet to be grasped[12] – is not an attitude worthy of those firmly grounded in knowledge,[13] whether they are men of science or men of religion. It is, assuredly, that of conceited and presumptuous minds, of the semi-educated, who are far more dangerous than the ignorant masses,

---

[12] Qur'an 10:39. (Ed.)
[13] Qur'an 3:7. (Ed.)

for their false knowledge is in fact compound ignorance. True impartiality requires that everyone be conscious of their limits and endeavour not to go beyond them, to bring objective and constructive criticism into the debate. It also requires everyone to keep an open mind towards new methods and arguments they may not have considered before.

Every day we see scientists who specialize in a given field, whether natural or rational, incorporate the findings of those who work in other sciences. They do not task themselves with redoing all the experiments or re-verifying all calculations. For if it were otherwise, the sciences would not have moved a single step on the path of progress.

Such, too, should be the relationship between scientists and the practitioners of religions.

Do not all scientists believe in the fission of the atomic nucleus, for example, and in the possibility of putting the mass of energy thus produced into astonishing practical applications, when none of them, except for a few individuals, actually witnessed the experiment? Why then should we doubt the existence of the spiritual feats of prophets and visionary sages that have recurred throughout the history of humanity and of which we have before our eyes the indisputable traces?

It is the duty of religions to peacefully coexist with the sciences without neglecting or rejecting them. It is in their interest to take advantage of all human knowledge and to arm themselves with the results of their researches. Likewise, it would be just as well for the sciences to let spiritual truths compensate for their shortcomings and to fill the void of discontent they leave in the human soul – or, at least, for them to adopt an impartial attitude towards religions by refraining from attacking them or denying them altogether. For to reject religions as a whole is to reject all the observed facts contained in them – chief among them the belief in a higher truth that is sanctified and glorified by believers – and which no science can grasp. 'But religion exists,' writes Durkheim, 'It is a system of given facts; in a word, it is a reality. How could science deny a reality? ... Science cannot take its place, since if it expresses life, it does not create it. It may well seek to explain the faith, but by that very fact it presupposes it.'[14]

---

[14] Durkheim, *Formes élémentaires*, p. 614.

The second instance is when religions and sciences provide contradictory answers to precisely the same questions. This happens when religions, trespassing beyond their spiritual purpose, tackle scientific problems or concrete observations verified by researchers, and adopt particular positions about them they then decide to force their adherents to accept. Although this attitude is marginal and rare on the part of religions, and religions tend to have recourse to it as a means to an end, it could still be retained as a criterion; one could measure the degree of soundness or deficiency in a given religion according to how far it adheres to the proven conclusions of the sciences and the sound assertions of reason.

If religion and science live up to their respective share of the truth, they should support and confirm each other. However, if their relationship is one of distrust and betrayal, they will, almost certainly, accuse each other of deviance and falsehood.

3

Humanity's natural religious inclination

Some questions persist more than others and call for satisfactory answers: When did the first form of religion appear on earth? What is the future of religion in the face of the evolution of scientific thought? What is the influence of faith on the human psyche? What function does religion have in society?

The antiquity of religions

Can we date the appearance of the first form of religiosity on earth? Did the religious phenomenon precede all forms of material civilization? Did it succeed them? Were they concomitant?

Some eighteenth-century writers, precursors of the French Revolution, have argued that religions, as well as laws, were relatively recent innovations and that their appearance was only incidental. Voltaire wrote that the human race must have lived a purely material life based on agriculture, stone cutting, ironwork and woodcraft before considering religious or spiritual matters.[1] He went so far as to assert that the idea of divinity itself was merely the invention of cunning, deceitful churchmen and priests who found men simple and foolish enough to believe them.[2]

A similar view was held by Jean-Jacques Rousseau, who maintained that the notion of laws served no purpose except that of practical governance. He explained that often the individuals who first seize control of the land tend to be driven by their avarice and lust for power to conspire among themselves

---

[1] Voltaire, *Essai sur les moeurs*, p. 14.
[2] Ibid., p. 133.

to establish laws and regulations the sole purpose of which is to deceive the masses and to exploit the poor.[3]

This cynical look at religions and laws is nothing new. It echoes an age-old impudence, a pastime of the Greek Sophists, for example, who propagated such views to sow doubts and fallacies in the minds of their audiences. The Sophists claimed,

> There was a time when there were no laws, no restraints, and no morals. Men obeyed only by brute force. Later, with the emergence of laws, public disorder tended to disappear. But if the obvious injustice could be repressed by laws, secret crimes were no less numerous. It was then that ingenious mortal minds succeeded in making the masses believe in an immortal genius who resides in the firmament, and who sees everything, hears everything, and directs everything with prudence.[4]

Thus was the view of the Sophists, who saw laws and religions as nothing other than shrewd designs whose sole purpose is to remedy the unavoidable ailments of social life.

The late revival and dissemination of these ancient theories across Europe were enabled by, on the one hand, the increasing moral degeneration among a faction of church leaders and, on the other, the inherent injustice of existing laws and the unequal distribution of wealth. It was then easy for the gullible masses to be persuaded that both religion and State laws had always been this way.

However, even before the eighteenth century drew to a close, these assertions began to be contradicted by the numerous scientific expeditions carried out outside the European continent. It became clear, through comparative examinations of newly discovered rituals, beliefs and mythologies, that the fact of religiosity was indeed a global phenomenon, and that at no time in history has any people, civilized or primitive, been devoid of it. It was then that people recognized just how this idea predates all forms of material civilization, that it was not invented by cunning leaders and deceitful plotters and that it did not originate in exceptional or singular circumstances, but rather that it expresses an authentic and fundamental disposition common to all men.

---

[3] Rousseau, *Discours sur l'Origine et le Fondement*.
[4] See Boullaye, *L'etude comparée des religions*, vol. 1, pp. 17–18.

It also became apparent that the pervasiveness of the religious inclination among all peoples does not mean that it is equally reified in the heart of every human being. There will always be individuals so overwhelmed by the concerns and demands of daily life that they have neither the time nor the peace of mind to allow them to look upwards and contemplate higher truths and ideals. There will always be, moreover, contemptuous sceptics to whom earthly life is nothing but the pursuit of pleasure and enjoyment, who consider religion as only illusion and superstition. They always remain a minority, however. They tend to be individuals from affluent communities, whose indulgence in luxury shields them from the real tribulations and calamities of life. Thus, words such as 'modesty' and 'humility' have no meaning for them, and they become incapable of asking questions about their origin and their destiny. But these exceptions to the rule do not in the least contravene the latent presence of the religious instinct in the human soul, in the same way that the universal instinct to preserve the human species has never prevented some individuals from living a life without marriage or procreation.

We do not deny that there may have appeared, here and there, and at different times, invented forms of belief justified by tenacious opinions. This assertion seems reasonable and is further corroborated by observed experience. However, as far as the fact of religiosity is concerned, there is indeed no evidence that it did not germinate in tandem with the appearance of the first man.

> The religious instinct is common to all human races. It has been observed in its elementary form among the most savage peoples, those closest to animal survival .... The interest shown in the supernatural and in the divine is one of humanity's most universal and perennial tendencies. It does not disappear, though it might weaken or fade in excessive material civilizations, and among a handful of individuals.[5]

On the same topic, Barthélemy-Saint-Hilaire writes,

What is the world? What is man? Where do they come from? Who created them? Who governs them? What is their purpose? How did they originate? How should they end? What is life, and what is death? What

---

[5] Larousse, 'Religion', in *Larousse du XXème siècle*.

is the law that must govern human reason in the short passage of earthly life? What future awaits us beyond this life? Is there anything after this momentary existence? How do we relate to eternity? These are questions that not a single nation, a single people, a single society has not attempted to resolve with formulated answers, whether good or bad, reasonable or absurd, fixed or tenuous.[6]

Chachoin adds,

Whatever the marvelous achievements of the modern age, in scientific, industrial, economic, and social developments; and regardless of the great ardor with which we pursue the practical goals of life, and the struggle and competition to secure the best for ourselves and our loved ones, our minds will always come back in periods of calm rest (whether we were arrogant or modest, good or evil) to contemplating the eternal questions of why and how did we and the universe come into existence, to meditating on primary and secondary causes, and to pondering on our rights and our duties in this world.[7]

Henri Bergson, for his part, expresses the same sentiment in the following words: 'We observe in the past, as we observe today, human societies with neither science nor art nor philosophy. But there has never been a society without religion.'[8]

The future of religion in the face of scientific progress

As we enter the nineteenth century, we see that the primordial existence of religion had become unquestionable, a truth held by the majority of the people and that no one dared to doubt. In fact, a new idea emerged which while admitting that religions are indeed as old as humanity itself, declared that this fact nevertheless does not grant them stability or sustainability in the future. On the contrary, it charged them with all the flaws of old age and archaism and therefore pointed to their inevitable decadence and immanent extinction.

---

[6] St. Hilaire, *Mahomet et le Coran*, p. 34.
[7] Chachoin, *Évolution des Idées Religieuses*, p. 158.
[8] Bergson, *Les Deux Sources de la Morale et de la Religion*, p. 105. [See Bergson, 1977, p. 102. Ed.]

This is the theory of Auguste Comte, who advocated that human reason is subject to a law which he called the law of the three stages: the theological stage, the metaphysical stage and the positivity stage. The last, he asserted, is the final and noblest of the three. To begin with, mankind tried to explain natural phenomena by postulating the existence of one or more external supernatural agents. It then set out to explain them using specific abstract ideas, such as expansive force, elasticity, vitality and so on. Lastly, having ended up rejecting all internal and external explanations, mankind was now content to observe these phenomena as they present themselves and to record their actual relations, without worrying about their sources or their purposes. In other words, Comte maintained, the theological stage represents the primitive condition that allowed humanity to be entertained in its infancy. As it aged further, it felt constrained in the vision of childhood and embraced a middle stance during adolescence. When it finally came of age and began to see the world by the light of reason, it decided to definitively assimilate the spirit of empiricism.[9]

The major error of this evolutionary scheme lies in the fact that its supporters wanted to formulate a law which reduces the whole history of mankind to a single linear trajectory. It implies that humanity today would have bypassed two-thirds of its evolution to which it will never return, like a middle-aged man who could never possibly return to his childhood or his youth.

Perhaps this theory would not have been so gravely deficient if Comte had envisioned it in cyclical terms, which allow a return to the initial starting point. But even then it remains unwarranted, not only because it lacks the foundation of reliable evidence but also because it distorts history and contradicts the obvious. Indeed, we continue to witness in every age, including our own, how some people take great interest in faith, spiritualties and universal truths, while others, meanwhile, ardently focus their research on epiphenomena and observable material facts. We cannot even say that awareness of cosmic reality, or lack thereof, marks the dividing line between the two camps, for just as we often find fanatic sceptics among the ignorant and the 'unaware', we also find fervent believers among pioneers of material science. Even today, in the midst of the twentieth century and in the heart of European civilization,

---

[9] Comte, *Cours de Philosophie Positive*.

we observe that alongside intense and multifaceted empirical research, wide-ranging spiritual investigations are being carried out by renowned scholars[10] in the fields of medicine, philosophy, the physical sciences and so on. These scientists employ methods that are based on verified evidence and rigorous analysis. They seek to strip observed facts of all distortions and deception that amount to delusions and hasty conclusions. Instead, they consider only the outcomes of careful research, which in reality reinforce scientific certainties.

The so-called three stages of Comte should not, as a matter of fact, denote irreversible chronological succession, but rather parallel trends and tendencies that manifest themselves concurrently among all peoples. Each of them may undergo periods of exuberance or stasis in any given society, and according to how that society responds to adversity and prosperity, misfortune and felicity.

Moreover, these stages can well coexist in the heart of the individual himself, each one complementing the others, all three playing an equal role in maintaining the human condition. Just as we explain ordinary events by their direct or definite causes and say, for example, that a certain man has been killed by the blow of a sword or by old age or by disease, we tend to attribute unexplained, extraordinary events to fate or to some mysterious, higher causes.

We could go even further and argue that if we accept this deterministic evolutionary succession of mankind, Comte's stage of material positivity should be placed not at the end but at the very beginning of his schema. It represents the stage of infant psychology rather than that of maturity because it corresponds to the period of immediate, vital needs and the demands of daily life. It is the function of the sense and not of reason. It belongs to the domain of passive reception and instinctive response, not to the domain of the construction of great ideas.

The stage of explanation of phenomena by abstract causes can only germinate in the mind afterwards, when the developed faculties of abstraction and generalization could enable sound conceptualizations and judgements. Reason will then no longer be satisfied with joining events to each other in an idle, sequential manner, as one gathers twigs to make a bundle of them; it will attempt to link them by an idea, as a string threads the pearls of a necklace.

---

[10] For example, Oliver Lodge, the British philosopher, William James, the American scholar, and Charles Richet, the French physiologist.

It must be emphasized that any form of human knowledge will not deserve the name of science without having, in one way or another, access to the faculties of abstraction and generalization which enable elements to collate into a fixed framework and to be classified under common labels which facilitate their retrieval and the discovery of their shared definitive properties. The manifold empirical sciences aspire nowadays to be integrated into some sort of universal system whose objective is to regulate all their branches and to subject them to a common law. This so-called scientific monism denotes a form of intellectual pantheism, an echo of the principle of the unity of existence. Whether or not they achieve their goal is not the point. The fact remains, however, that this tendency to extrapolate universal categories is gaining ground and is not about to go away.

What remains is the spiritual or religious stage. It is evident that this phase will be born in the human mind only when it has widened its horizon by going beyond the interior and exterior appearances of the material world. This purview is undoubtedly the most all-embracing, and its aspirations transcend all others.

The stages of evolution proposed by our 'philosopher' Comte have thus been turned upside down, and each of the three needs of the human psyche seems to have taken its rightful place: the needs of the base instincts first, followed by the needs of reason and lastly the needs of the soul. In other words, the stage of the senses, then that of modest rationality and lastly that of sublime reason which transcends itself.

Yet what concerns us here is not so much rearranging these 'stages' into new schemata but to underscore their simultaneous presence in the hearts and minds of people. And just as we perceive no convincing sign pointing to the imminent disappearance of the inductive approach or the analytical method, we find no warning signs that the fact of religiosity will shortly disappear, or at least not before the disappearance of man himself from the face of the earth.

In this regard, Salomon Reinach writes, 'Not only do religions have an indeterminate future, but we can be certain that their traces will always be with us, since there will always remain hidden mystery in the world, and because science will never be able to fully accomplish its sworn task.'[11]

---

[11] Reinach, *Orpheus*, pp. 35–6.

Dr Max Nordau adds, 'This authentic and deep-rooted feeling is present in primitive man as in the most astute and cultivated intellectual. It will persist as long as humanity lasts, it will evolve with it, and will always adapt to the developments of the rational culture of societies.'[12]

Ernest Renan declares with regards to the history of religions that 'it may be possible that everything we love will disappear, that intellectual freedom and science will also disappear, but it is inconceivable that the religious inclination will one day disappear. It will remain a living proof of the insufficiency of materialist theories that seek to imprison human thought in the vulgar harassments of earthly life.'[13]

A similar view is eloquently expressed by Mohammad Farid Wajdi in the entry on *Din* in his *Encyclopedia*. He writes,

> Religious thought cannot diminish, for the simple reason that it represents the noblest inclination of the human soul and the most gushing of its feelings; we need not mention its propensity to make man raise his head high above all creatures. On the contrary, it will always increase. The religious instinct will accompany man as long as his reason is able to distinguish good from evil. It will become all the more essential as his consciousness evolves and as his knowledge is enhanced.[14]

Let us pause for a moment to consider the last statement. It may indeed seem strangely paradoxical to assert that progress in science and the widening of knowledge could in turn sharpen the religious instinct, an instinct driven by a quest for something hidden and mysterious. Yet if we think carefully about it, this apparent 'paradox' ceases to have currency. We will realize that the more scientifically advanced we become, the closer we come to admitting our ignorance, that our knowledge, our shortcomings aside, is like a drop of water in a vast and deep ocean. Each new door that science manages to open and which makes us see the vast expanse and the grandeur of our universe in a new light will give rise to countless new problems brought about by hitherto unsuspected perspectives, thus exposing humanity to new and unfathomable mysteries.

---

[12] Nordau, *Réponse au Mercure de France*.
[13] Source unspecified by the author. (Ed.)
[14] Wajdi, *Da'irat ma'arif al-qarn al-'ishreen*, vol. 4, pp. 106–12 (Ed.)

Consider, for example, our solar system, with the sun and the planets that revolve around it: they are so numerous that only a handful is visible to the naked eye. In the era of Laplace, only forty-two stars, around which planets and satellites revolve, were known. Later observations managed to enumerate more than a thousand. Eventually, however, we came to learn by undisputed evidence that this galaxy of ours is only one among millions, each with its own constellations, its own stars, its own satellites and all of them differing in their composition, their age, their atmosphere, their movement and trajectory, their geology and the forms of life they might sustain. All of this is unknown to us, and we can only begin to approximate an understanding with the help of our imagination. Not to mention the baffling immensities of the empty void or the dense space that lie beyond. Even if we could one day determine how the interstellar gas clouds that generated the planets were condensed, we would still have to find out where the gas clouds themselves came from.

Thus, the expansion of our knowledge is in itself an expansion of the realm of mystery, a deepening of our ignorance. Our ever-growing knowledge is encompassed into wider and wider circles, which at the same time expands the radius of the unknown. We can only surrender to the fact that beyond every advance we make in the knowledge of the visible world, there will eternally be long, new journeys to be made in the world of the unknown, a world whose end will never be fathomed by man – unless the infinite becomes finite, or the contingent and ephemeral become eternally existent. Indeed, this is confirmed by the Qur'an:

You have only been given a little knowledge. 17:85

If we turn from macrocosm to microcosm, and if we consider the progress achieved by science in the analysis of matter, its elements and the utmost divisions of those elements, we will come to exactly the same conclusion. The atom has long been believed to be the most elementary, indivisible and indestructible principle in matter – that the atom's mass and properties remain intact despite all the natural forces and all the chemical reactions it could be subjected to. It was then discovered that this very atom was in fact a complex 'world', comprising a stable nucleus surrounded by a cloud of particles which revolve around it like the planets around the sun; that this sort of shell, which forms an integral part of the atom, is nothing more than an electric sphere comprising free electrons; and that it could be separated from the nucleus with the help of radiation and thermal energy.

Even the nucleus, which for a long time was thought to comprise identical elements – that is, positively charged protons – was found to contain two opposite forms of energy: positive and negative. It was also proven that the nucleus could itself be split into several fragments[15] and that the colossal energy thus freed by fission could be used either to make the world a better place or, on the contrary, to spell its destruction and annihilation.

The material world has finally revealed its true nature, and the old façade of ascendency seems no longer sustainable. If matter is ultimately an 'energy', a pure abstract force, it would be necessary to seek the origin of this energy elsewhere, beyond the corruptible frames of nature and the fallen idols of materialism. Thus, the concrete world is drawing nearer to the world of abstraction. The visible world could soon merge with the invisible one at all levels. Scientists cannot deny the existence of this mystery, even if they are unable to see it with their own eyes. They believe in it because they feel its traces and sense its consequences.

Science is absolutely convinced today of the existence of forces which cannot be perceived even with the help of the most powerful equipment and the most precise measuring devices. Simply put, insofar as science recognizes that direct sensory experience cannot be the only measure of truth or of existence, it lays with its own hands the same cornerstone on which all religions have been founded.

All the scientific theories explored thus far, whether ascending to the complex or descending to the simple, and which depict matter as vanishing in the glimmering mirage, have in fact forced material science to descend from the heights of pride and arrogance and to return to humility and surrender. What these sciences represent in reality is the practical and applied side of knowledge, an activity closer to the arts and crafts than to science itself.

---

[15] Nuclear scientists assert that the lightest and simplest of atoms is the hydrogen atom, which consists of one proton and one electron, and that the heaviest atom is uranium, which bears the atomic number 92. They also claim that the hydrogen atom is found in all the nuclei of elementary bodies, like aluminum and so on, so that the analysis of these bodies will always end up in the hydrogen atom. Here, one cannot avoid the clear Qur'anic allusion to this scientific observation: 'His Throne was upon the water' (11:7). In other words, water was the origin of creation, even before heaven and earth were created.

Science cannot be reduced only to analyses and syntheses without sustaining at the same time a vision which links the effects to their causes, which infers general laws from partial observations and which provides an explanation for the entirety of existence likely to appease the mind and reassure the heart. Can we find in the very nature of experimental science, or in its methods or means of investigation, anything to make it adequately respond to this expectation of the human mind, so that it no longer needs to seek elsewhere for other explanations? Alas, we are very far from this![16]

It is not enough to say that these sciences, despite their almost spellbinding achievements, have only succeeded in unravelling a tiny part of the laws of nature beyond which lies a world of anomalies and exceptions which defy all rules and all physical laws.

Neither is it enough to say, while remaining within the same limited confines, that as soon as the sciences leave the domain of simple elementary materials and reach a point where elements and effects begin to entangle themselves and the complexity of their problematic interrelations deepens, that these scientific laws immediately abandon their rigor and precision, or that they are transformed into mere approximations based on estimated probabilities whereby, even if they succeed in calculating exact arithmetic means, they leave the extreme ends fluctuating in the ebb and flow of uncertainty. These general assertions could easily be demonstrated by examples known to experts in biology, psychology and the social sciences, among other fields.

Rather, we maintain that in the language of natural science itself, there has never been, nor ever will be, general laws obtained solely by the strict application of the rules of experimental methods. No matter how often an experiment is repeated, and despite the use of various new samples, each reaction remains a particular case, conditioned by a precise moment and by a determinate place.

There will always be, between the sum of the results, on the one hand, and the formulated general laws which should by definition transcend time and place, on the other, an abyss that separates the supposedly 'infinite' character of laws from the 'finite' nature of practical experience. To fill this gap, science takes refuge in two patchwork 'methods' based on a kind of analogical

---

[16] Qur'an 23:36. (Ed.)

thought, but interwoven with conjecture, fantasy and chance. The first of these methods (interpolation) consists in extending a phantom bridge between the facts actually observed during the experiments. Thus, all the missing links, unverified by observation, are assumed to uniformly follow the same pattern as the recorded facts; they become part of a connected chain, a seemingly straight path unaffected by anomalous incidents or contradictions. The second method (extrapolation) allows the scientist to make a giant leap, past the connected chain of experimentation and into a time and space unknown to him. He will then decide, by simple conjecture, that the conclusions he has reached in a partially verified domain will be found, similar and unchanged, in the new domain where he has not verified anything at all. In other words, science decides what has been as well as what will be. No doubt, any law which overly relies on concrete and exact observations, as is the case with all the laws of natural science, is obliged to have recourse to a kind of mental faith in unverified intellectual assumptions which add to the testimonies of the senses unsuspected 'concrete' realities without which no law could claim to be truly universal or inclusive.

Even according to the higher principles of thought itself, or the rules or reason, we can affirm that any attempt to explain the effects only by their natural and immediate causes carries within it the seed of its own deficiency and error, and only if the rules of logical thinking were rooted out of our minds could we take such an approach seriously. For if effects were to necessarily follow from the same causes, the effects would have to be no more than a prolongation of those causes. The effects resulting from the same causes would have to be similar in all respects, so that discovering the slightest difference among them, in their nature, quantity or quality, would open up new questions which the experimental method would fail to answer. Indeed, the smallest variation in time or space would lead us to ask, Why are some things placed before others and why after them? Why is one on the right and the other on the left? If we follow this course of reasoning to the end, the universe will be reduced to a final indivisible point, and all notions of otherness or difference would disappear from our minds only to be replaced by the principles of sameness and identity. Yet thought has no life except in multiplicity and in difference because it is a movement between several possibilities that eventuates in bringing about continuities or oppositions. Thus, the explanations provided by natural sciences leave us standing between two fires: either they declare their defeat and bankruptcy in meeting our expectations and abandon us without quenching our thirst or they persist and retain their promises until we end up in failure and at a deadlock. Since human reason cannot ignore the disappointments and contradictions brought about by science, nor will it ever be satisfied with them, the only option would be to go beyond these mechanistic explanations, to seek a higher cause endowed with an absolute and incontestable will, and which has the freedom to decide that the same causes may not always produce the same effects.

All rational and natural sciences, whether theoretical or practical, are unanimous in admitting that their exhaustive pursuits of immediate and primary causes will always culminate in a notion of invisible existence. Thus, they themselves pave the way for the continuity and eternity of religions.

So far we have described the sciences as looking at one end of an equilibrium while turning back on the other; they try to appease part of the human quest for rational knowledge and ignore the other part. Now, the human mind's desire to understand what surrounds it is not satiated by simply ascending to the primary causes of things. It must also descend to ascertain their ends and purposes, their objectives and goals. To have a well-rounded knowledge of something, it is not enough to know where it comes from if we do not also know where it is going, nor what it is if we do not know why it is. This insistent demand of the mind does it not in fact point to a conviction firmly rooted in our nature – that all phenomena occur within a prearranged grand design, that they proceed along a path decided by the force which governs the universe and that they do not result from blind coincidence or arbitrary chance?

Let us now consider the attitudes of contemporary sciences towards our persistent intellectual need to know the destinies and ends of things.

In fact the sciences have already, at a certain point in their evolution, washed their hands of these inquiries, arguing that as long as their overriding role was to study the visible causes of phenomena and the mechanisms of their effects these openings should remain closed. To determine if their interconnections had a purpose or to study the nature of such a purpose was not considered the business of science – it was beyond its powers. The sciences thus readily admitted that they would not meet our expectations and would not accomplish their avowed mission of research in a complete, satisfactory manner since they decided at the outset to stop halfway along its course. However, this supposedly 'neutral' position could not be sustained for long, since the natural scientist, himself a human being, could not ignore the urgings of his own mind. This is why every time he encounters a series of consolidated phenomena which manifestly reinforce each other, each occupying a position precisely needed to fulfil its role in the grand scheme of things, we see him compelled to look for mysterious ultimate causes without daring to call them by name. He goes from investigating each cell in an organ to the study of the workings of organs in each apparatus, to the role of each apparatus in the body and so on. He then decides to describe them as physiological 'functions' in order to avoid calling them 'goals' or 'objectives'. As we can see, this is only a thin façade that can hardly conceal the facts with which the scientist refuses to come to terms.

What is essential is not the names given to things but the things themselves whose existence the scientist implicitly admits in practice. The more science presses onwards along the path of inquiry, the more it is forced after only a few steps to come to a standstill. This is because the scientist feels obliged to admit the incapacity of his material means to penetrate the thick barrier that stands between him and the understanding of ultimate causes and final ends which, while sensing their presence, he is nevertheless powerless to explain.

But then again, what greater testimony[17] to the fact that the far reaches of human knowledge, far from dealing a fatal blow to religious instincts, have, on the contrary, helped increase their brilliance, than the words of Comte, founder of the positivist theory, and those of his disciples, who came to recognize this based on their own experiences and expressed it directly and indirectly in their writings. Here is Comte himself, who had announced that the death of religions would be the inevitable consequence of scientific progress, having entered towards the end of his life into a bizarre phase of mysticism, deciding to crown his eminent career with the founding of a new 'religion' modelled on the ecclesiastic laws of Catholicism, with all its beliefs, rituals, festivals and the hierarchy of priests – as one rewrites a work of fiction by changing only the names of the characters.

And here is Spencer who, for his part, defines the 'unknown' as 'that force which does not yield to reason but which is the starting point of all that is

---

[17] Qur'an 6:19. (Ed.)

rational, the source from which flows all that exists'. But isn't this 'unknown' precisely the object of religions, which is now returning to us disguised in the language of science?

Émile Littré wrote a beautiful account of the day he resolved to put an end to his commitment to the service of the exact sciences. He described how he found himself surrounded on all sides by a vast, abysmal sea[18] made of unsolved mysteries, with neither a vessel nor a compass. What was his attitude in the midst of this dire ocean? It was neither that of a mystified poet, nor of a dejected lover, but of a humble believer, a pious man who takes refuge in his divine creator.[19]

Sources of the religious sentiment in human nature

What kind of force is it then which only grows fiercer and more blazing in the face of opposition and resistance, and which always defeats its supporters and enemies alike? Could it be anything but the force of innate instinct which is nourished on every occasion, as a tree foliates and bears fruit by the light showers of spring, or perhaps a single drop of rain is enough, as the passing glimmer of insight is enough to awaken our consciousness or to shake our resolve so that our imagination takes flight and floats in the mysterious realms of our origins and destinies?

If this instinctive belief in the invisible and the fascination with the mystery of our beginning and of our ultimate end were merely attributes of religious faith, their denial would indeed be a mark of heresy and atheism. If, as we have seen, they were the inevitable outcome of the very progress of science and the broadening of its horizons, then the refusal to believe in them would be nothing more than a sign of deficiency and myopia on the part of the sciences. But since these questions and the perplexity they bring about are inborn and innate in human nature, to reject them would be even more perilous. It would suggest the defeat of man, who would find himself debased, not even to the level of the oblivious child, but to that of the unconscious animal. For even

---

[18] Qur'an 24:40. (Ed.)
[19] Quoted by Sabatier, *Esquisse d'une Philosophie de la Religion*, pp. 11–12.

children, who possess a slight rational sense, do not contend with what they see with their eyes, nor do they stop halfway along the chain of causes. On the contrary, they always aspire to ultimate explanations through their reiterated questions about the primary sources and final ends of things. This is only a quick glance at the vitality of this intellectual human inclination that invariably fights against all that could stifle or paralyze its activity.

This natural aspiration towards final knowledge is the basis of both science and faith, and those who restrict it to the domain of sensitive matter would be obstructing the path of human perfection; they would deprive the world of great potential, not to mention upsetting the harmonious nature which God instilled in mankind.[20]

Having said that, we must recognize that when our minds project their lights beyond the bounds of sensory experience, in an attempt to look for the original source of things and their fate and purpose, they do not all proceed at an equal pace. Some minds are modest and uninspired. Their search for the meaning of existence, its mysteries and its aims, halts abruptly at the threshold. They attribute the origin of each group of similar phenomena to a regulating and moving principle of which they only have a brief glance, and explain the goals and functions of the same phenomena by their progression in a certain direction, towards their culmination. They seldom inquire into the beginning and end of each principle, or the beginning and end of all beings as a coherent whole with a common mission. They will be content to multiply the governing principles of nature, which are represented as active powers, as authorizing gods: a god for the wind, a god for fertility, a god for life, a god for death, a god for poetry and so on.

Other minds, however, are more perceptive, freer, and more aspiring. They carry out their reflections unchecked, without losing sight of the ultimate objective of their mission, and without contradicting themselves in their judgements. They are convinced that the object of their quest is an entity far too sublime to be contained within the confines of time and space. So much so that if one listed for them all the scientific, technical and artistic achievements of humanity, and all the physical and spiritual pleasures imagined by men, the two extreme ends of existence would remain inexplicable for them using

---

[20] Qur'an 30:30. (Ed.)

both the sciences and the arts. They would still feel an abysmal void that could be filled neither by all the material past, nor by all the present, nor by all the future combined. Nothing could diminish their ambition, nor their need for transcendence; nothing could calm their anxiety and turmoil, nor the dogged pursuit of their goals, except this truth, which is the alpha and omega of all truths; a truth which resists fading into the horizon of the contingent and the possible; a truth which does not appreciate the assumption that anything could be before or after it, neither in time nor in space. These enlightened minds always yearn for harmony behind contradiction, for unique oneness beyond multiplicity. This is why they refuse to settle for relative standards and partial explanations. They are not prepared to succumb to a law among laws, but are ready to rise up to the Law of all laws. They scan the horizon in the hope of seeing the hand of the one who established, gathered and organized these discrete laws, laws that work in unison to sustain the cosmic structure. Is not this beautiful harmony, which governs all terrestrial and celestial creations whose natures and roles are in flux, a testament to the one great Being who watches over the universe and who subjects all parts of this astonishing machinery to its own unique course and plan? Praised be that Being!

In short, these aspiring minds are driven by the desire to look beyond fleeting and transient appearances towards the apprehension of a universal eternal truth, a truth that no framework of science can encompass and to which all sciences and all knowledge aspire. This is the very truth identified by the great religions as being worthy of the veneration of men and which no confession of faith denies, even if some of them may occasionally associate this higher truth with lower created beings.

This natural and instinctive yearning for absolute eternity and this insistent demand of our minds to fathom infinite immensities point to two vital principles. The first relates to the nature of the bond that connects us to our desired object. This bond is not, as Aristotle imagined, a kind of forced movement towards a centre of gravity. Rather, it resembles the traces that the creator leaves in his creation, or, in the words of Descartes, that the designer stamps on what he makes. The second clearly indicates that there is a noble, celestial element in the human being that destines him for eternity, even if men sometimes seem oblivious to or sidetracked from it in their delight with the vain attractions of a mediocre material life.

Religiosity, especially in monotheistic faiths espousing belief in eternity, is therefore an essential element of the faculty of abstraction in man. It is exclusively by this sentiment that rational minds are satiated, whereas without it they could never reach higher aspirations.

The religious sentiment is, furthermore, an indispensable element of the power of conscience in its quest for human perfection. For when we no longer find in terrestrial objects or in humanity a resonance of the noble feelings of love, passion, gratitude, humility, decency, hope and so on, and when we see their sources drying up in a passing, dissipating world, it is in the religious domain that we find for them boundless expression, a mainspring whose outpouring never dries up.

Lastly, religion is a necessary element for the exercise of our will, as it equips it with the strongest drives and impulses that shield the soul against the drudge of despair and lethargy.

The religious idea enables the human soul to express its manifold impulses and inclinations. Just as man has been called a 'thinking animal' or a 'social animal', we can also define him as being intrinsically a 'religious animal'.

The social function of religions

The religious instinct is therefore the ideal nourishment for our spiritual inclinations and the inexhaustible fuel of their vitality. In addition to these contributions at the level of individual psychology, religion plays an equally important role in the social sphere.

We cannot overstate the fact that no society can exist without a level of solidarity among its members, that this solidarity cannot do without a law which governs their relations and determines the rights and duties of each one of them, and that this law cannot be established without a type of incentivizing and deterring authority which guarantees respect for the law and prohibits its violation.

It would indeed be fruitless to pursue such truisms any further. This 'authority', however, requires our close attention: What is its true nature? Does it have real powers?

We affirm here that there is no power on earth that can equal or even approach that of the power of religiosity in terms of guaranteeing adherence to the law as well as stability and social cohesion, and of ensuring peace and security in a society.

This is because human beings stand out from the rest of creation by their voluntary conduct, which depends on something that cannot be seen or heard. It is not something that they wear around their wrists or around their necks; it does not run in their veins or trigger their muscles or their nerves beyond their control – it is the human spiritual values of understanding and faith. Some people fall into serious error when they reverse these values and imagine that thought and conscience have no influence on material life or economic conditions, that they are, on the contrary, fully dependent on them. Such is the Marxist analysis. This mindset leads man to discard his crown of dignity, to regress towards a state of animal existence. It is a claim that contradicts the obvious and distorts the true behaviour of individuals and societies. Even when men choose to live a purely material life in which the heart and the spirit are absent, they convince themselves that this life will bring them happiness. Man is forever disposed to adjusting his conduct in accordance with an idea, whether good or bad, and all his life's successes and failures will depend on this idea.

Man acts under impulses which come from within himself and not from without. Neither social norms nor the powers of coercion, which States arrogate to themselves, will suffice to establish that virtuous city where laws are respected and where each individual fulfils his moral responsibility to the utmost. For he who fulfils his civic duties entirely from fear of the whip or of serving time in jail or of paying a fine will neglect his duty as soon as he is assured that he can escape the law with impunity.

It is manifestly wrong to believe that only by investing in science and culture, as a substitute for moral discipline and religious education, can we ensure peace and prosperity. We must keep in mind that science is a double-edged sword, capable of destruction and devastation as well as building and cultivation. Therefore, a kind of moral authority is necessary both to direct humans towards goodness and success and to restrain them from the evil ways that lead to corruption. This authority is belief and faith.

But faith comes in two forms. The first is the faith one has in the value of virtue, in human dignity and in other abstract principles which impose themselves on good souls and which they cannot ignore or escape, even were they granted a reprieve from punishments or penalties. The second is faith in a superior being who watches over the secrets of our inner selves. The law thus draws its moral authority from the commandments and prohibitions of this being. Men become enamoured of the divine issue of these laws; they observe them as much out of burning feelings of love as out of fear. It is undoubtedly the latter which has the greater dominion over human minds. It is from this faith that souls draw their strength to resist the storms of temptation and the upheavals of impulses. It is the fastest way to find the surest place in the hearts of everyone, learned and lay alike.

That is why religiosity is deemed the best guarantee of establishing just and equitable relations among human beings. It is as much a social necessity as it is a natural human instinct.

Would you then find yourself[21] in doubt as to the necessity of the religious sentiment in the building of societies and nations? Would you, too, find yourself deceived into thinking that the great nations of the world could have been so firmly grounded in an ideology other than religion?

We do not wish to precede events and forestall the doom of these edifices, which are founded on the absence of pious faith and in fear of the Creator.[22] What we would like, however, is to offer the reader a sample of statements whose authors are not men of religion, but rather celebrated scientists, politicians and military leaders.

Here is Robert A. Milliken, the American natural scientist, who writes, 'The most important thing in the world is belief in the reality of moral and spiritual values. It was because we lost that belief that the World War came, and if we do not now find a way to regain and to strengthen that belief, then science is of no value.'[23]

And here is what Woodrow Wilson, former president of the United States, wrote,

---

[21] Qur'an 47:22. (Ed.)
[22] Qur'an 9:109. (Ed.)
[23] Quoted in *al-Din wa al-'ilm* by Izzat Pasha, p. 173.

The sum of the whole matter is this, that our civilization cannot survive materially unless it be redeemed spiritually. It can be saved only by becoming permeated with the spirit of Religion.[24] ... Here is the final challenge to our churches, to our political organizations, and to our capitalists – to everyone who fears God or loves his country.[25]

Marshal Pétain, the former French president, concluded a speech delivered on 25 June 1940, after signing the ceasefire with victorious Germany, with the following declaration: 'I invite you above all to a moral revival.'[26] Field Marshal Montgomery, in a speech to the Eighth Army on 4 March 1951, said,

I consider the moral[27] factor the greatest and the only factor in war. It is impossible for a commander to push his troops to full potential if they are not acting in accordance with their conscience. I feel strongly that an army that acts against God's pleasure is a defeated army. The danger of the moral degradation of an army is more dangerous than the enemy itself. We cannot emerge victorious in battle without first achieving victory over ourselves.[28]

* * *

The great service offered by religion to society does not stop here. Its role is not limited to being the best impetus for maintaining morals, social relations and the rules of justice, nor to being an effective weapon in the fight against anarchy and corruption. Its positive role and function have deeper roots in societies. Religion brings the hearts of its followers closer together and creates among them bonds of brotherhood and compassion that no ties of race, language, neighbourhood or common interests could match.

Indeed, all these bonds, no matter how effective they may seem in ceasing wrongs and in ensuring mutual cooperation, remain, nevertheless, artificial unions. They gather social actors as one ties together a bundle of sticks that continue to be separated by gaps and breaks, and by all the psychological

---

[24] Wilson used the word 'Christ' in the original English text. Its replacement with 'religion' appears in the Arabic translation (from Ottoman Turkish) of Pasha's *al-Din wa al-ʿilm*. (Ed.)
[25] Quoted in ibid.
[26] The French press on 26 June 1940.
[27] I have been unable to verify whether Montgomery was referring here to 'morale' rather than 'morality'. The speech was reported in the Egyptian press in Arabic translation, and my attempts to find the original English version have been unsuccessful. Special thanks to Dr Will Hanley of Florida State University for his assistance in this inquiry. (Ed.)
[28] The Egyptian press on 5 March 1951.

barriers that may exist among them. Only in the brotherhood in faith and the mutual respect for higher values will they be bound tightly together. Multiplicity then turns into uniformity and, like opposing mirrors, each person's soul is reflected in the soul of another.

We even note that this unity of hearts often takes precedence over other causes of accord and harmony. It creates the strongest unfailing bonds among individuals of different races and tongues, from distant lands, and despite conflicting interests. We also see how societies, which are founded on the basis of common national interests irrespective of their members' religious diversity, tend to appeal to all the moral influences of these faiths in order to restore mutual harmony in the face of external threats and aggression. Therefore, one can assert and with good reason that any form of nationalism deprived of moral and religious stimulus would be tenuous and on the verge of collapse.

Let us close by saying that religions, on the whole, occupy in societies the place retained by the heart in the human body. Whoever undertakes to study the history of religions would in fact be writing down the lives of people and retracing the evolution of civilization.

4

On the origin of belief in God

Underlying factors in the human mind

We noted in the foregoing chapter that the religious sentiment arises from two intuitive principles that are deeply rooted in our mind – namely, the principles of causality and finality. We restate here that these principles, if properly understood, will lead to the highest religious ideals of monotheism and eternity; that polytheistic, fetishistic or nihilistic theories would only be born out of a kind of inattention or laziness of the mind, which causes it to stop halfway.

The principle of causality postulates that a thing, taken among possible things,[1] cannot exist by itself because it does not have the necessary cause needed for its existence. Neither can it cause another thing to exist because, just as zero cannot engender a positive integer, a thing cannot give another what it is incapable of giving itself. In order to exist first, then be able to have an effect on others, it needs a cause external to itself. If this external cause, in turn, cannot give itself its own existence, it will need another cause and so on, until one invariably ends in a first cause, which is the necessary cause of all other causes.

---

[1] This expression is better known in the following formulation: 'Nothing comes from nothing.' We have added 'among the possible things' in order to delimit the field where this formula may be applied, and to avoid the erroneous conclusions which could result from taking it in absolute terms. Necessary principles, or axioms, such as 'the whole is greater than the part', or 'a thing is identical to itself', or 'one and one equals two', or 'adding zero to zero equals zero' and all the rest of the Laws of Identity, carry in their very concepts the cause of their existence; they exist without a cause external to them. In contrast, impossible or illogical principles – such as 'the part of a whole is greater than the whole', or 'a thing is not itself', or that 'a thing is the essence of another thing' and so on, as well as all the other examples that defy the Law of Contradiction – carry in themselves the cause of their nonexistence; they cannot exist by themselves or by any other external cause. As for the possible things which admit both existence and nonexistence, and whose nature supposes neither, their existence is contingent on an external cause. For if their existence were inherent in their nature, they would cease to be possible and become necessities, which would amount to a paradox and self-contradiction.

As for the principle of finality, it dictates that any stable, well-ordered and complex system cannot exist without intention, that all intentions necessarily tend towards an objective, and that if an objective only covers partial, superfluous ends, the mind will automatically seek another objective beyond it, until it arrives at a universal, final goal which will be the ultimate goal of the whole system.

But man is by nature incapable of pursuing, step by step, the extended succession of causes and objectives in order to reach the source of the universe, on the one hand, and its final end, on the other. For this reason, experimental sciences fell back into despair and declared at the outset their incapacity to attain this knowledge. They reduced their ambition to moving a few calculated steps, forward or backward, throwing everything else which is laid beyond them into the domain of mystery where the most ignorant and the most learned stand on equal footing.

This human hopelessness in ascertaining the origin and destiny of beings, phase by phase and in their details, is nevertheless counterbalanced by a certainty of which every human mind is convinced (willingly or unwillingly) that, no matter how long the chain of causes and partial objectives, there must be at both ends of this chain – if we want to vindicate, understand and explain the existence of each of its links – an original cause and a final destiny. They must carry in themselves the cause of their own permanent existence. They will be the first principle before which there is nothing, and the final objective after which there is nothing. Otherwise, all contingencies would either remain in the state of nothingness and non-being (if deprived of an independently existing original principle), or they would forever be a riddle, irrational and futile (if they lack a genuine sense of purpose enough to appease the demands of reason).

The existence of this absolutely first and last truth is an inescapable rational necessity that none can in their right mind dispute, as long as they are able to contemplate for a moment the consequences of denying it. We suggest, in fact, that any attempt to challenge this truth can only come from a fool who delights in transgressing the rules of reason and arithmetic, who recklessly abolishes all the principles of common sense.

By setting out to investigate the origin of belief in God, we do not wish to look into the existence or non-existence of this unquestionable fact that resides in the depth of our being. This question would be superfluous. Rather, our inquiry concerns the factors and circumstances which allow this fact to rise to the level of consciousness, the factors taking this idea out of the domain of abstraction and transforming it into a living reality, a burning feeling the object of which is a Superior Being to whom human souls turn, full of love and fear, supplication and surrender.

***

Mainstream specialists who engage in such research tend to shift their attention from the observable facts, which readily explain the awakening of religiosity in man and the endurance of this phenomenon through the ages. They understand the 'origin of religions' in terms that relate only to the form in which religions made their first appearance on earth. The 'antecedence' which they seek to prove is not of a logical order (in the way premises are placed before conclusions); nor is it an historical precedence (which relates to established and familiar timelines). It is an absolute temporal antecedence that is yoked to the initial appearance of man on the planet.

To achieve this, they engage in excavating the remains of past civilizations and in exploring peoples that have remained primitive to this day. As they arrive at what they believe to be the earliest form of religious expression, having traversed the dark alleyways of history and roamed distant exotic lands, they conclude that the religion of the first man was necessarily the same as that which they had been able to discover.

But since their conclusions were not always concordant (one scholar's 'first form' of religion often confuted that of another), they split into two great schools, each of which developed in an opposite direction.

The first group supported a theory that claims that the earliest religions were discrete forms of superstition and paganism which refine and perfect themselves, generation after generation, until they arrive at the belief in one God. Thus, they take the same evolutionary path followed by science and technology. Some scholars went so far as to argue that monotheism is a recent idea, born out of the particular mentality of the Semitic people.

This theory was advocated by supporters of the progressive (or ascending) evolutionism that proliferated in Europe during the nineteenth century and left its mark on many scientific disciplines. It was also applied to the history of religions by scholars such as Spencer, Tylor, Frazer, Durkheim and others, who nevertheless disagreed among themselves over the precise nature and the object of the earliest expressions of faith.

The other group sought to undermine this theory by presenting counterarguments in order to prove its incongruity. They maintained, on the contrary, that the belief in a supreme creator was indeed the oldest and most pervasive form of human religiosity, since it is found without exception among all peoples, ancient or modern. As for the various identified forms of idolatry or paganism, they were considered nothing more than temporary dysfunctions or lesser epiphenomena next to this imposing and timeless belief in a single God.

Many ethnologists, psychologists and other specialists in the human sciences defended this view and endorsed what could be described as the theory of the 'primordiality and authenticity of monotheism'. The most famous of them were the following: Lang, who established the existence of a 'Higher God' among the primitive tribes of Australia, Africa and the Americas; Schroeder, who confirmed its presence among the ancient Aryan races; Brockelmann, who found it among the Semitic tribes of pre-Islamic Arabia; LeRoy and Quatrefages, who found it among the pygmies of Central Africa; and Schmidt, who found it among the pygmies and the inhabitants of south-eastern Australia. The last also concluded that the 'idea of a Supreme Being is found among the most archaic human races'.[2]

Even if the primordialist approaches differ significantly from those of evolutionism in terms of outcomes, primordialists seem to agree, nonetheless, on the object of their research, which is to find the precise form of man's first expression of faith. They also agree on the method of investigation allowing one to achieve this – namely, the study of extant primitive tribes, on the one hand, and of vanished civilizations, on the other.

For our part, we suggest that to pose the problem in this way and to try to solve it by these methods stems from a double error: an error in defining the research goal and an error in the means of attaining that goal.

With regard to the object of research, which is to define the most original form of religion and its manifestations in the most primordial time, we need only recall that science had declared loud and clear that this so-called

---

[2] Schmidt, *Origine et évolution de la religion*, p. 30.

originary condition falls outside its field of inquiry and therefore had refused to take interest in it. To return now to this domain in the name of science is to try to dispose of counterfeit money, or to promote old agendas under a new guise. Any judgement issued under this banner would be pronounced by a disqualified judge who has since lost all claims to legitimacy. In fact, historians of religions themselves recognize that the artefacts associated with the religious forms of the Palaeolithic age remain largely unknown to us, and that we can only examine them by speculation and conjecture.

Regarding the working method, which consists in attempting to infer humanity's earliest forms of religion from those of the backward peoples who remain outside the pale of modern civilization, it assumes that these populations have always been, from the beginning of their existence, frozen in the state in which we find them today. Indeed, this is unfounded. What history tells us, and what the excavations of ancient remains confirm, is that the periods of stagnation and regression believed to precede the times of prosperity and florescence that follow were themselves often established on the ruins of civilizations that would have disappeared at an indeterminate past, near or distant.

This cyclical movement of history, which recalls the succession of the seasons, makes it highly improbable that we will one day be able, given the abstruse nature of our evidence, to decree with certainty which form of belief preceded all others.

We can still assert, however, that it is indeed possible that the myths and legends of the past gave birth to certain cults and beliefs. But it is just as possible that they were the result of the dissolution or distortion of great religions whose followers would have been torn apart by wars or by social upheavals. Then, as they become increasingly willing to lend an ear to impostures and false prophets, and as tales of fancy and superstitions are passed down over the generations, people eventually adopt them as sacred beliefs.

Høffding rightly remarks,

> It is improbable that the history of religion will ever succeed in solving the problem of the first dawn of religion in the human race. ... History nowhere shows us the first beginning of religion. What we find is a series of different lower or higher forms of religion. ... Even the lowest savages with which we are acquainted have passed through a long process of development.[3]

---

[3] Høffding, *The Philosophie de la Religion*, pp. 126–7 (see also Høffding and Meyer, *The Philosophy of Religion*, pp. 131–2. Ed.).

We can see now the frailty of these hypotheses and how contemporary approaches are founded on a shifting sand cliff, ready to crumble.[4]

The evolutionary theory is distinguished by another, equally unfounded, postulate, which consists in drawing a parallel between the evolution of physical and intellectual capacities, on the one hand, and the development of man's spiritual dispositions, on the other. For just as the human body passes from the frailty of infancy to the strength of adulthood, and just as his intellectual development passes from ignorance to knowledge, mankind's spiritual life may also appear to have begun in absurdity and superstition and to have arrived at unblemished faith only after long and painful efforts.

To begin with, we are entitled to wonder about the rational basis of such an analogy.

Is it true that all human mental aptitudes develop in the same uniform manner? Is it then true that spiritual life flourishes in correlation with physical and material development? Do we not see them in fact as moving in opposite directions along the path of evolution? If it is true that the first man was satisfied with a cave for shelter, animal skin to cover himself and a few wild plants to appease his hunger, would it not be reasonable to assume that such meagre material ambitions would have given him the peace of mind, and ample time, to engage in a kind of contemplation of the world conducive to sharpening his religious sense, and to the cultivation of elevated spiritual feelings? In a similar vein, when humans are preoccupied with material luxuries, as is the case in advanced civilizations, we find them pushed towards assimilating opposite attitudes. Human propensities tend to sharpen and intensify at the expense of their opposites, like the two arms of a scale – when one goes up, the other can only go down.

It takes only a little thought, however, to realize that any attempt to understand religion in correlation with the arts, the sciences or forms of technology is an attempt to bring together two distinct fields that differ as much in their essential natures as in their means. While scientific truths are indeed a vast treasure that the mind yearns to reach and to uncover, and whose acquisition requires much effort, diligence and often the help of external physical means,

---

[4] Qur'an 9:109. (Ed.)

religious truth resides in the depths of our being. Its sure signs are readily presented to our senses; even a brief moment of clarity is enough to apprehend it instantly – as quick as a flash of lightning. The acquisition of this immense truth is not the laborious result of the prior gathering and accumulation of detailed observations and thorough understanding of the universe, nor is it 'more difficult than the human quest for science and material development', as has been claimed.[5] Rather, it is the light of faith which precedes all, and which engulfs our thoughts and reflections until we conclude the detailed study of the phenomena of nature. Hence, all men, whether versed in the sciences or uneducated, stand on equal footing before this innate human feeling; anyone can find in the universe, and in his own way, something that dazzles his mind and overwhelms his senses.

It would seem more sensible, if we wish to know the primeval state of religiosity that existed at the dawn of time, to establish parallels, not with the evolution of material civilization, but with the evolutionary patterns of the known religions. It is then that we will realize just how religions begin with pure and simple beliefs in a single deity and that corruptions and deviations from the original teachings grow with the passage of time. We can conclude, therefore, that this is the actual progression of all religions – their beginnings are always better than their endings.

If, however, we insist on studying the evolution of beliefs by equating them with the advancements of the arts and sciences, we should not stop at superficial resemblances and misleading philological associations, but go to the heart of things. It would then be clear that this comparison in fact confirms the point of view held by supporters of the instinctive nature of religious feeling. This is because 'evolution' in the domain of the arts and sciences, as with any other aspect of human existence, implies a kind of progression from a simple, naïve harmonious conception towards a fragmentation and complexity which only increase as one moves away from the original state. If we wish to apply this evolutionary approach, in the strict biological sense, to religions, we must conclude that religions, like the arts, have followed a path which takes them from unity to multiplicity, and from

---

[5] See the opening page of *Allah: Kitab fi nash'at al-'aqidah al-'Ilahiyyah* [*On the Origin of Belief in God*] by al-Aqqad.

purity, simplicity and ease to intricacy and complexity, which result from the introduction of legends and whims of the imagination, which in turn suffocate reason and common sense.

If we understand 'evolution' in moral terms – that is, as a progression towards perfection – we will quickly see that this 'evolution' does not proceed in a sustained natural manner, nor does it adhere to predictable scientific laws. Mankind's march towards progress cannot be described in strictly evolutionary terms. It is, at best, an objective, an aspiration towards which the efforts and wills tend, which men sometimes reach, and from which they often turn away. Of course, every reformer must be convinced that he can, and will, achieve his noble goals. Without hope and faith in the perfectibility of morals and beliefs, all legislations would be obsolete and any attempt at reform would be in vain. But there is a large gap between the possibility of perfection, on the one hand, and the realization of perfection, on the other. Only those who have paid their dues of hard effort and unshakable will can achieve it. The history of mankind, as far as the progress towards perfection is concerned, does not proceed in a straight line.[6]

We can therefore see that neither the study of the psychology of belief, nor of historical facts nor of the concrete stages of social evolution, supports the theory denoted by the term 'evolutionism', which claims that myths and superstitions were the undisputed origin of all religions. On the contrary, everything seems to point to the opposite point of view. Be that as it may, all these assertions of the second school do not rise to the level of incontestable historical truth. They remain, at best, partial proofs. They do not give us assurance of any kind, neither logical nor practical. They do not prove to us, for example, that events always occur as we are used to seeing them occur, even less how we would have liked them to occur.

---

[6] Studying the developments of the three great revealed religions will show definite progressions from one to the other. But this progression is not continuous (as the evolutionary theory suggests), since they are all, in the eyes of their respective adherents, perfect dictations 'from above'. This sense of progression is evident, however, if we focus our inquiries on their formal expressions of faith and their legislative systems. But, even then, it is not a progression in a straight line from the false to the true (as advocates of the evolutionary theory of religion would have us believe); rather, it is a series of ascending degrees of good faith, holism and perfection. We may have an opportunity later on of illustrating this unity among the three religions by referring to their sacred texts themselves.

There remains a third hypothesis that should be considered in this debate. It suggests that common sense and folly in the religious idea not only follow each other in a kind of sequence, where one of them could, over time, overtake the other and replace it, but also are, rather, simultaneous facts that manifest themselves at all times and in all places. Their respective impact seems to evolve according to the variables of sound moral reason and the spiritual elevation of individuals. For no human generation is ever short of clear minds that can distinguish between truth and the corruptions of superstition, and of minds that cannot make that distinction. This last hypothesis may well be the closest representation to the reality that we can observe around us.

Let us restate here what we have established elsewhere in this book, which is that all reliable historical authorities agree that even the most savage and pagan populations are convinced of the existence of a creator of the world who is the god of gods. Let us not forget, moreover, that between our knowledge of the short span of human history uncovered thus far, on the one hand, and of the timeline that stretches to the first appearance of man on earth, on the other, there is a wide gulf that has not been, nor is likely to be, filled. Therefore, no one can claim that the existence of historical facts, the evidence of which has been lost or destroyed, could be irrefutably demonstrated by mere conjecture. Speculations based on possible comparisons and superficial resemblances with known facts cannot exempt us from verifying and analyzing the circumstances and conditions under which each element of the either side of the comparison developed.

Thus, the methods of the empirical sciences have been unable to provide a satisfactory answer concerning the religion of the first man. Now, those people who allow their mind to be guided by revealed books will find in them something to reinforce the opinion of those who lean towards the primordiality of divinely inspired religions, not only in terms of innate instincts but also in their temporal developments.

This is the natural disposition God instilled in mankind. 30:30

These texts attest that, at the beginning, men lived by rational and upright principles, and that dissentions were incidental and only came at a later stage:

All people were originally one single community, but later they differed. 10:19

These persistent divergences, and the widening gap between them, have been aggravated by the influence of 'inherited tradition', as each generation passes down its beliefs onto the next, often by means of indoctrination: 'Every child is born with the true faith, then his parents convert him to Judaism, to Christianity or to Magainism.'[7] Be that as it may, the holy books agree in asserting that the first human community was not left to itself, in vain, solitary reflection, without guides or preachers. Rather, it was cared for by the light of revelation from the very outset. Adam, the father of humanity, was the first among the unrivalled men of inspiration, the first to declare his faith in the one unique God and the first to turn to God in supplication and in veneration.

The fact that we find ourselves obliged to have recourse to these texts is itself an implicit admission of the inability of the human sciences to lead us, along a path of certainty, towards the exact starting point of religion. This is because, in truth, the only answer to this question will come from revelation itself. It takes us into the realm of the unknown, which is the object of faith, and not of the sciences, no matter what form they take.

On the whole, then, all these theories, which tried to present us with an image of the religion of the first man by equating it with the religions of the distant past or with those of the savage populations of today, did so in ways that are either slightly credible, or sorely deficient or altogether fabricated. Most of the time, these are only hypotheses built on other hypotheses. They do not deliver the 'truth' – which is, by definition, the avowed goal of science – but only probable possibilities that, in one way or another, resemble the 'truth'.

We now propose to present a survey of some of the theories that have dealt with the first triggers of the belief in God in the minds of men. It must be made clear, however, that we will stop following these theories the moment they claim to portray the primary state of religious life, which they are incapable of, as we have just seen. Instead, we will limit ourselves to an analysis of their arguments and of the historical references on which they are based.

---

[7] Prophetic tradition. See in *Sahih al-Bukhari*, 'Book of Funerals' (*Kitab al-Janaa'iz*), written by al-Bukhari.

Naturalism

a. Peaceful nature

Some scholars have argued that the primary impulse in the awakening of the religious idea in the human mind is the observation of nature, especially the spectacles of the celestial spheres and elements.

Contemplation of the unfathomable vistas of nature gives man the feeling of being surrounded on all sides by a superior, overpowering force over which he has no control. It is a force that subjects the entire universe to its will, and man finds himself impelled to recognize his inability to undo or modify anything in the course of things. Thus, enamoured by feelings of awe and admiration, man begins to see the world as a miracle. In truth, it is a great miracle, for nothing is less natural than nature itself.

The most famous defender of this theory is the German philosopher Max Müller in his book *Comparative Mythology*. He does not limit himself, however, to this mental response of man to cosmic infinities. He enriches it with various philological investigations inspired by his comparative studies of ancient myths and traditions, particularly his analysis of the Vedas, the books of the Brahminic religion. He notes in these texts how the names of the deities tend to be the same as those of natural forces, such as the sky, fire and so on. He adds that the letters that form the names of these deities are similar to those that compose the names of these natural elements across most of the so-called Indo-European languages. Thus, Müller concludes that the first humans, before leaving their original motherland, and before branching off into different races, used a uniform language to express their reverence towards these natural elements. The religious idea, therefore, would have emerged long before the appearance of any specific culture or civilization.

The fact that religion, in the precise sense of the term, cannot exist without belief in active, living beings, endowed with reason, to whom we address our worship, imposes the question of the cause of such a mental leap from the contemplation of the spectacle of the visible world to the formulation of the ideal of the necessary existence of invisible forces.

This, too, replies Müller, is explained by the influence of languages, since they tend to attribute to the different elements of nature actions and behaviours similar to those observed in humans. We say, for example, that the river 'runs', that the sun 'rises', that the wind 'groans' or 'roars', that the fire 'breathes' and so on. However, these expressions, originally figurative and allegorical, were taken in the long run for their real and literal meanings. So much so that the elements themselves ended up taking in the minds of men the form of living and thinking beings. It is from this point that we began representing celestial bodies and elements by human or animal forms. With imagination playing an important role, we resorted to the symbolic representation of the same ideal using different forms, depending on the number of names attributed to it or, on the contrary, to the depiction of multiple diverse facts as one and the same, under one shared symbol which applies to all, and so on.

The reader will surely realize by now that while this theory may succeed in explaining myths and legends, it cannot be suitable for explaining religions.

Max Müller himself acknowledges that the kind of thinking which represents the elements in the form of thinking animals can only come from a troubled mentality, caught in the net of fantasies and delusions, sunk in the depths of lunacy and delirium.

We will add, for our part, that this analysis does not come from a strictly religious mentality. This mentality, as already demonstrated, places its faith in an independent spirit that governs the world, not in a substance trapped in nature and subject to its whims.

It would seem more sensible to understand this mental transfer from the contemplation of material forms to the conception of the idea of an invisible mind as a kind of natural progression from the created to the creator, which proceeds by the rules of logic, without needing the intervention of language. For just as the person who admires a work of art cannot help but think of the artistic skills of its creator, or the person who inspects the nuts and bolts of a complex machine cannot help but be astonished by the ingenuity of its designer, the admiration one feels upon contemplating the wonders of the universe will lead, quite naturally, to marvelling at the majesty of the intelligent force that begat and sustained them. If the mythological point of view (which ascribes speech to inanimate objects and is persuaded that an intelligent spirit inhabits them) is neither natural nor religious, then this inferential logic is, on the contrary, both religious and logical. The human brain can hardly imagine or accept that agglomerates of matter, devoid of soul and sensitivity, can move, by their own volition, along well-defined orbits, in between other mobile bodies with which they work in unison towards achieving a pre-ordered, intelligent objective. Such flawless choreography can only be orchestrated, directly or indirectly, by something endowed with will and feeling, and which organizes and regulates all these movements with utmost precision and diligence.

Imagine, if you will, a finely built residence, richly furnished and decorated, situated at the top of an inaccessible mountain, or enclosed in an impenetrable forest. Imagine that one day a man succeeds in reaching this dwelling and, having seen no living soul either inside or around, concludes with certainty that the rocks of the mountain were cut off and then pieced together, by themselves, to build this magnificent residence, with all its alcoves and arcades, its rooms and amenities; that the trees of the forest were also transformed into planks which were then assembled into doors and partitions, seats and pedestal tables, and that these were distributed, each taking its intended place, to furnish rooms and lounges; that the plants, as well as animal furs, were spontaneously woven to make carpets and curtains, and were delivered to every room in the house to provide luxury and comfort; that the lamps grew out of the ceilings in bunches to ensure perfect lighting .... Would you not think that such an explanation could only come from a mind affected by delirium, hallucination or mental confusion? What if now this palace had the heavens for its ceiling, the entire earth for its foundation, the mountains for its pillars, the plants for its decoration, and the sun, the moon and the stars for its illumination? Could this miracle be easier to explain than this inferior and insignificant structure? Should not the creation of the universe be more likely to awaken our minds to the necessary existence of a master maker, a living god, who created all things in due proportion, who determined their destinies and guided them?[8]

If our admiration for the beauty of a work of art makes us instinctively wonder about the artist who created it, and to seek ways to express our appreciation and admiration, even if he remains unknown to us, would not our admiration of the wonders of the world make us more likely to address its creator in supplication, to confide in him and to try to show him our gratitude, our deep deference and our fervent veneration? Is worship of God, after all, anything other than that?

---

[8] Qur'an 87:2–3. (Ed.)

If we attempt to analyze the kind of obedient supplication that characterizes the believer's attitude towards the divine, we will find two crucial observations:

1. It supposes that the thing to which this intimate prayer is addressed is willing and capable of receiving it.
2. It supposes that this thing is a being superior to man and more powerful than him, since it can do what man is incapable of.

We must therefore exclude the possibility that this thing is raw matter, blind and deaf, which does not feel, nor see, nor hear our prayers. Otherwise, this adored object would be deprived of life, reason and sense, all of which are enjoyed by the entities he created. Clearly, this would be a contradictory and self-refuting proposition.

Faith in God and the act of worship arise from the union of two innate elements in the human psyche. The first is the kind of mental instinct that makes man aspire to understand the natural world that surrounds him. The second is his emotional sense, an aesthetic sensibility that makes him react in the presence of the beauty and majesty of the universe.

That the idea of God proceeds from the contemplation of nature, that there is an unbreakable link between religious thought and sensitivity to the natural universe, is what the testimonies of all people of all times constantly confirm.

> Exalted is He who holds all control in His hands; who has power over all things; ... who created the seven heavens, one above the other. You will not see any flaw in what the Lord of Mercy creates. Look again! Can you see any flaw? Look again! Your sight will turn back to you, weak and defeated. 67:1–4

This theory certainly remains among the most convincing explanations of the source of religious thought, despite the objections that may be raised against it.

Objections to this theory

Some critics reject the claim that the contemplation of nature can lead to the awakening of deep religious feelings. They argue that the repetitious and monotonous unfolding of the spectacle of the world, on the contrary, creates invariable complacency to the point that it no longer attracts attention or demands rational explanation. Even if one supposes that it can provoke wonder and humility in intelligent minds, this could not be the case in naïve[9] minds, which go so far as to arrogate to themselves special abilities to change the laws of nature, to invoke the winds, to call down rain and so on. These critics add that it is religious belief itself which ingrains these ideas in the minds of simple men, since it teaches them that 'with faith, they can move mountains'.

Faith, therefore, finds its source in man's power to confront the elements of nature, and not in his weakness or surrender to it.[10] If the triggers of faith, the critics add, were only the feeling of our weakness and insignificance in the face of nature which makes us search for ways to attract its benevolence and ward off its misdeeds, then all religions would be incoherent nonsense, because clearly it is neither prayer, nor fasting nor the offering of sacrifices that causes the rain to fall, or waterways to flow, or that eradicates famine, misery or disease. Lived and observed experience would have conclusively demonstrated to all men that these means, for the most part, are futile and ineffective. Then again, if it is the spectacle of the universe that awakens the religious feeling, and if the purpose of prayer is to implore the mercy of nature, man would have quickly relinquished his faith the moment he is convinced of the frivolity of these attempts. But since religions have not disappeared, nor will ever fade away, we must concede that their causes and purposes must be found elsewhere. The fact remains, however, that even if we are able to explain the reverence certain individuals feel towards the imposing forces of nature as the result of the feelings of awe and bewilderment that these forces leave in them, how can we account for the worship of standing stones, trees, insects and other trivialities which do not give rise to the same reactions? These critics, then, raise a final problem: How can we explain the phenomenon of

---

[9] It is worth mentioning here that most researchers differentiate between enlightened and ignorant minds in the reverse order. They consider the attitude whereby this moving feeling leads to explaining natural phenomena by the presence of an invisible higher force to be a mark of naïve minds that are guided by bare instincts, without any awareness of logic or scientific laws. Indeed, this point of view may seem closer to observed reality than its opposite. However, it remains no less erroneous, because we are only too aware that learning does not attenuate this feeling but rather reinforces it. This is directly attested by some of the most influential modern philosophers. Pascal writes, 'The eternal silence of infinite spaces terrifies me'; Kant also says, 'Two things fill the mind with ever new and increasing admiration and awe, the more often and steadily we reflect upon them: the starry heavens above me and the moral law within me.'

[10] Some contemporary authors have taken up this argument and broadened it. But, given its problematic nature, they quickly ran into self-contradiction. See al-Aqqad, *Allah: Kitab fi nash'at al-'aqidah al-'Ilahiyyah*, pp. 10–11.

the clear separation established by religions between the lawful and the illicit, the sacred and the profane?

These are the main objections that Émile Durkheim[11] raised against the theory which maintains that a transfer can take place from the observation of the concrete elements of the universe to the abstractions of the religious feeling.

Response to objections

There is no denying that sameness and habituation efface the sharpness of reactions, that the monotonous repetition of sensations can drive away the impulse to ponder their origins and sources. However, cosmic phenomena, despite the regularity of their occurrence, perpetually reveal before our sensory perception alternate images and ever-renewed formations. For example, the changing phases of the moon, the various positionings of the stars,[12] the rising and setting of the sun, the spectacles of dawn and dusk, the alternation of night and day,[13] the fluctuations of winds, seasonal variations and the blooms and droughts that they bring, all of which carry new reminders for whoever listens attentively and whoever sees with clarity.[14] We do not mean to say, however, that everyone must necessarily indulge in reflections about the origins and mysteries of these phenomena, but we affirm that whoever pays attention must inevitably be struck by wonder and feel a deep sense of reverence and humility.

The assertion that the minds of 'savages' are incapable of this awareness because they tend to attempt to subjugate the natural elements to their personal ends or their pleasure would be based on a misreading of lived reality, particularly if applied to every individual at all times. Simple ordinary people are far too destitute to dare grant themselves such powers. Moreover, even if a select few – practitioners of sorcery and magic – give the impression of influencing certain earthly forces, this does not prevent them from humbly submitting to higher forces that no mortal hand can reach. God brings the sun from the east; who can bring it from the west?[15] Every soul will taste death;[16]

---

[11] Durkheim, *Forme Elémentaires de la Vie religieuse*, pp. 112–21.
[12] Qur'an 56:75. (Ed.)
[13] Qur'an 2:164. (Ed.)
[14] Qur'an 50:37. (Ed.)
[15] Qur'an 2:258. (Ed.)
[16] Qur'an 3:185. (Ed.)

who then is able to secure eternity? Who could part from his shadow, or go back in time or make his offspring grow to his likeness? Who has ever managed to create a fly or any insect?

We have already demonstrated how magic and religion are two wholly different activities, both in nature and in purpose. Feeling oneself capable of subjugating certain natural forces might be observed in a magician or an alchemist, but it cannot in any way cross the mind of a believer. One cannot, in fact, venerate something which he feels capable of subduing, nor can one subjugate something which he, at the same time, claims to adore and worship.

The maxim 'faith moves mountains' does not mean that man's strength is the source of his faith. There is a difference between saying that faith is the source of strength and saying that strength gives birth to faith. Confusing the two is to reverse their roles; it is to put effects in the place of their causes, to present conclusions before their propositions. Thus, we can see how haste and overindulgence can only lead to opinions critically lacking in rigor and precise expression. But, then again, what is this strength that faith generates? Is it not the strength rooted in confidence and certainty that comes to us in compensation for our intrinsic feeling of weakness and bewilderment, which are the original impulses of religious sentiment itself, and from which proceeds the strength of faith? Does it not spring from the trust that the believer places in this higher spiritual power in which he takes refuge? Lastly, we must be careful not to confuse the ability to understand and admire the world with the ability to change or influence its course. The most powerful minds and the most eminent scientists are at the same time the most aware of man's weakness and pettiness in the face of the grandiose universe, as well as of his dependence on and subordination to its higher laws, laws that no one can modify. It is this feeling which constitutes the inception of faith as well as the primary impulse of deification and devotion.

Here, we wonder about the meaning of this mysterious mental sequence which passes from reflection and contemplation to reverence and admiration, ending in veneration of and verbal supplication to the creator. Should there be a logical purpose behind all of this? When you ponder a work of art and find yourself overwhelmed by its beauty and artistry, do you not feel within yourself an irresistible impulse to express your enthusiasm to its creator, as if you owed him a debt of honour for which you expect no reward or benefit in return, except the satisfaction of being able to translate your admiration into words of gratitude?

What then would be your reaction to the most extraordinary of masterpieces? Would it not provoke in you an irresistible attraction towards its designer to express your admiration and gratitude to him, to praise him, to adore his majesty, without expecting anything in return? What then if you realize that you are, yourself, part of this magnificent creation and that you are indebted for your intelligence, your strength, your very existence, to this master maker who created and shaped you, who gave you sight and hearing, who granted you reason and eloquence, who put at your service all the bounties of heaven and earth; would you not feel drawn to him with all your heart and senses, full of gratitude, humility and submission? All these are the noble goals unfailingly delivered by religions. How can one say, then, that humility before the magnificence of the universe, and the surge of devotion towards its creator (which is often derived from inner impulses), can be explained away as mere calculated decisions which aim to extract some material advantage or to avoid some calamity or misfortune?

In his critique, Durkheim clearly confused two different hypotheses: the hypothesis of 'admiration', which we are currently discussing, and that of 'desire and fear', with which we will deal later on in this chapter. He thus opposed one of the hypotheses based on the objections associated with the other.

Suppose that the motive for worship is only the expression of a need, and that the meaning of prayer and supplication turns from glorification and praise of the creator to the simple appeal for protection. Even if this were the case, the devotee knows very well that he cannot regard his prayer as an irreversible means of attaining his goals, as if it were an operation involving mathematical calculation or logical deductions or a scientific experiment, the results of which would be guaranteed. This is because religious faith is always directed towards a force that acts only according to its own will. Hence, we find in the invocations of the faithful a double feeling: an amalgam of submission and ready acceptance towards the known and of hope and anxious expectation towards the unknown.

If the intrepid athlete, who sees himself losing time and again, cannot easily succumb to final defeat, and maintains the hope that, sooner or later, luck will smile upon him once more and grant him victory, we have all the more reason to be convinced that the believer will be able to remove from his mind any cause of despair, to be filled with hope and optimism throughout his life and beyond the grave. Moreover, the honest believer who turns to the object of his adoration, to implore him and to confide in him his desires and his fears, will in fact find in these very appeals and invocations a remedy for his anguish; they become more precious to him than the grievances for which they are invoked in the first place. It is enough for him to know that, by these outbursts of faith (in his words, his movements and his very being), he presents a sincere account of his awareness of reality, of the clarity of vision with which he separates the impotence of the creature from the omnipotence of the creator. By his awareness and his way of expressing it, he fulfils the highest duty that has been entrusted to man on this earth. Hence, it makes no difference to him whether or not his prayers are met with the approval of his master, for he will have achieved, in advance, thanks to his humble devotion, his noblest objective, which is to conquer his pride, to put himself in his rightful place in the universe and to purify his soul to achieve the maturity of his spiritual disposition. These are indeed the supreme goals of believers, the delight of their eyes.

Let us turn now to the objection which proposes that if the point of departure of the religious sentiment is the contemplation of the grandeur and magnificence of nature, then devotion should have been directed, first and foremost, to its most impressive elements: the sun, the moon, the seas, the mountains, the winds and so on, and not to minor elements, such as the plants or animals, which the author of this objection deems to be the older and more frequently observed form of worship.

We have already pointed out that historical research and excavations by archaeologists in this field have produced contradictory results which cannot be fully trusted; that Durkheim's conclusions, based on what he believed to be the oldest and most primitive, have since been contradicted by other research that revealed older forms of belief; and that the increasing possibility that science will one day discover earlier epochs, which in turn could reveal to us novel and unsuspected religious formulations, undermines our confidence in historical and archaeological research, since our knowledge would be based on something shifting and susceptible to constant change and modification every time a new discovery is made. We also noted that although the theories which assert the primacy of those religions grounded in the worship of a single god, who is the master creator, have not been sustained by definitive and irrefutable arguments, we must still recognize that they are, at least theoretically, more credible than others.

The definition we proposed earlier for the word 'religion' makes us raise yet another doubt about this objection, particularly in view of its unwarranted assumption that devotion for the elements of nature takes place in a literal sense. Historians of religions have demonstrated that objects of worship, material or invisible, large or small, have never been venerated for themselves. They are often considered, in fact, either as receptacles and reference points, or as symbolic representations, of higher mysterious forces, of their attributes and their actions. This last point is surprisingly confirmed by Durkheim himself in more than one passage in his book. The believer's reaction in the face of these concrete objects is very similar to that of a lover who stops by the traces of the beloved's abandoned campsite. He does so, not out of love for the place itself, but out of nostalgia for its now-absent inhabitants. We could add that the devotion directed towards small and trivial creatures, as symbolic representations of that higher dominant force, rather presupposes the recognition of the effects of this force in other grandiose entities. Thus, it would be reasonable to argue that the ability to apprehend the subtleties of smaller beings is a sign of a more evolved intelligence than that which is astonished by impressive natural events that anyone can see with their eyes. This interest in the small things of nature denotes, at the very least, a capacity for deep reflection, a precision and rigor of reflection capable of seeing exceptional signs of wonder in every part of the universe: 'And in everything you will find a sign of His power.'[17]

It remains to examine the distinction between the sacred and the profane proposed by Durkheim. According to his theory, this distinction boils down to the difference between what is divine and what is human; in other words, between what is sublime and extraordinary, and what is banal, trivial and negligible. Yet the fact remains that things do not produce the same effects on all men, neither in the attention they attract, nor in the beholding of the eye, nor in the edification of spirits nor in the capture of hearts. What you consider

---

[17] Part of a line from a famous poem attributed to the ancient Arab poet Labid (c. 560 – c. 661). See Brockelmann, 'Labid b. Rabiʿa', in *Encyclopaedia of Islam* (2nd ed.), vol. 5, pp. 583-4. (Ed.)

beautiful and wonderful may not always be the same for me. A flower or an insect may catch your eye and occupy your thought, while others may pay no attention to it, and may not be in the least spiritually inspired by it.

All things are divided variously between what is, in the eyes of people, minor and does not deserve attention and what is major or divine and inspires the idea of the 'sacred'. That is to say, which gives rise to the most intense feeling of submission and the strongest spiritual drives which lead to glorification.[18] This glorification is not for these creatures themselves but for their maker and creator.

b. Violent nature

The English scholar Jevons also considers the observation of natural phenomena to be the primary impulse of religious belief. However, he declares in his *Introduction to the History of Religion* that the regular and uniform aspects of nature are not sufficient to give rise to religious belief, because the fact of habituation, resulting from constant repetition of phenomena before our senses, does not provoke the mind to reflect or seek an explanation for them. Sudden earthly turbulences or rare atmospheric phenomena, on the other hand, disrupt the monotonous unfolding of the course of nature. Lightning, thunder, storms, thunderbolts, avalanches, floods or earthquakes, all of these occurrences act as alarm signals to awaken the inattentive and the oblivious. This is because it is ingrained in the minds of men as in the instinct of animals that something cannot come out of nothing (even birds and wild beasts are frightened by unusual disturbing noises and turn in their direction with the intuition that such noises must have a cause). It is therefore only natural for

---

[18] Durkheim, in his attempt to explain religion, first desisted from defining it in terms of the sacred: 'The sacred is not necessarily the most superior and dignified' (*Forme Elémentaires*, pp. 51–2). He retained from the sacred only its practical side, and from the latter only its negative sense – that is to say, taboo, prohibition and untouchability. He then returned to implicitly assert the view, which he had already denounced, that 'the idea of majesty is essentially a religious one' (ibid., p. 87). In our judgement, the 'sacred' in fact draws its influence from the theoretical domain, not from the practical. Not everything that is forbidden is necessarily sacred; but what is sacred among the forbidden things is what the divine authority has forbidden. Sanctifying the taboo by prohibiting any attempt to approach it, for example, would be senseless if one were not convinced of the existence of a force which protects it, which prevents its violation and which surrounds it with a fence of exclusion, of sanctity, that one must respect out of veneration for this protecting authority. It is this kind of reverence and consideration that constitutes the cornerstone of the meaning of the 'sacred'.

abrupt and violent phenomena to disturb he who witnesses them and push him to inquire into their source. And if no apparent cause is found, he will come to suppose, out of rational necessity, that they must have an invisible cause endowed with extraordinary powers. Indeed, the human mind has no way out of these two extremes.

Jevons, nevertheless, does not reject the idea that ordinary phenomena and consistent natural occurrences can also give rise to religious sentiment. But, according to him, this can only be achieved by deep reflection, when there is peace of mind, maturity of thought and total absence of distractions. He thus contends that the feeling of fear and anxiety takes precedence over that of admiration in the awakening of religiosity.

Clearly, all the questions raised by the first theory, that of peaceful nature, and the answers to them, could be repeated here, since they both belong to the same category.

However, this theory of Jevons, which managed to escape the objections that had been raised against Max Müller, attracted the criticism of Auguste Sabatier,[19] who argued that the feelings of awe and fear inspired by superior forces do not alone suffice to explain the birth of the religious idea. They must be joined by other feelings that can counterbalance them and attenuate their sharpness.

This is because, he explains, when fear takes hold of an individual, it will obliterate his will; it will paralyze him and put him in a state of despair. If we fall prey to panic, while losing hope in the possibility of salvation, we will not attempt to call to be rescued from the perils we find ourselves in. Therefore, in order for the religious sentiment to emerge within us, fear and panic must be offset by an equal measure of hope and fervent wishes that can inspire invocation and prayer, both of them the very essence of religiosity.

Animism

We have just seen how thinkers working in the naturalist paradigm attempt to defend the view that belief in God in fact arises from contemplation of the

---

[19] Sabatier, *Esquisse d'une Philosophie de la Religion*, p. 13.

exterior material universe, so much so that some have claimed that the first form of religion practiced by men was the worship of nature itself.

We now turn to expounding the opposite doctrine, the theory of Animism, which asserts that the first religions consisted in the worship of the souls of the dead and not of concrete nature.

As we see it, this dichotomous framing of spirit and matter rests on a confusion between the element which gives rise to religiosity and the very object of veneration, since we have said, time and again, that worship always proceeds towards an abstract spiritual principle. We have already seen Max Müller, chief advocate of the naturalist theory, declare that our observation of the wonders of the spheres and elements will, before long, pass from these natural forces to spiritual forces endowed with private will and reason, and that, without this transition, they could not be admitted into the domain of religion.

In reality, the difference between the two approaches does not lie as much in their logical arguments as in their understanding of the nature of this transfer, as well as their designation of the precise moment of its appearance. The naturalists maintain that belief in an ineffable force (or forces) dominating the world arose from the kind of intuitive contemplation of the material world which infers from the splendour of creation and its inconceivable character the skill and intelligence of the spirit which created it; in the same way, one can assume the existence of the rational faculty in a human being by simply observing the traces of his capacities for reasoning, expression or coherent conduct, and so on, without physically seeing or touching them in himself. The animist doctrine maintains that the idea of the existence of mysterious, invisible but active forces is likewise based on experiences of a similar nature, directly observable by men in their immediate social settings. The two approaches lead to the same result, even if the logic uniting the premises to their conclusions may seem, at first glance, less rigorous in the animist doctrine. In naturalism, the passage takes place from visible material objects to the postulation of abstract spiritual ideas; in animism, we pass directly from one spiritual realm to another.

The animist theory was pioneered by Edward Tylor in his book *Primitive Culture* and was adopted, with some modifications, by the English philosopher Herbert Spencer in his *Principles of Sociology*.

We must begin by first pausing for a moment on the meaning of the word 'soul', a potentially problematic term given its homonymic nature. After all, proponents of animism conclude that activities associated with this 'soul' sufficiently explain the awakening in man of the belief in a higher spirit worthy of worship. We will then turn to elucidating the true meaning of this theory and its logical implications before closing with a discussion of some of its additional aspects which deserve closer scrutiny.

The question here is certainly not one of the principle of animal life (even if the field bears the ill-fated and misleading term of 'animism') – that is to say, of the principle from which emanate growth, respiration, sensitivity, movement and so on, but rather of the higher principle which inspires thought, organized will, feelings and consciousness. In other words, the principles of superior rational life.

Everyone can easily conceive of the difference between these two categories and conclude that this soul, which is specific to man, differs from the other, which is common to man and animal. We observe that the individual who is sleeping, or who has lost consciousness or who is suffering from dementia continues to breathe, to nourish, to walk; thus, he is in possession of his 'animal' life until the moment he recovers this special power or 'soul' which will give him back control over his consciousness and the consistency of his reasoning. These experiences, and the resulting idea of the separation of the two functions, have been generally accepted by scientists to the present day.

But, if we let our mind wander freely beyond these preliminary observations, it will pass over this practical distinction between the two functions to the intrinsic separation of the two elements; it will conceive of two very distinct principles, two independent essences. This independent character, once established, will allow us to move one step further.

Having observed that when consciousness is detached from the body during sleep it does not become pure nothingness, since it is regained when awakening, we begin to wonder why it would then not be the same when they are separated at the time of death. It is true that the alternation of life and death has not been verified by scientific experiments, unlike that of the waking and sleeping states. However, asking whether the soul actually returns to the body or not is one thing, and to declare that its detachment from the body after death means that it has been reduced to nothing, is another. Indeed, this conclusion is not supported by any evidence, and humans naturally repudiate such a thought.

Our survival instinct connects us, on the one hand, to a past that we cannot forget and whose memories we seek to preserve and, on the other, to a distant future in which we hope for the return of absent ones, no matter how prolonged this absence may be, in which we await a reunion with the departed, no matter how long it may take. The prospect of soul extinction is also disparaged by the conventions of our reason, conventions that rely on concrete and repeated observations. Just as we do not accept the idea that something can be generated by nothing, neither can we easily accept the idea that something can be reduced to nothing. All that our minds conceive of upon the disappearance of something is an alteration of form, a transformation of temporal and spatial qualities. We naturally view the idea of death as a separation of the two principles, the body and the soul, each of which will then return to its own nature and to its element of origin; the body returns to its material world, and the soul takes on a new invisible form in the realm of mystery. This is the origin of the idea of the existence of free souls, independent of bodies.

We thus arrive at the fourth link in this chain, or at the fourth of the concentric circles of the animist theory, which suggests that the passage of souls from the perceived world of forms to the realm of mystery, from the visible to the invisible, does not necessarily reduce their powers but, on the contrary, reinforces them. As long as the soul is tied to a specific body, it remains, more or less, imprisoned in this frame, occupied with its governance and lacking any influence over anything except the physical frame in which it resides. While in this state, it can only be described as an enslaved and controlled soul, and not free or autonomous. But as soon as she departs the body, due to sleep, or death or for any other reason, she again becomes a free spirit, occupying a wider sphere, capable of her own initiative, whether good or evil, without anyone even noticing.

Do not think this last step is the product of the whims of imagination or of simple intellectual abstraction based on mere wishful thinking and conjecture. Men do have recourse to it to explain certain phenomena for which they find no other explanation. We often encounter in the realm of human activity behaviours that are strange, that stand out, for better or worse, from established social norms, behaviours that some find laudable and others reprehensible. We see, in every age, exceptional and anomalous phenomena to which no one has been able to provide plausible explanations, and which have been linked to the intervention of mysterious forces – the adept soothsayer, the inspired poet, the charismatic orator, the fearless warrior, the unerring hunter, the prodigious mathematician who, without pencil or paper, solves the longest and most complex problems, or 'the illuminated seer who guesses you better than if he had seen and heard everything about you'.[20] It is said that all success and genius came to these individuals thanks to the support of a favourable spirit which endowed them with superhuman qualities. In contrast, those who are afflicted with lunacy or madness, or who find themselves in the grip of vice, perversion or criminal impulses, will be said to be possessed by an evil and malevolent spirit.

We could also add curious cases of true visions – of precise acumen, of judicious inspiration, of seeing events in distant places once they occur – or seeing ghosts, or hearing voices or any other phenomena that cannot be properly ascribed to concrete or rational causes.

It makes no difference to us whether these observations or experiences and the deductions that can be drawn from them are sound and reliable. What matters is that they reinforce each other and allow this hypothesis to explain the rise of two forms of belief:

1. Belief in the existence of creatures endowed with thought that our senses cannot perceive. These entities can be souls that have departed their human bodies, or originally and intrinsically independent souls – such as jinns or angels – or even higher and more sublime entities.
2. Belief that these nonmaterial hidden beings can, with their unique supernatural capacities, penetrate the domain of human perception and leave in the consciousness of men lasting, inexplicable effects.[21]

These simple assertions are deemed sufficient to explain the rise of the idea of the divine.

---

[20] From a poem by the pre-Islamic Arabian poet ibn Hujr, see *Diwan Aws ibn Hujr*, p. 53. (Ed.)
[21] We must remember here that these inclinations to believe in mysterious forces, and in their influence, are not exclusive to one particular nation or religion; they relate to all people, whether civilized or not. None of the known religions is exempt from it. Spiritualist schools are currently exploring ways of approaching them through experimentation and advanced scientific means.

This mysterious being, hitherto supposed by naturalists to originate from observing the elements of the material universe, is now wholly deduced from the same abstract domain to which it belongs, from lived human experiences which lead the mind to imagine him, to conclude he is a great spirit capable of creating wonders and mysteries. This spirit, which can, by its own will, grant men enlightenment or deprive them of it, is undoubtedly a superior, active and creative spirit.

Some might object by saying that the unmistakable infinite diversity of created beings could be a proof of the multiplicity of creators, just as each river flows from its own unique source. That if we admit the existence of several gods, instead of one supreme Creator, would they not all equally deserve honour and veneration?

The answer to this objection will be shaped by the varying degrees of acuteness or dullness of people's minds.

Limited intelligences, those of men suffering from mental myopia, will equate the number of their venerated gods with the concrete and particular phenomena they have observed. They will restrict the powers of each of these gods to the relevant sphere in which the phenomenon occurs – the spirit of the holy man or the patron saint in whose presence my prayers have been answered and lavish blessings felt will be a god, the diviner or soothsayer whose predictions and foresight come to pass will be another god, the spirit that comes to the aid of a poet or orator and loosens his tongue will be a god, the angel who reveals divine communication to Prophets[22] will also be a god and so on.

Thus, oblivious men will be rendered speechless as they stare with dismay[23] at each of these wondrous effects. They will prostrate themselves before the first direct cause or before an intermediary cause whom they take as the true initiator of that great power. They will seldom free themselves from the shackles of immediate causes, remaining attached to narrow solutions subject to incidents of being and nothingness, appearance and disappearance, incapable of opening themselves to the possible existence of a higher Being, the invisible, the pre-existing, the eternal, who has full power over souls and

---

[22] Qur'an 53:10. (Ed.)
[23] Qur'an 21:97. (Ed.)

spirits. They are like he who, seeing a source in each river, does not realize that all rivers originate from a common source – water – which the Creator sends down from the sky and guides along to form gushing springs.[24]

As for the penetrating intelligences of men who wish to touch the heart of things and reach the root of problems, they will not stop at these fading shadows and fleeting forms. They do not allow themselves to be distracted by the vitality of the lesser forces of heaven and earth from the ultimate object of their efforts, which is to approach the Supreme Master, the God of gods, the Cause of causes, whom all beliefs, even extreme forms of paganism, recognize and revere, though they may rarely invoke him.

***

Let us now sketch a brief outline of the path taken by Tylor and his followers to demonstrate the emergence of belief in God from spiritualistic observations.

According to them, this belief took shape in two stages: The first is the faith in the eternal subsistence of the souls of the dead, and the second is the conviction that the stars and the other elements of the universe also have a soul.

They agree, in their explanation of the first stage, that the idea of eternal souls comes essentially from the experience of 'dreams', particularly the approach to this phenomenon found among 'primitive' peoples who are persuaded that the image of a person seen in a dream constitutes a real appearance of that person's soul. It appears in the form of a transparent image, an exact duplicate that has flown from the body and appeared in phantom form, as one sees a reflection in a mirror. As dreams reveal the dead as well as the living, in other words, as the souls of the dead as well as those of the living come to visit the dreamer, this proves that many souls of the dead abound in the world and that they can come into contact with the living, to help or harm them. All this requires that individuals endear themselves to them in order to avoid their misdeeds and solicit their sympathy.

It is at the second stage, however, which concerns the veneration of the souls of the stars and of other natural elements, that their explanations diverge.

For his part, Tylor, pioneer of the theory in question, considers the mentality of the primitive to be far too childlike and naïve to be capable of distinguishing between raw materials and living bodies, and considers them equally endowed

---

[24] Qur'an 39:21. (Ed.)

with life. He approaches them like a child who plays and speaks to his doll as if it had a soul. Spencer, however, rejects this explanation on the basis that it does not apply to the mentality of the child, or to that of animals, let alone to that of 'primitive' peoples. For him, this veneration of natural elements does not come from a mental confusion, as claimed by Tylor, but from a linguistic confusion which has to do with the names of venerated ancestors. These, in fact, sometimes bear the names of natural elements or animals, calling one of them 'star', another 'tiger' and another 'rock', so that the veneration is transferred from those who bore these names to the things for which they are named. It is a confusion between the names borrowed for the purpose of personification and the objects signified by these names.

As one can see, this second explanation is hardly better than the first: Both comprise the belief that the elements of the universe possess intrinsic supernatural qualities forming the basis of veneration, both consider this belief to be ultimately premised on ambiguity or confusion, and both decree that veneration is addressed to 'souls' supposed to reside in celestial bodies, and not to an independent mind that has control over them.

Insofar as ancestor worship is sustained, according to the animist thinkers, solely by the experience of dreams and the superstitious analysis they make of them, we can maintain that their theories are in fact as frail as the thread of a spider's web.[25]

Durkheim turned all his polemical powers against this weak point in the theory, arguing that the primitives do not need to interpret or analyze their dreams for themselves, and that if they ever experience this need, they would certainly not do it in the manner suggested by animist theoreticians. However, we will retain one aspect of this theory that, in our view, presents the most plausible and acceptable explanation of ancestor worship since it deals with the real causes of this phenomenon. Even if we grant that the experience of dreams is capable of initiating belief in 'souls', it cannot on its own provide a satisfactory explanation for their divine source and character. For some people, dreams can be nothing but hallucinations and incoherent chimera; for others, they are simply visions of past memories. Indeed, none of this seems to call for the need to have faith in a deified being. The only kind of dreams likely

---

[25] Qur'an 29:41. (Ed.)

to provoke this belief are those which display things of a specific inspiration or unveiling; the kind that could envisage unexpected events or facts that could not be attained by the light of human reason alone. Moreover, we do not know of a people whose respect for their dead led them to the veneration of *all* their dead or *all* their ancestors. Rather, the ones among them who became objects of sanctity were only those known during their lifetime to possess exceptional forces or powers, those who would have left a lasting imprint on nature or in society. Death, therefore, is neither the condition nor the cause of veneration. The criterion of sanctity is this mysterious power, this divine effulgence, whose effects can be found in the unusual and extraordinary activities observed in exceptional human beings.

The other points of criticism, thought by Durkheim to refute the very basis of animism, are mostly trivial and superficial controversies which debate the mentality of primitive peoples and the superstitious character of their thought. Aside from that, the essence of animism remains intact and emerges without much damage from these extended critiques.

The mysterious world of spirits is no less capable of inspiring the idea of the divine than the wondrous world of nature. In fact, it has closer associations with it since they both belong to the same domain of mystery. We have previously pointed out that the belief in the existence of spirits is not specific to so-called savage peoples. It is far-reaching, much older and more deeply rooted in the minds of all men than in this perceived primitive formulation. Durkheim himself admits this by stating that 'just as there is no known society without a religion, so there exist none, howsoever crudely organized they may be, where we do not find a whole system of collective representations concerning the soul, its origin and its destiny'.[26]

Psychology

This is another group of theories whose core concepts may be summarized in the fact that belief in the existence of God does not require the contemplation

---

[26] Durkheim, *Forme Elémentaires*, p. 343. [See Durkheim, *The elementary forms of religious life* (London, 1915), p. 243. Ed.]

of the beauty of nature, nor to be terrorized by its upheavals, nor to be troubled by the inexplicable manifestations and mysteries of the spiritual realm. It is rather our inner psychological reflections and our personal and daily experiences that compel us to admit the existence of a higher truth.

a. Sabatier

In the first chapter of his *Outlines of a Philosophy of Religion*, Sabatier attempted to base belief in God on a number of psychological observations. He argued that this belief begins to evolve from a very early stage in human life, precisely when man begins to feel in himself the intrinsic tension between his sensitivity and his will, which are two of the most basic elements in human psychology.

Our psychic life, he explains, is based essentially on two opposed movements: one acting from the outside to the inside (from the periphery to the centre) and the other from the inside to the outside (from the centre to the periphery). The first represents the influence that the environment exerts on us through the conduits of our sensitivity (the self's receptivity and passivity). The second is the reaction of our will to these influences (the efficacy of the self's activity). However, the effect of these two movements is not one and the same. Their conflicting actions are neither synchronous nor comparable because our sensitivity suppresses our will and crushes it.

Each time our human will tries to move towards the outside world, like a wave rising to new heights, it always breaks on the rocky shores of external reality and returns to where it started, disappointed and miserable. These repeated shocks and constant struggles between our being and the external world are the main cause of our pain. However, at the same time, they are also the source of the light of consciousness within us. For the repeated ebbs of this wave of broken will and its return to its base creates in us a focus of heat and energy similar to that produced by the wheel turning around its pivot. Before long, this heat will release a spark that will illuminate our whole being. This is the kind of awareness, or acute insight, which makes the person both understanding and understood, governing and governed. It becomes a twofold self, comprising a mind aspiring to the ideal and a stifled soul contending with its own reality.

This is how our psychic life begins: with the agonies of pain and defeat. Yet is not every birth accompanied by the tears and pains of labour?

Sabatier adds that every other human psychic state would seem, in light of this observation, to arise from one contradiction and vanish in another. The desire for knowledge ends with the admission of ignorance; pleasure and enjoyment end in revulsion, as if they carry the seeds of their own destruction; and devoting excessive efforts to the pursuit of worldly happiness results in a loss of serenity and, on the contrary, can augment pain and misery.

Where then do we go from here?

According to Sabatier, it would be wrong to count on our scientific advancements to save us from this misery and frustration because science, instead of easing these imposing contradictions, will, on the contrary, sharpen them and make them more lethal. Each new scientific discovery in fact forms an additional link in the long procession of causes necessary to explain things, their organization and permanence. Hence, the sciences only tie us with additional heavy chains that limit our freedom, until we arrive at the decisive separation between knowledge and action, thought and movement, and natural laws and moral laws. It is amidst this internal struggle, this raging battle between the faculties of our psyche, that we will find ourselves despairing of attaining the very meaning of life.

But it is from this internal crisis, too, that religiosity is born, as springs of fresh water erupt from a cracked rocky surface following an earthquake. This sort of faith will not provide a theoretical solution to our crises, because the answers that religions provide are always purely practical. Religion may not open new horizons of knowledge, but it will surely and effectively lead us back to the higher principle that comprises our very being. It gives us faith and confidence in Him who is the source and final destination of all reality. Though the vital role played by this confidence in the realm of the human psyche resembles that of the survival instinct in the physical world, it remains, nonetheless, far more noble. In the physical world, our instincts are propelled by an oppressive blind force, while in the psychic world, they are inspired by both the light of consciousness and the rational will. This confidence is also based, adds Sabatier, on experiences in the real world, on a feeling concomitant with the nature of every human being, which is the feeling of subordination, of absolute surrender to the one common law which rules over all creation.

Who could ever escape this feeling of helplessness? Has not our share of fate been decided for us without our being consulted? Has not our existence, here and now, been mandated for us by someone else? Have we not been endowed, in spite of ourselves, with special capacities and distinctive characteristics? Indeed, no matter how much we seek, we do not find, whether in ourselves or in any other class of created beings, either the reason for our existence, or the justification of our utility or the explanation of our finality. This is why we find ourselves forced to seek these justifications outside of ourselves – that is to say, in the vast expanse of existence. Then again, religiosity is nothing but our admission of these feelings of helplessness and humility.

This feeling of dependence, according to Sabatier, comprises the empirical basis of faith in God. No matter how deficient and incomplete the idea of God may be in our mind, it never ceases to be felt by our senses. It is always present in us, so strongly that it makes us feel justified to pose the following formulaic equation with full confidence: Our feeling of absolute dependence proves that the divine mystery resides within us. It is from this that the idea of the existence of God emanates, with irresistible force, as from a deep spring.

However, there remains the question of knowing how human reason can accept its subordination to this supreme, all-encompassing principle. This rebellious reason, which considers itself to be of a nature different from that of matter, which is aware that its role is to understand, to dominate and to subject things to its own ends, how can it accept being placed in a position of inferiority? 'Man', wrote Pascal, 'is a reed, the most feeble thing in nature, but he is a thinking reed. ... If the universe were to crush him, man would still be more noble than that which killed him, because he knows that he dies. ... The universe knows nothing of this.'[27]

Thus, it can be seen that the principle to which man must submit is not matter but the universal spirit that governs the world of matter. The rational faculty can only submit to an authority similarly endowed with reason that dominates it and the world alike. We thus see that our mental life, which was born out of the conflict between self-consciousness and the concrete experience of the outside world, finds its complement and its resolution in

---

[27] Pascal and Rawlings, *Pascal's Pensées; or, Thoughts on Religion*, p. 120. (Ed.)

a third factor which unifies the other two – their common submission to an authority which reigns supreme over them.

This beautifully written page by Sabatier remains among the most meticulous attempts to analyze the idea of God in revealed religions. But can it be applied to all religions? Could we say that its philosophical complexity and its high degree of abstraction make it an unlikely candidate for a universal theory that explains the religiosity of mankind?

Sabatier anticipated this criticism and responded by saying,

> Those who raise this objection have not sufficiently marked the permanent nature of the initial contradiction which constitutes, at the beginning as at the end, the empirical life of man. ... To experience it and to suffer from it, man did not need to wait until he became a philosopher. It manifested itself in the terrors of the savage in the presence of the cataclysms of nature, in the midst of the perils of the primeval forest no less than in our troubled thought in the presence of the enigma of the universe and the mystery of death. The expression of human misery and the consciousness thereof are different things; the religious thrill which brings relief, at bottom, is the same. ..... [When people] cease to reason in order to decide to live, do they not feel forming within themselves, and in spite of themselves, a sigh which is the beginning of a prayer?[28]

b. Bergson

This theory is somewhat similar to the previous one in that it proposes that belief in God is triggered by man's psychological experiences in his daily life.

But while Sabatier's theory deals with man's relationship with the fixed and permanent laws of the external world, and with the consistent failures of the human will to overpower these laws and its consequential surrender to the power which established them and imposed them, Henri Bergson, on the other hand, in his work *The Two Sources of Morality and Religion*, engages in the analysis of two other aspects of the same daily life. The first relates to the moral laws imposed by society and its established customs and norms. The second concerns man's projections of the future, which open up gates of indefinite

---

[28] Sabatier, *Esquisse d'une Philosophie*, pp. 14–22. [See Sabatier, *Outlines of a philosophy of religion based on psychology and history* 1902, pp. 24–5. Ed.]

possibilities, which cause uncertainty, since they are often unpredictable and subject to chance.

Let us now attempt to explain how belief in God, according to Bergson, arises from a feeling of social responsibility. Given that the rules of social cohesion require the individual to give up certain desires, to sacrifice part of his freedom, to bear burdens which are of no direct benefit to him because they are necessary for the good of others; given that it is not easy for a person to willingly accept all these sacrifices and deprivations because his sense of civic responsibility is never strong enough to make him forget himself while serving the common good, or to make him act like the ants or the bees in their selfless service of their kind; and given that even a simple intelligence would show men that contributing to the collective good imposes greater costs than benefits, and that their personal interest must come first, all this calls for the need of another authority capable of maintaining equilibrium among the varied and associated interests of the individual and society. This authority, says Bergson, was naturally and deeply integrated in the human mind in the form of the religious idea. It depicted social prohibitions as a frightful affair, fraught with danger, since any violation of them entailed severe consequences. This representation was enacted many times over, to the point of convincing men that social taboos are protected by an invisible and mysterious, authoritarian and repressive, guardian who holds transgressors to account and who threatens them with brutal punishments. This is the very meaning of 'belief in a divine being'.

Bergson adds that while it is true that this image of the guardian of social laws is not born out of logical thinking (but rather from illusions and imaginative attempts to personify the invisible or to turn abstractions into material objects), it would seem that it is not the product, either, of the fantasy and musings of painters, sculptors or other creative artists. These works are nothing but expressions of indulgence and affluence that one can easily dispense with. Images of the divine, on the other hand, are forged by social necessity. Even if they were products of an illusion, it would be an illusion imposed by the reality of human life, which demands the invention of symbolic meanings.[29]

---

[29] It should be noted that this explanation applies, according to Bergson, only to the masses who choose to live a life strictly governed by the laws and customs of their societies, such as tribes, peoples or nations, which Bergson terms 'closed' societies. But it does not apply to exceptional men of genius

Coming to the second part of this theory, Bergson asserts that if we observe the course of one's everyday activities, we will find in them an emptiness so deep that only the idea of the divine can fill it. The hunter who fixes his arrow towards the aimed prey, the trader who labours for greater profits, the patient who swallows his medicine in the hope of recovery, the farmer who awaits the fruits of his cultivations, the parents who anticipate the birth of their child, the sailor who hopes for rescue aboard a sinking vessel, the gambler who, caught between despair and hope, looks for a stroke of luck, and all those who wait in anticipation without knowing the kinds of success or misfortune that await them, if all those people used their mind and attuned their activities according to the definite, or probable, fruition of their anticipated outcomes, they would definitively cease making any effort, and the wheel of life would stop turning.

But the powerful impulse of life defies inaction. This is why life needs a weight to be put on the other side of the scale, to ensure the endurance of human activity despite uncertainties and anxious calculations. This counterweight is nothing but hope and faith in the possibility of good fortune. By incentivizing this hope and by encouraging it, the human spirit eventually comes to imagine that there is a hidden and mysterious will which soothes the heart of man, and in which he can place his trust. This is the will of God, the Being whom we seek for help, and whose authority directs and judges our actions.

We can see that this theory produced the idea of the divine, in its two appearances in the human mind, as a symbolic meaning only fit for the kinds of tales we invent to scare or amuse children. The first part of Bergson's theory is implausible unless we are prepared to consider all the laws and norms in societies, whether religious, economic or any other, to be equally capable of generating an awareness of the divine in the minds of men. It would be fair to say, then, that their particular idea of divinity does not indicate faith in the real existence of a divine being but that it is purely symbolic of man's awareness of the awesome power of society and the fears it instils in him. The individual who accepts to live like this, subjecting himself to all the norms of his people,

---

and excellence who do not derive their beliefs from social laws or norms and who do not need these measures of utility. These men draw their inspiration from the pure and inexhaustible spring of life, and, instead of being subjected to the rules of their societies, they make their own rules and incite everyone else to follow them. They view society in universal human terms, a society that knows neither limits nor borders, whose laws are respected on the basis of love, not through the utilitarian calculations of costs or benefits.

however repressive, all their customs, however savage, all their laws, however unjust, or who reaches such a degree of passive surrender that he convinces himself that these vile and corrupt settings are willed by God, that the soldiers of the heavens ensure their protection, ready to intervene should the soldiers of the State flee or falter, the least that could be said of this individual is that he is foolish and delusional, that he does not call things by their rightful name. However, a more robust and logical approach would be to take the moral law for what it really is and to consider the secure and intimate place it occupies in the minds of men as a source of inspiration for faith in God, and as a proof of the majesty of the initiator and creator who guides man along the right path and who gives him the choice between evil and virtue.[30] Indeed, the latter view is more plausible, and we will soon see how the German philosopher Immanuel Kant made the moral law the first foundation of any reflection on the existence of God.

By the same token, we contend that the attempt to infer the pre-existence of divine will by means of the uncertainty of future events whose outcomes are unknown to man and to which he must nevertheless succumb, events that can arise in unexpected and haphazard ways, is likewise a sound and convincing argument which does not slip into ambiguity or artifice. This argument is based on two premises. The first is that these events imply the presence of an unknown and invisible force. This is a particularly decisive and detrimental point, for anything that has no cause in the visible world must have a cause in the realm of the invisible. There is no other alternative. The second premise is that this invisible cause is also a rational force which acts by its own will and which knows and contrives events before they transpire. This, too, is an argument based on not only sound reason but also unanimously attested by the experiences of all nations. We have come to know, quite well in fact, that although the secrets of future events remain untenable by the light of reason alone, they may still be accessed by certain inspired individuals who show themselves capable of predicting them with utmost precision, and whose prophesies, once verified, no one dares to doubt or question. Obviously, these events are not the product of chance or mere coincidence, nor are they the mechanical consequence of the unrelenting blind wheel of life, as Bergson

---

[30] Qur'an 91:8. (Ed.)

claims.[31] They are undoubtedly part of a preconceived plan, drawn by the hand of a mysterious organizing force that is as aware of its decisions as it is of everything that occurs in its domain.

c. Descartes

It will surely seem as if we have ventured somewhat beyond the scope of this chapter by incorporating into this series of psychological explanations of the rise of religiosity one of the approaches followed by the French philosopher René Descartes to prove the existence of God. Indeed, his intention was not to undertake a study of the evolution of religious sentiment, nor to explain its birth in the minds of men in general. He simply wanted to record his personal thoughts on the matter. However, since he himself declares that the basis of his arguments was rooted in the domains of human intuition and psychology, we feel justified in including his theory alongside the others discussed here.

In his *Meditations*, Descartes decisively affirms that belief in the existence of God is based on an experience in the human psyche that is more direct and immediate, and less abstruse and complex, than any of the experiences we have reviewed thus far. He says that even if we close our eyes, plug our ears, cut all ties with the world and with other humans and then withdraw into ourselves and dive into our inner thoughts and feelings, we will find the key to unlocking this belief present in the folds of our being. It appears whenever we are made aware of the difference between doubt and certainty, ignorance and knowledge; in short, whenever we perceive the reality that our wanting nature still lacks the supreme ideal of perfection.

According to Descartes, the idea of absolute perfection is not inferred from yet another idea, but rather is a primary, immediate and intuitive fact. It even precedes, in our mind, the feeling of our imperfection. For how could I feel the absence of that which I do not already know? How could I know that I am imperfect if I did not have within me an image of a perfect entity in relation

---

[31] It has been suggested that Bergson, who was born into a Jewish family, declared towards the end of his life that he had converted to Christianity. But all his philosophical reflections suggest that he was, in reality, neither a Jew nor a Christian, but rather an agnostic. For him, life is embodied in a volatile force concerned with its own volition, oblivious to the harmful consequences of its haphazard acts and impulses.

to which I could recognize my imperfections? My desire for perfection is, in itself, proof of the pre-existence of the object of this desire in my mind. Furthermore, this idea is not negatively correlated with its opposite (as stillness is the opposite of movement, or darkness the opposite of light) but the union of all positive truths and the summation of all categories of perfection.

Where does this idea come from, wonders Descartes? It cannot come from the abyss of nothingness because the existent cannot be born from nothingness, just as no positive number can be generated from zero. Neither can it spring from the deep ends of my conscious self because this self is the very cause of the imperfection which I vainly seek to escape. Neither can it be said that although this idea of perfection which I have not attained in actuality is, nevertheless, present within me in potentiality, that I could thus reach it by my own assiduous efforts and by gradually rising towards it on a scale of intermediate perfections, or that the natural attraction which I feel towards perfection suffices to implant its idea within me.

To say this would be wrong on two counts. First, because this concept of perfection does not portray for my mind the possible degrees of perfection that I could ultimately attain, but that at each degree of perfection that I imagine in me or in others, I immediately imagine another degree, higher still. Second, the idea of higher perfection that I find in myself at once contains all the degrees of perfection in the real and actual sense of the term, which cannot, by definition, be realized by partial or insufficient means. Otherwise, it would not be absolute perfection. It is not possible, in fact, to acquire this perfection by fractions. My limited powers and insufficient means cannot generate that which is only partially and contingently present within me in such complete and dazzling totality; for it is inconceivable that I might grant to others qualities which I do not possess myself. This idea, concludes Descartes, is neither the invention of my fantasy nor a hypothesis produced by my imagination; it is a fact that imposes itself on my intelligence and all other intelligences.

All that is left, therefore, is the image reflected in the mirror of my soul, of an external objective reality, which is the very substance and the source of absolute Perfection, of the supreme Ideal. This image is deeply engraved onto the canvas of my mind, as a craftsman stamps his work with his mark, or as the writer signs his name on his correspondence.

Even if Descartes was not the first to undertake this reasoning, it was he who delineated it to such an exceptional and prolific degree, as we find it in the third part of his *Meditations*. Nevertheless, in his lifetime, his ideas were met by fierce criticism.

The German philosopher Kant thought that he could destroy the basis of Descartes's theory, once and for all, with the following refutation: While the properties of mental concepts can be perfectly deduced from the very nature of these concepts, just as one can deduce the properties of the geometric shapes from their definitions, the quality of 'existence', in particular, cannot be deduced from purely mental conceptions. For example, even if we come to recognize, by the logic of geometry, the specific properties that determine a triangle, it does not necessarily follow that a triangle actually exists outside our mind. All it suggests is that if a triangle existed, it would have this appearance and properties. The same applies to all intellectual concepts – the fact that my mind can conceive of them does not effectively prove that they exist in the external world. In fact, my mind can also conjure up absurd notions, such as a palace made of water, or a human being shaped out of air and so on.

This example by Kant shows that Descartes's critics tend to disregard the wide gap[32] that separates the imaginable and contingent elements, on which they base their objections and whose non-existence would not entail absolute impossibility, from that indispensable rational element which forms an integral part of the human mind, and whose non-existence would mean the abolition of all reason and all knowledge. Reason can only recognize the existence of this entity outside of itself, since it is from it that reason will derive all the possible forms, whether concrete or abstract.

Morality

The German philosopher Kant argued in his *Critique of Practical Reason* that the existence of God is not the subject of science or knowledge, which is explicable by reason or by empirical experience. It is a conscious intellectual

---

[32] As pointed out by Descartes himself.

faith, the first datum without which reason cannot confirm our deeply rooted moral principle. Kant develops his arguments in three stages.[33]

1. All human beings, young and old, find in themselves reasons to appreciate certain behaviours and to reproach others, in that we are supposed to perform certain actions and avoid others. This moral law is similar to that of nature in the sense that both are necessary and inescapable. But moral law differs from natural law in that it does not relate to a concrete reality, verifiable by observation and experiment, but to an object the realization of which is fervently desired, and whose existence, possible or otherwise, is always external to us. It could even be claimed that nothing in the world indicates that this ideal has ever been properly realized. Indeed, all men are sinners, purity and infallibility being the attributes of God alone. Even those who seem to act in strict accordance with the rules of moral duty, one cannot ensure that they conform to these rules in spirit as they should – that is, for the sole purpose of sincerely performing their duty, without the blemishes of egotism or self-interest, and without the need to call upon other noble and natural inclinations in addition to what already exists within themselves.

    Thus, our prescribed duty, says Kant, is to carry out duty, for the sake of duty, through the fulfilment of duty. That is to say, under the powerful influence of the idea of duty itself and not out of love of duty. All attempts to fulfil duty would be vain and obsolete at the slightest undermining of any of these principles. What human being could ever achieve this degree of selflessness? And yet, this is the power of the moral law which imposes itself on us, says Kant, despite the resistance and opposition of the laws of nature which dominate our being and which reign supreme over our senses, our faculties and our will. From this we learn that human beings affiliate with two spheres: that of reason and that of nature and the senses. Each of these spheres pulls us in its own direction, each demanding its fair share. The moral law is but a messenger of pure reason, speaks in its name alone and ignores the prevailing power of nature.

2. If reason demands with such insistence the fulfilment of this absolute good, it is because the means to accomplish it must already exist. For if reason obliges us to do something, it is because this thing is possible;

---

[33] Kant, *Critique de la raison*, Parts II, IV and V.

otherwise reason would not be what it claims to be. And since we recognize the impossibility of man attaining this absolute good during his brief sojourn on earth, he thus has only the possibility of achieving it, step by step ad infinitum... This is the basis of the presumed eternal life of man, a life in which he can accomplish this perpetual progression towards the moral ideal, which is the ultimate goal of his reason and his will. Hence, subsuming the immortality of the soul becomes indispensable for the conceptualization of the moral law in the mind. Indeed, the claim that man can attain holiness and absolute virtue during his earthly life is as fallacious as the claim that the moral law can be satisfied by seeking lesser, imperfect human virtues.

3. Even if we come to achieve the absolute good by acquiring perfect virtue, says Kant, there would still be a final requirement of reason to be fulfilled, which is to attain the supreme good. This, far from being a simple idea, is compounded from the union of two elements: One is virtue, the other is happiness. It enables man to obtain all that he wishes in his life by satiating his desires. Yet we see that these two requirements (virtue and happiness), in fact, follow distinct paths that scarcely ever meet. We often see that modest virtue, steadfast and diligent, endures a life of misery and depravation, and an afterlife marked by contempt and oblivion, whereas we find that ambitious vice, rowdy and flattering, enjoys all the advantages of power, fortune, and the good life, as well as lasting renown and prestige. Now, the dictates of sound reason demand that felicity and virtue accompany each other, that vice be inseparable from wretchedness, and that the degrees of misery and happiness be fairly distributed among men according to their deeds and intentions. This is why it is necessary that there be a higher principle that achieves and maintains this equilibrium, a principle to which nature would be subject and which would manage the universe according to a just law. This principle can only be the creator of nature and of man. It can only be Almighty God.

The existence of God, concludes Kant, is therefore an ultimate object of human reason. It is the necessary condition for the rational possibility of moral legislation.

Beholding this rich tapestry of ideas and insights, one can only delight in its masterful and innovative construction. But if you undertake to unwrap the bonded layers of this texture, you will find fragile threads and foreign elements concealed in exceptional skill and artistry. Moreover, we will discover that the three stages comprising Kant's overall argument are neither evident, nor conclusive nor do they, in fact, properly achieve their objective.

Regarding the first stage, even if we generally agree on the idea that the moral law is ingrained in the depths of our mind, the image Kant gives us calls into question whether it can be imposed on everyone. It is more likely, rather, that many people with honest dispositions will reject it, not only because it is implacable and demanding, not only because it does not differentiate between vital and subsidiary duties, but also because it overturns familiar and recognized standards and settings. It decrees, in fact, that the one who abides by the law with pleasure and munificence will not have fulfilled his duty, and that true conformity to the law can only exist if one does so in spite of himself, in suffering and in agony. Thus, we will see that upright and honest souls distance themselves from the high ideals of virtue while those whose characters are marked by malice and ruthlessness will approach their duties forcefully, as one takes on an enemy or a rival.

Concerning the second stage, even if the required duty (which seeks the fulfilment of the pure good for itself, without being tarnished by the desire for personal benefit or having been correlated with any other feeling, noble or otherwise) were not humanly possible, it cannot be obligatory, as Kant himself recognizes. If it were possible, here and now, then postulating eternity would no longer be necessary, and if it were deemed possible at some future time, then the immortality of the soul would no longer be justified, since its continued existence, for even one moment, past the accomplishment of duty, would be superfluous.

If the perfect fulfilment of this moral ideal cannot be achieved at any moment in this life or the next, then proposing the idea of eternity would be inadequate. This is because when the slightest inclination towards the good comes to mingle with a kind of indifferent obedience to moral duty (which by definition invalidates the basis of virtue), it would no longer be a case of progression from imperfection to perfection but a relentless succession of negative values which cannot engender positive results. Indeed, any accumulation of failures, even infinitely, cannot bring about success.

However, perfectibility in the hereafter, as understood by Kant, leads us to a very strange situation, for we are supposed to accept that we must strive in our future life to suppress our noble and generous inclinations, to wage against all goodness a violent struggle which gets fiercer over time, so that fulfilment of duty is only the fulfilment of duty, in spite of ourselves and our internal conflicts. What a marvellous paradise is that which only lets demons in!

As for the third stage of Kant's argument, it injects in the name of moral law an element totally foreign to it, in that it defines man's quest for happiness in simple laymen's terms (i.e. as the realization of his wishes and the satiation of his natural desires and instincts). However, virtue and happiness, thus defined, are in fact two different things. The first is a rational obligation imposed from above, the second is a materialistic disposition that solicits and implores in the hope of satisfying its desires and needs. Requiring that these two opposing extremes be joined together, in the human aspiration towards the formulation of a universal law where moral and natural laws reinforce each other in perfect harmony, would seem nothing but an aspiration towards an imagined façade, a nominal geometric entity. It is neither a rational necessity nor a moral obligation. It is not a rational necessity because one cannot enforce that which is presumed to be impossible. Neither is it a moral obligation, because we know very well that virtuous men, even in the midst of misery and wretchedness, even as they suffer privations and offer great sacrifices, rejoice in satisfying their conscience and in fulfilling their duty, and they find in this a true pleasure unmatched by all the delights that life brings.

Moreover, if it is absolutely necessary that virtue be compensated with a material reward, why should it have to be dispensed to us in the next life? Why cannot we consider that we have reaped our reward in advance in the form of innumerable bounties and benefits of which we avail ourselves during our earthly life? Would not our moral duty then be to repay this old debt by expressing our gratitude towards the Creator for all his favours, rather than initiating a new transaction that awaits recompense?

It would seem that all these pitfalls could have been avoided if the German philosopher had cut the path short, passing directly from the moral law to the discovery of the legislator himself, the one who instilled the law in our mind, as Descartes did in his demonstration of the idea of perfection. Kant, on the contrary, based his reasoning on convolutions, trickery and manoeuvres that lengthened the path and led him, in the end, to what he himself considered an unverified hypothesis based on a shaky foundation.

Sociology

The French sociologist Durkheim departs from all the theories we have discussed so far, which argue that religious sentiment is a psychological state that emerges in the minds of men whenever they contemplate the distant horizons or whenever they dive into themselves. He argues instead that religions are in fact born of purely social causes.[34] He goes further and maintains that all the elements of thought, and all mental structures and knowledge, are only the product of life in society, and that they are created by society in accordance with its own schemes.[35] Since our concern here is not to critique the basis of Durkheim's theory of knowledge, we will limit ourselves to expounding, then critically examining, his point of view on the origin of religiosity.

Durkheim sets the stage by declaring that the best way to explain a phenomenon as complex as the religious one is to study it in its most elementary form, before it is tainted by foreign elements, and that this can only be achieved by examining 'primitive'[36] peoples in whom, he suggests, the family unit is not clearly discerned, and who are grouped, instead, into tribes, phratries and clans.

We know that the clan (which is the smallest component of these societies) is defined and distinguished by a common name shared by its members. This name is usually the name of an animal or a plant, and less often of inanimate objects or celestial bodies. The clan is convinced that it has a very ancient relationship, physical or spiritual, with the element whose members are named after it (either that they descended from the element in question or that it had been, from time immemorial, the protector or ally of the founding ancestors, and so on). This is why it is respected, represented on the walls of their dwellings, on their tools, their weapons and their pennants. Some even imprint it on their bodies in the form of a tattoo, used as a sign of recognition, like an identity card, to prove that they belong to one clan and not another.

---

[34] Durkheim, *Forme Elémentaires*, p. 132.
[35] Ibid., Introduction.
[36] Gone are the days when the word 'primitive' was readily used to designate peoples who live today as they did in their earliest modes of habitation, without advancing a single step on the path of civilization. Today, this misconception has vanished, and no self-respecting author would allow himself to use this term without quotation marks, which indicate that it is a conventional term, used by some authors, but one that he does not necessarily agree with.

This system is known as totemism and derives from the word 'totem',[37] which is a kind of clan mark, or patronymic. It is common among ancient peoples (Egyptians, Ethiopians, Arabs, Greeks, Romans, Gaels etc.). Even today, traces of it are found in European folktales or in the names of certain cities. It is also widespread among the uncivilized tribes of America and Australia, the latter being, according to Durkheim, the most fertile ground for the study of this phenomenon. It is there, he believes, that we find the least evolved humans who remain closest to their natural, original state. Hence, he derived from them all the data that allowed him to establish his theory.

In summary, Durkheim declares that when these peoples honour the name they bear, they, at the same time, honour the referent that this name designates. Since the name is common to the animal, the founding ancestor and to the members of the clan, and since the relationship among these three elements is, in their view, one of perfect unity and harmony, they come to refer to the same substance whereby honouring one is also honouring all three. But these people reserve the greatest share of veneration for the name itself, or for the unifying image – that is, for the sign represented by the imprint or the tattoo. They would even ascribe to it extraordinary magical powers, claiming, for example, that whoever wears it to war is assured of victory, that his arrow never misses a target, that it can treat wounds and quicken healing and so on.

This respect, however, does not go as far as adoration, and does not inspire the idea of religiosity, or of sanctification or of deification. Therefore, we see members of these societies lead mostly unexcited lives, each busy rummaging for food, or alone in the mountains, collecting wood, or at the edge of ponds, catching fish. We do not notice, throughout their uninteresting lives, any sign of religiosity, except the fact that each one takes care never to violate certain prohibitions. Religion, however, will only manifest itself, in full force, on specific dates and seasons, when joyous and loud celebrations are held. Then, we see clan members unleash themselves in frantic movements and deafening cries, punctuated by drums and musical instruments, while the pole that carries the clan's emblem is fixed in the middle of the festive crowd. All these loud and

---

[37] This term is adopted from the language of the native peoples of North America. However, its form and exact meaning remain imprecise. It is most commonly written as 'totem', but we also find 'totam', 'toodaim' or 'ododaim'. It is sometimes defined as 'the place where the clan resides', and sometimes as the clan's most distinctive sign (Reinach, *Orpheus*, p. 23; Durkheim, *Forme Elémentaires*, p. 144).

wild festivities produce in them a state of unconsciousness and delirium. It can even lead clan members to break sexual taboos for which they normally reserve the greatest respect. They may even explain these strange outbursts by the presence of the spirit of the ancestors who would have invaded them through the emblematic monument, because their veneration is in fact for the spirit it designates, and which they suspect to be the cause of their outlandish mystical transformation.

It is only then that Durkheim's theory intervenes to open their eyes and to draw their attention to the fact that their feelings had deviated from their true source and their original objective. That if they wish to offer their worship to the cause which provoked this spectacle, they should know that this cause is neither the monument which they have erected, nor what it symbolizes, but the raging assembly itself. The nature of such gatherings is such that participants detach themselves from their individual traits, all of them dissolving into the common identity or spirit of the assembly. Thus, human association becomes the very origin and purpose of belief. Society, in fact, worships itself.

***

This theory exposes itself to countless criticisms. First of all, and like all theories about 'primitive mentalities', it is based on questionable facts that should only be considered with extreme caution. They are generally drawn from information on the beliefs and customs of exotic and savage peoples, collected and reported by travellers and explorers, and which prove to be feeble for several reasons. To begin with, not all travellers are sufficiently familiar with the psychological, logical, religious, moral knowledge and so on, nor are they equipped with the necessary techniques and the relevant methods of investigation that enable them to ask the right questions and to make and record observations with depth and precision. Rather, it appears to have been the least of their concerns. Moreover, this information is not based on any written document because it is assumed that peoples under observation have no written record of their culture or their arts. Therefore, they are exclusively drawn from oral traditions of peoples who have yet to reach the stage of cultural refinement that allows them to analyze their ideas or accurately express their feelings in relation to these questions. Most likely, they were quick to respond with 'yes' or 'no', without engaging in deep thought or analysis. No matter how accurate and precise, objective and well-intentioned both questions and answers may have been, there would still remain the language barrier. The resources of the 'primitive' languages of these peoples have not reached the degree of maturity to accurately express subtle and obscure meanings and ideas that defy even the richest and most advanced languages. In addition to all this, we can easily assume that the opinion of a member of the group does not necessarily represent the point of view of the entire clan or tribe, because impressions differ from one individual to another, and the same individual can maintain contradictory impressions and perceptions. Indeed, there can be no better proof of the weakness of these travel accounts than the ones gleaned from the authors themselves, who, in their accounts of the same tribes, often contradict[38] each other.

Let us now go beyond these general considerations and turn to the basis of the theory itself. Durkheim declares that the religious phenomenon must be studied in its earliest historical manifestations, and in forms closest to its original nature. According to him, tribal and clan structures are older than the family unit, and since the tribes of Central Australia provide the oldest specimen, therefore, these tribes should comprise the first step in the study of the first appearance of the religious phenomenon.

Although the first postulate seems to be largely sound in the context of purely historical investigations, to decree that the outcome of our research into the allegedly oldest social groups is to be taken as a universal fact that illuminates the truth of human religiosity is an offense to logic and sound reasoning. For, would we be justified in deducing the original state of mankind from the observation of the first stage of a human embryo, or from the early stages of a living organism or before its bodily systems take shape, before the functions of its various organs are defined, before it begins an autonomous life, before the awakening of the faculties of understanding and expression and so on? To give religion such a vague and ambiguous image, which resembles the first stammering of the child who is not aware of his feelings or of the consequences

---

[38] The work of Man, for example, who spent many years on the Andaman Islands, studying the customs and beliefs of their inhabitants, and who published his observations in 1882. In later years, the ethnologist Radcliffe-Brown also went to the Andaman Islands and in 1922 published a new book consisting almost entirely of criticisms of the account given by Man (Saurat, *Histoire des religions*, p. 19).

of his acts, is to adopt a method no less flawed than that which claims to define humanity based on the early formations of an embryo. Høffding rightly states,

> It is not always possible to draw much information about the true nature of a being from the examination of its origins because the transformations and the varied systems that develop in the course of its existence can produce qualities which were not present at the beginning. The true nature of a being consists in its complete development, from its origin until its final form.[39]

The second postulate, which asserts that tribal social formations represent a stage of human evolution historically older than that of societies adopting the structure of the family unit, remains unsubstantiated. In fact, the evidence of history and archaeology tends to prove the contrary. The ancient remains of the Aryan or Semitic peoples reveal that they were already organized according to a family system wherein all members shared the same rights and duties, and where the father retained the highest authority over other members of his family. If we read the descriptions that Aristotle and Homer gave of other nations who flourished during the time of ancient Greece and who had remained closer than they had to the naïve state of nature, we would see that the criterion by which these authors distinguished these peoples from those who were more civilized was that they had no advisory councils, and that each man assumed absolute authority over his wife and children.[40]

Regarding Durkheim's third postulate, which affirms that the tribes of Central Australia represent the oldest known tribal system, it, too, does not stand up to scrutiny. Robert Smith, one of the great researchers who conducted meticulous first-hand studies in Australia, confirms that these tribes studied by Durkheim are, in fact, among the most recent and most evolved tribes on the continent, and claimed that the oldest tribes are found in Southeast Australia. Among the latter, however, the system whereby clans carry the names of animals does not exist, and they clearly demonstrate that they believe in a high god. Moreover, the portrait that Durkheim paints of the life of the tribes of Central Australia proves by itself that we are dealing with a people far removed from the natural naivety and simplicity of primitive cultures, one that has made great strides in the development of their social and

---

[39] Høffding, *The Philosophie de la religion*, p. 126.
[40] Badawi, *Abhath al-tarikh al-'am lil-qanun*, p. 15.

economic systems. This is clearly evidenced in the rules that govern marriage, descent, property ownership, the regulation of hunting or fishing seasons and so on. The system of codification of names alone would have required long periods of development before becoming established and adopted, and before being upheld by everyone through successive generations. Indeed, this system evolved into a precise framework in which each tribe is always divided into two moieties: the tribe must have a generic name and the distinct names of the two moieties must contrast one another as opposites and remain within the meaning of the tribe's generic name. Each moiety then branches off into numerous clans, each bearing a distinctive name, and like the branches of a tree, no two clans will ever share the same name. Thus, a number of specialists have considered the totemic structure to be more of a civil, legal and economic system than a religious one.[41] Others, like Lang and Frazer, saw no trace of religion in it whatsoever and declared that the idea of religion and divinity emerged among these people independently of the evolution of the kinship structures of totemism.[42]

The latter is our preferred point of view. We are convinced that these names and emblems serve no more than as ethnic or tribal signs that remind clan members of their ancestral origin, which foster in them a sense of pride and belonging, which maintain solidarity and respect for the law of property distribution and all other laws that govern their community. They worship neither the signs nor what they signify. They believe in the existence of a spiritual being to whom they turn in their largest and smallest endeavours, from whom they seek inspiration or advice, even about selecting names for their children. As for the source of prohibitions, they tend to refer to religious myths inherited from their ancestors to which they ascribe a divine origin and which they turn into divine commands.

Strangely enough, the founder of the French school of sociology himself states that many Australian tribes have in fact arrived at the idea of a 'supreme' or 'unique' god. This is an eternal and infinite being who commands the sun, the moon and the stars, who instigates lightning and sends thunder, to whom

---

[41] Hubert, *Introduction à la traduction française du Manuel d'Historie des religions, par Chantepie de la Saussaye*, p. xxxix.
[42] Durkheim, *Forme Elémentaires*, p. 294.

one turns for rain or clear skies, who created the animals and plants, who made man from a piece of clay and breathed life into him, who gave him speech, taught him skill and industry, who instituted the manners of worship, who judges men after their death and who distinguishes the good from the wicked.[43] Durkheim even declares that these beliefs were not borrowed from the Europeans, as Tylor had asserted, that they long predate the arrival of Christian missionaries and that they are expressed through real acts of worship during which the hands of men are raised high in prayer and supplication.[44]

Durkheim recognizes all this. However, when it comes to formulating his theory of divinity, he deflects his attention from these manifestations of true religiosity and only retains a form of obscene festivity observed in certain tribes that has nothing to do with religion or worship, and during which tribal members allow themselves to indulge in vile acts in violation of their own established codes of morality, which they respect at all other times. He retains only these crazed and manic sprees, sketching from them a salient portrait that he places before our eyes, saying, 'If you want to know what religion is, this is its source, and here are its manifestations!'

This is the kind of respect that the great researcher grants to the intelligence of his readers, and this is the attitude that allows him to divert them from the facts by giving them false names and misleading descriptions. His intention is clear – he wants to tell us that any hysterical fever raised by a raging crowd, any degenerate impulse which provokes, by contagion or imitation, the release of unrestrained impulses, whatever the intention or cause, is a form of religion, even if the wave of uninhibited passions washes away all barriers imposed by reason and breaks through every last bastion of morality normally respected by the people themselves.

It is therefore incumbent upon us to draw attention to a manifest error in the method Durkheim invented and which it appears that he himself fell into.

According to the rule established by France's leading sociologist, Durkheim,[45] whoever undertakes to describe the normal state of society must begin by examining the behaviour of the majority of its members and

---

[43] Ibid., p. 412.
[44] Ibid.
[45] Durkheim in his famous work *Le Règles de la méthode sociologique*, ch. 3, pp. 69–70.

in as many times and places as possible. Since it is generally accepted that religion pervades nearly all aspects of life in primitive societies, would it not be a heinous violation of logic to study the manifestations of religion based on such exceptional and exaggerated states, which occur only sporadically in the course of the life of these people, while disregarding all the beliefs, rituals, moral codes and customs comprising the real framework of their lives?

Durkheim was right to distinguish between two contrasting aspects of the primal mode of life. But he turned things upside down by making anomalous and exceptional social expressions universal standards, of which he selected only the most degenerate and least religious-like and presented it as the truth of religion.

It would not have been difficult for him to find the explanation for this brazenly strange behaviour had he placed it within the context of the social and moral systems of these societies, which are, for that matter, based on the segregation of the sexes and on respecting the privacy of each domain. It is, for example, forbidden for a woman to see the dripping blood of newly circumcised young boys. Likewise, the adolescent is kept from participating in adult affairs until puberty. Only then, particularly on the occasion of his circumcision, will he be introduced to the idea of sexual intercourse. To them, this marks an important milestone for which they organize jolly celebrations, similar to those observed until recently in Eastern cultures. When the indigenous Australians exaggerate the expression of their festivity, they use the opportunity to present their teenagers with a fanciful image of what awaits them in their future lives, reminding them that this is the habit and practice of all the ancestors to whom the tribe owes its existence. If we scrutinize what goes on during these festivities, we will see that they all revolve around play and the indulgence in licentious pleasures, and we will notice the great difference between these farcical seasonal displays and the seriousness and sacredness which dominate all other activities of their daily life. It is thus a great mockery to present these depraved dramatics as expressions of the revered sanctuary of religion.

It is no less strange, moreover, to see Durkheim who considered the sanctity of things as measured by the yardstick of their prohibition present the violation of these same prohibitions, or at least crossing their limits, as the expression of the very essence of religion, and further declare that nowhere else could the religious phenomenon be better studied.

However, let us assume, for the sake of argument, the validity of all the components of Durkheim's theory we have just discussed. Let us admit the reliability of the travel accounts of tourists and explorers; let us admit that they have never disagreed or contradicted each other; let us admit that their descriptions of the facts are accurate; let us admit the soundness of the approach which infers the universal idea of religion from the study of primitive religiosities; let us admit that the tribal structure of primitive peoples bears an absolute resemblance to the systems found in primary societies, and that the system found among the tribes of Central Australia, in particular, is indeed the oldest; let us admit, also, that the totemic system is imbued with religious significance; and let us even admit that these gatherings and these vulgar festivities are purely religious in their essence and in their functions.

Even if we admit all of these 'facts', it remains to be known whether they can in their entirety lead to the same conclusion affirmed by Durkheim – that religion is, above all, a social system, in the sense that it is the product of social causes whose function is maintained through becoming itself an object of worship and veneration.

The wide gulf between Durkheim's assertions and premises, on the one hand, and the conclusions of his reasoning, on the other, is unmistakable. His deductions seek to transport us directly from meagre and fragile facts to overblown and far-fetched conclusions. In this connection, let us quote a noteworthy confession of one of the members of the same school of sociology who asserts the following:

> It is not enough to say that religious phenomena are produced by and differentiated across social groups to conclude that they are the product of societies... On the one hand, social phenomena have an objective existence, independent of individuals, as we find in established laws and rules of economics. On the other hand, the activity of the individual in the social domain is often determined or modified by the proximity of his fellows without his adhering to it or becoming aware of it. Can we say, in this case, that religious phenomena and social phenomena are one and the same?
>
> Doubtless, many religious phenomena appear in the form of institutions that consist in practical expressions of faith, which are fixed rules thanks to oral or written formulations, and which subsist outside the will of individuals and independently of their tacit approval.

But are these group settings and conventions religious facts per se? Are they the primary forms of all religious feeling and expression? We will be tempted to answer in the affirmative if we limit ourselves to the history of ancient or primitive religions, because their remoteness from us erases the uniqueness of individuals and absorbs them into a uniform social mass. However, if we study religious phenomena as they appear to us in the present state, and in a religion whose ideas we share, albeit faintly, we will naturally be led to place more emphasis on individual initiative and innovation.[46]

Such is the way the disciples reappraised the theory of their master by pronouncing that it should adopt an approach of differentiation and not of generalization, and that while we may consider the superficial or external aspects of religion – that is, its symbolism and community organization – to be concrete social facts, since they bear the mark of collective obligation and in whose conception the individual has no role, the fundamental aspects of religion, which comprise beliefs and spiritual insights, cannot, by nature, be imposed by an inevitable external force that does not respond to our thoughts, emotions or sensitivity.

If we look closer, we will also see how the heavy yokes of external rites and ceremonies are felt and experienced even by the most committed and convinced follower of an already established, stable religion. But explaining this will take us beyond the focus of our study, which is the birth of religion and its first appearance on earth. Has anyone ever heard of an established society forcing its members to convert to an emerging religion that introduces new and unfamiliar beliefs and rituals? Would it not rather resist and show great hostility towards these alarming ideas and even persecute their proponents?

Let history speak for itself! Let the facts and experiences reveal themselves, so that those who claim to construct their theories on history, facts and experiences can take heed!

Here, we arrive at the greatest wonder of all. The founder of the theory, not satisfied with his claim that religion, with all its varied beliefs and practices, is a kind of moral obligation imposed by society on individuals, insists on arguing that the object of this faith and the final target of all devotion is none other than society itself. He tells us that the religious feeling of each individual is

---

[46] Hubert, *Introduction à la traduction de Chantepie*, pp. xxvi–xxx.

nothing but the spontaneous imprint of the image of society on his conscience, an image surrounded by an aura of sanctity, since it is society, after all, which supports his very being and ensures his protection.

This would also explain the differences in the nature of the divine and the limits of its powers observed across societies and why they tend to be proportional to the size of the community of believers. Thus, if several clans are joined together to form a phratry, if several phratries unite to form a tribe and then several tribes coalesce into a single people, the idea of god will evolve accordingly until this divine being becomes the God of the whole people.[47]

If so, then let us be told, 'Where did humanity get the idea of an almighty, unparalleled God, creator of heaven and earth?' To the size of which community have we fashioned it? Let us be told, 'How could the belief in a supreme divine being arise in the minds of members of the most modest societies when the size of any conceivable society could not even begin to suggest his unfathomable magnitude?' It would seem that there will always be between the all of humanity, indeed, between the whole universe and this conception of an Almighty God, a vast abyss which no society, real or imaginary, can ever close.

Let us quote yet another assertion by Henri Hubert, one of the advocates of this theory, who declares that 'a satisfactory demonstration of the social character of religion remains impossible'.[48]

Certainly, it must not be understood that we deny, once and for all, the influence that societies have on religions.

Religion (like language, ways of thinking, means of transaction or other institutions that form the foundations of societies) is an important element of society, if not its essential lifeblood. Who could deny the role that society plays as the guardian of these institutions – that it is the fountain from which current generations draw these resources and that ensures their continued presence in future generations?

The question here, however, is not of the preservation or the perpetuation of extant religions, but of the initial birth and subsequent formation of religions.

---

[47] Durkheim, *Forme Elémentaires*, p. 412.
[48] 'Une démonstration pleinement satisfaisante du caractère social de la religion n'est pas encore possible' (Hubert, *Introduction à la traduction de Chantepie*, p. xxvii).

We do not deny the vital role that societies play in preparing and enabling this emergence. When nations find themselves at a particular juncture in their history, torn between an antiquarian past and an undefined future, they can decide to change the course of their history by accepting or rejecting new religious teachings. If the apostle were to fall short of appreciating the dispositions and the capacities of the people whom he evangelizes, he would be like the one who plants a seed in a swampy land whose shoots will be, in due time, uprooted from the surface of the earth, with no power to endure,[49] or like the one who gives the diseased man food that his stomach cannot tolerate and will soon reject.

All this, however, does not justify the assertion that it is the collective consciousness which creates religion and gives rise to its idea in the minds of men; otherwise, one would also be justified in saying that the stomach is the creator of food, that sight is the source of light or that the patient is the maker of his remedy. Indeed, each of these conditions is necessary, but none of them is, as the logicians say, sufficient or perfect on its own. Surely, cooperation is necessary between the doctor and the patient, between the one who gives and the one who takes, between the active and the receptive. If one can say that nations create their leaders, it would be just as accurate, if not more so, to say that leaders shape their nations. The nation gives natural birth to the one who will become its future leader and provides him with all the necessary means to realize this leadership. The nation will then be reborn, thanks to its leader, through a complete spiritual, political, military and artistic regeneration. The nation offers the fertility of the soil and the adequacy of the instrument; the leader plants the seed, waters it and commits to ensuring its growth. He holds the reins and directs their movement; he points the way and stops when the specified goals are reached. In fact, it is often he who specifies these goals and clarifies them. But when the needs of the people are confused and the pathways that lead to them are tangled and vague in their 'collective consciousness', they await with full anticipation the emergence of that exceptional individual, the man of the hour. The man through whom they recover consciousness and in whom they recognize their needs. The man who would deliver the good news, through intuition or inspiration or revelation. The man with the

---

[49] Qur'an 14:26. (Ed.)

required resolve and determination to take the reins and guide the people to the journey's end. If the people finally identify him and entrust him with the reins, they will have done themselves a great service and will have opened a new page of power and glory. However, if the paths branch out and diversify, if the leaders are deeply divided and if people cannot choose, or if they make the wrong choice by forsaking their inspired guide, who they reject or condemn to failure or death – not because his call is incompatible with their nature but because they have yet to know their own nature, since their minds are still astray – they will then have, unconsciously, taken the path of wretchedness and chosen death over life.

Hence, it would be an act of obstinacy and self-deception to reject the influence of individuals on the religions of societies and their structures. It would also be an act of obstinacy and self-deception to reject the influence of societies on religions.

What we fear most, however, about the exaggeration of the role of the group at the cost of the role of the individual is that it risks inducing in people a fatalistic, demoralizing spirit which would push individuals to wait, in idleness and passivity, for the potential powers and hidden impulses of the collective consciousness to reveal themselves, instead of waiting for that ardent chant inviting unique individuals to seek unrivalled eminence, one that fills them with hope that one day they will be able to move their nation forward.

Revelation

All the foregoing doctrines develop the view that man is supposed to arrive at the idea of God by himself, and that this can be achieved by human means, either by relying on his own observation and personal reflections, or by being subconsciously persuaded of it under the yoke of social obligation.

At the opposite end of the spectrum is the theory of revelation, which maintains that man did not go to religions but that religions came to him, that he did not ascend to them but that they descended to him, that people did not discover God by the light of reason but by the light of revelation.

This theory, which Europe adopted throughout the Middle Ages and which was supported by respected historians well into the nineteenth century, remains widespread among the most prominent clergymen. We also find confirmations of the positive side of this approach in all revealed scriptures.

These sacred books attest that when God created Adam, the father of mankind, he honoured him and taught him the truth of all things. God taught him that he is the Creator of the heavens and the earth and all that is in them, that he is the creator of man and of his means of sustenance, that he is the Lord to whom we owe obedience and veneration, that he will bring all men back to Him and will be the judge of their deeds. God then assigned to Adam the duty of teaching these truths to his offspring, which he did. These spiritual truths thus became humanity's inheritance from the first man. Certainly, not all men have been faithful to this sacred covenant. Indeed, many have gone astray and became tangled up in polytheism or disbelief. But traces of this heavenly instruction have never been lost to humanity, and the idea of God and his veneration held out among all nations in the world.

The heavenly care given to this spiritual instruction did not end with the first man. It endured, and the message was frequently delivered to nations at brief or long intervals, as reminders, by means of envoys of revelation – the prophets and messengers. All sacred books of the great religions testify to this heavenly origin of the religious idea.

Conclusion

Now that we have explored the opinions on the original source and early formation of belief and the intricate pathways that scholars have taken to arrive at them, let us take a panoramic look that will allow us to piece together these various theories and to reconcile their seemingly divergent approaches.

To achieve this, we will retain from each of these theories[1] its positive side (i.e. the logical reasoning underlying their arguments) and ignore its negative side (i.e. their rejection of other doctrines). Thus, differences among them will emerge less as irreconcilable disagreements than as complementary divergences in which theories reinforce one another.

Let us recall the undeniable fact that the quest for the discovery and the understanding of God has been the overriding concern of many schools of thought, whether based on philosophical reasoning or on prophetic inspiration; that the proofs of the existence of God are found as much in the depths of the human psyche as in the spectacle of distant horizons; and that the psychological triggers which give rise to it are rooted both in reason and in feelings. However, people do not stand on an equal footing when it comes to their mental capacity to follow the paths of these arguments, nor with respect to their willingness to admit the proofs that they furnish. Some, beset by a tendency to introversion, will be more readily persuaded by their interior reflections than by reflections inspired by exterior phenomena. Among the latter, some may be spellbound by the beauty and majesty of the spectacle of the world, while others will only be agitated and alarmed by the calamities

---

[1] We will rule out two theories: Symbolism, which explains all forms of religion as products of the 'imaginary', and Deification of Society, which, on the contrary, sees religion as a concrete and objective reality. The latter, however, replaces the being to which the believer turns with his mind and his heart with an unconscious entity (society). These two theories differ fundamentally from all others, and any attempt to reconcile them would be futile and beside the point.

and vicious forces of nature; some will be concerned with the effect of these events on their private thought and sensibility, others with their universal material dimension; and in some, reason will prevail over emotions, while in others, feelings will always take precedence over reflection and so on. For some, a passing vision or a cursory glance is enough to awaken their conscience, while for others it requires a violent shock or a severe crisis. Some will only admit faith under the combined action of multiple factors. For others, however, all the rational proofs in the world will not give rise in their oblivious and distracted mind to any impulse of faith, an impulse only likely to be awakened if these proofs are meticulously explained, or if they are inculcated into them.

Now, all these thinkers whose ideas and theories we have surveyed are they not human beings like everyone else, each convinced by the arguments that best correspond to his capacity for deduction, and by approaches more in tune with his disposition? It was only natural, therefore, that each of them should begin his investigation with the path he is most familiar with, with which he has the most affinity and by which he is most easily persuaded. All other arguments will simply come later. Thus, one person – that is, the scholar – found his religious inspiration by contemplating the spectacle of nature, the second by his spiritualist experiences, the third by seeing his religious consciousness awakened by his psychological observations of his daily life, the fourth by analyzing some rational data, the fifth by deducing it from moral laws and the sixth by rising to the challenge of these big questions only after receiving divine instructions and reading sacred books.

All these are means that lead to the same goal. But the mistake of the thinkers whose theories we have studied is that each one of them, when delineating the path which he followed, shunned all other possible paths and made the point of departure that he chose for himself, based on his own partial judgement, a general rule applicable to all, and hastily made himself a universal criterion. If each researcher had been content with the conclusions that his chosen approach enabled him to reach, he would have naturally concluded that his approach explains the birth of faith for him and for those whose inclinations resemble his. But they turned their relative facts into absolute truths, which could only provoke conflict and disputes.

Conclusion

The truth of this question is simple and can be summed up in two points:

1. The signs of the divine are found everywhere.
2. Some people tend to be inspired and guided by certain signs rather than by others.

This twofold truth is clearly attested in the Qur'an. Regarding the first point, it says,

> *There are signs in the heavens and the earth for those who believe: in the creation of you. 45:3–4*
>
> *On earth there are signs for those with sure faith, and in yourselves too. 55:20–1*
>
> *We shall show them Our signs in every region of the earth and in themselves. 41:53*

Regarding the second,

> *We have assigned a law and a path to each of you. 5:48*
>
> *Each community has its own direction to which it turns. 2:148*
>
> *[Earlier] communities each had their guide. 13:7*

Undoubtedly, it was due to this variety of the means of persuasion among individuals, that the Qur'an diversified the means by which it advocates its divine message. The verses which elaborated these means are so logical, so articulate and so inclusive that if we wanted to review the methods used by the Qur'an to guide men to faith in God, we would find that they encompass all sides of the arguments mentioned above and that they appease all human dispositions. We might even find that they enhance each method by furnishing new elements unnoticed by the researchers we have studied.

If the reader wishes to verify these claims, here are some extracts taken from the Qur'an, arranged according to the successive order of their respective theories.

The Naturalist doctrine appears in verses such as these:

> *Do they not see the sky above them––how We have built and adorned it, with no rifts in it; how We spread out the earth and put solid mountains on it, and caused every kind of joyous plant to grow in it. 50:6*
>
> *Watch their fruits as they grow and ripen! 6:99*

> *He makes the dawn break; He makes the night for rest; and He made the sun and the moon to a precise measure.* 6:96
>
> *Say [Prophet], 'Just think, if God were to cast perpetual night over you until the Day of Resurrection, what god other than He could bring you light? Do you not listen?' Say, 'Just think, if God were to cast perpetual day over you until the Day of Resurrection, what god other than He could give you night in which to rest? Do you not see?'* 28:71–2

The Qur'an adds in this connection a new element – the fact that we find variations within the identical. These variations remain unexplained because human science has yet to know their causes, or control their effects or predict their occurrence. This is because, says William James, these variations are related to processes that take place at the atomic level and which cannot be subjected to any kind of observation, and which do not depend on any known natural condition. They can arise under all kinds of possible circumstances and, despite all of this, seem to operate in a system of their own which is most coherent and precise.

The Qur'an draws our attention to instances in which rich diversity can result from identical natural conditions and factors:

> *There are, in the land, neighbouring plots, gardens of vineyards, cornfields, palm trees in clusters or otherwise, all watered with the same water, yet We make some of them taste better than others.* 13:4
>
> *Another of His signs is the creation of the heavens and earth, and the diversity of your languages and colours.* 30:22
>
> *Have you [Prophet] not considered how God sends water down from the sky and that We produce with it fruits of varied colours; that there are in the mountains layers of white and red of various hues, and jet black; that there are various colours among human beings, wild animals, and livestock too?* 35:27–28

Lastly, the Qur'an pays special attention to a phenomenon in the domain of creation which has mystified and tormented scholars – namely that of life:

> *How can you ignore God when you were lifeless and He gave you life.* 2:28
>
> *Consider [the semen] you eject, do you create it yourselves or are We the Creator? ... Consider the seeds you sow in the ground, is it you who make them grow or We?* 56:58–9, 63–4

Look, then, at the imprints of God's mercy, how He restores the earth to life after death: this same God is the one who will return people to life after death. 30:50

All these statements relate to the peaceful aspect of nature. Of the violent aspect, the Qur'an states,

Among His signs, too, are that He shows you the lightning that terrifies and inspires hope. 30:24

The thunder sounds His praises, as do the angels in awe of Him; He sends thunderbolts to strike whoever He will. 13:13

The Qur'an not only highlights astonishing phenomena whose occurrences are frequent and predictable but also adds warnings of unsuspected or unforeseen ones:

Do the people of these towns feel secure that Our punishment will not come upon them by night, while they are asleep? Do the people of these towns feel secure that Our punishment will not come upon them by day, while they are at play? 7:97–8

Do they not think about what is in front of them and behind them in the heavens and earth? If We wished, We could make the earth swallow them, or make fragments from the heavens fall down upon them. 34:9

As for the arguments of animism, we find echoes of them scattered in numerous Qur'anic verses. The principle of the independence of the human soul and its separation from the body, and from animal spirit, during earthly life; the principle of the continued subsistence of the human soul after death, which remains in limbo, between this world and the hereafter; and the principle of the obsession of the souls of the dead with affairs of the living, all this is confirmed in Qur'anic verses such as these:

It is He who calls your souls back by night, knowing what you have done by day, then raises you up again in the daytime until your fixed term is fulfilled. 6:60

God takes the souls of the dead and the souls of the living while they sleep. 39:42

[Prophet], do not think of those who have been killed in God's way as dead. They are alive with their Lord, well provided for, happy with what God has

> given them of His favour; rejoicing that for those they have left behind who have yet to join them. 3:169–70

The Qur'an also describes the condition of the damned while still in their graves:

> They will be brought before the Fire morning and evening. 40:46

Not to mention the many references in the Qur'an to the existence of other types of spirits, independent of the living world though in relation to it, spirits that God can direct, sometimes to support humans and lead them to felicity, sometimes to the opposite effect. Read the story of the Jinn in the chapter that bears its name, or the chapter of the Prophets, or that of the Ants or that of Sheba. Read, also, the account of the Angels in the Creator chapter, or in chapters such as the Family of 'Imran, or the Livestock or the Battle Gains, among others.

Regarding psychological approaches, the Qur'an underscores the deficiency of man's efforts to realize his goals and his impotence vis-à-vis the divine will to which he is forced to submit. To this effect, the Qur'an says this:

> Is man to have everything he wishes for, when the present life and the life to come belong only to God? 53:24–5
>
> Your Lord creates what He pleases and chooses those He will; they have no choice. 28:68
>
> Do you have a Scripture that tells you that you will be granted whatever you choose? Have you received from Us solemn oaths, binding to the Day of Resurrection, that you will get whatever you yourselves decide? Ask them [Prophet] which of them will guarantee this. 68:37–40

Still in the context of psychology, we find that the Qur'an furnishes us with a new idea (drawn from our daily life) that strongly proves God's omnipotence. This is the fact that our feelings can be fundamentally changed without the presence of natural or logical causes – when the hatred in our hearts is transformed into love, enmity into fondness, reprimand into acclaim and agitation into tranquillity.

> Remember God's favour to you: you were enemies and then He brought your hearts together. 3:103

[He] brought their hearts together. Even if you had given away everything in the earth you could not have done this, but God brought them together. 8:63

God sent His tranquillity down on to His Messenger and the believers. 48:26

The Qur'an encompasses all this, and related insights, in the following formula:

Know that God comes between a man and his heart. 8:24

The moral theory is not absent from the Qur'an, for we find that its most fundamental concepts are summarized in verses like this one:

By the soul and how He formed it and inspired it [to know] its own rebellion and piety! 91:7–8

Indeed, even social theory itself, if we retain its most relevant principle, which is the affirmation of the profound influence of the environment and traditions on individuals, and the way in which they shape ideas and beliefs, is also affirmed in the Qur'an as a fact of life:

We follow the ways of our fathers. 2:170

We saw our fathers following this tradition; we are only following in their footsteps. 43:23

However, the Qur'an only affirms this fact in order to express reproach and blame. It deplores the masses who delight in the enslavement of their reason and the abdication of their human dignity. Thus, men will be like a herd of cattle that heeds the screams of any wild beast.

What! Even though their fathers understood nothing and were not guided? 2:170

This is why the Qur'an calls on people to distinguish the genuine from the reverse and to solicit the best opinions from men of virtue.

So [Prophet] give good news to My servants who listen to what is said and follow what is best. 39:17–18

Those were the people God guided, '[Prophet], follow the guidance they received.' 6:90

The same meaning is confirmed in the following wise prophetic narration: 'Do not let yourselves be 'yes-men', saying: If the people are good then we will be good, and if they are wrong then we will be wrong. Rather, make up your own minds, if the people are good then you are good, and if they are evil, then do not behave unjustly.'[2]

As for how our minds can break free from this social incarceration, the Qur'an proclaims that there is only one way to achieve this: individual reflection, tranquil and free from all restraints, except those of common sense and sound reason.[3]

> *Say [Prophet], 'I advise you to do one thing only: stand before God, in pairs or singly, and think.'* 43:46

We come at last to the theory of revelation, and references to it abound throughout the Qur'an. Along with its persistent exhortation to believers to learn the lessons of the evident signs and all the proofs they can find in the depths of themselves and in nature's infinite horizons, the Qur'an decrees that divine mercy did not limit itself to providing signs intended for reason, but reinforced them by the testimony of revelation, thus providing no excuse for the oblivious and the resigned. The Qur'an reminds us that God has sent

> *messengers bearing good news and warning, so that mankind would have no excuse before God, once the messengers had been sent.* 4:165
>
> *So you cannot say on the Day of Resurrection, 'We were not aware of this,' or, 'It was our forefathers who, before us, ascribed partners to God, and we are only the descendants who came after them: will you destroy us because of falsehoods they invented?'* 7:172–73

Thus, we find grouped in the Qur'an all the approaches, ways of thinking and methods of research and inquiry we observed to be divergent and ramified in the writings of the specialists whom we considered for this study.

---

[2] Narrated by Tirmidhi in the chapter 'Charity and Forgiveness' [Translation in *Jami` at-Tirmidhi*, 2007. (Ed.)]

[3] This wise counsel must be carefully considered. It contains both the diagnosis of the ailment and the prescription of the remedy. First of all, it presents an implicit affirmation of the fact that the minds of individuals are stamped by the collective consciousness with the same seal which makes them think differently depending on whether they are together or alone. The verse thus exhorts every individual to retire from the group and to reflect on his own or with a companion, in order to free himself for a moment from the influence of the environment and its sweeping currents. Recognizing the authority of this collective consciousness and its impact on personal thought, the verse suggests that what the mentality of this community decrees is not always the most sound or reasonable. This is why it recognizes each individual's right to intellectual freedom and to unbiased criticism of what the group might prescribe, in order to rectify any deviation or aberration, and to preserve virtue and righteousness.

Any fair-minded researcher, ascertaining this extensive and conclusive examination, will only be able to see it as further proof of the fact that the Qur'an is not the reflection of the psyche of an individual, nor the mirror image of the mentality of a people nor the record of a certain historical period, but that it is indeed humanity's open book and the spring to which all men are led to quench their thirst. Everywhere in the world and at all times, despite the multiplicity of races, colours and languages, despite conflicting sensibilities and inclinations, the seeker of truth will always find in the Qur'an a clear and laid out path, one that will lead him towards God in full knowledge and in perfect clarity.

We have made it easy to learn lessons from the Qur'an: will anyone take heed? 54:17

Editor's Bibliography

Abdel Haleem, Muhammad (2004). *The Qur'an: A New Translation*, New York: Oxford University Press.

Arjmand, Reza (2017). 'Islamic Education in Egypt', in H. Daun and R. Arjmand (eds), *Handbook of Islamic Education* (pp. 577–92), Cham: Springer.

Asad, Talal (2003). *Formations of the Secular: Christianity, Islam, Modernity*, Stanford: Stanford University Press.

Badawi, Mustafa (1992). Book Review of Donald Reid's *Cairo University and the Making of Modern Egypt*, Journal of Islamic Studies, 3(2), 273–7.

Bayard, Dodge (1958). 'The International Islamic Colloquium', *Muslim World*, 48(3), 173.

Bayyumi, Muhammad (1983). *Al-Azhar bayna al-siyasah wa ḥurriyat al-fikr*, Cairo: Dar al-Hilal.

Bergson, Henri (1977). *The Two Sources of Morality and Religion*, Notre Dame, IN: University of Notre Dame Press.

Braybrooke, Marcus (1996). *A Wider Vision: A History of the World Congress of Faiths, 1936–1996*, Oxford: Oneworld Publications.

Bréhier, Émile (1926–32). *Histoire de la Philosophie* (2 vols), Paris: Alcan.

Brodeur, P. C. (1989). 'Contemporary Muslim Approaches to the Study of Religion: A Comparative Analysis of Three Egyptian Authors', MA diss., Institute of Islamic Studies, McGill University, Montreal.

Brodeur, Patrice (1999). 'Arabic Muslim Writings on Contemporary Religions Other Than Islam', in J. Waardenburg (eds), *Muslim Perceptions of Other Religions: A Historical Survey* (pp. 240–9). New York: Oxford University Press.

Al-Bukhari, Muhammad bin Ismail (1903). *Sahih al-Bukhari*, Cairo: al-Matba'ah al-Maymaniyah.

Burleigh, John (ed.) (1980). *Augustine: Earlier Writings*, Philadelphia: Westminster Press.

Delgado, Javier (2016). 'Religions, Lifeways, Same Difference: Defining Din in the US, the Middle East, and South Asia', *American Journal of Islamic Social Sciences*, 33(1), 1.

Draz, Muhammad (1970). *Al-Din: Buhuth mumahhida li dirasat tarikh al-'adyan* (2nd edn), Kuwait: Dar al-Qalam.

Draz, Muhammad, and Bekir Karlığa (eds) (1987). *Din ve Allah İnancı*, Istanbul: Bir Yayıncılık.

Draz, Muhammad, and Abd al-Sabur Shahin (eds) (2006). *Dustur al-akhlaq fi al-Qur'an*, Cairo: Mu'assasat al-Risalah.

Draz, Muhammad (2011). *Introduction to the Qur'an*, London: I.B. Tauris.

Draz, Muhammad (2014a). *Dirasat Islamiyya fi al-'alaqat al-'jtima'iyya wa al-duwaliyya*, Cairo: Mu'assasat 'Iqra'.

Draz, Muhammad (2014b). *Nazarat fi al-Islam*, Cairo: Mu'assasat 'Iqra'.

Darz, Muhammad, and Basma Abdelgafar (eds) (2018). *Morality in the Qur'an: The Greater Good of Humanity*, Kuala Lumpur: Islamic Book Trust.

Draz, Muhammad, and Mohsen Draz (eds) (1999). *Les hommes à la découverte de Dieu: Prologue à une histoire des religions: 'Ad-Din'*, Beirut, Lebenon: Éditions Al-Bouraq.

Draz, Muhammad, Rebecca Masterton and Danielle Robinson (eds) (2008). *The Moral World of the Qur'an*, London: I.B. Tauris.

Draz, Muhammad, and Adil Salahi (ed.) (2017). *The Qur'an: An Eternal Challenge*, La Vergne: Kube Publishing.

Durkheim, Émile (1915). *The Elementary Forms of Religious Life*, London: Allen & Unwin.

Fadliyya, Ahamd (2007). *Muhammad Abdullah Draz: dirasat wa buhuth*, Cairo: Dar al-Qalam.

Fadliyya, Ahmad (2010). *Awraq Muhammad Abdullah Draz*, Cairo: Maktabat al-Iman.

Gautier, Émile-Félix (1931). *Mœurs et costumes des musulmans*, Paris: Payot.

Gibb, Hamilton, et al. (eds) (1954–2009). *Encyclopaedia of Islam*, Leiden: Brill.

Goldschmidt, Arthur (2000). *Biographical Dictionary of Modern Egypt*, Boulder, CO: Lynne Rienner Publishers.

Gorce, Matthieu-Maxime, and Mortier, Raoul (eds) (1948). *Histoire générale des religions. [Tome 1], Introduction générale. Les primitifs. L'ancient Orient. Les Indo-Européens*, Paris: A. Quillet.

Gul, Andleeb (2017). 'Current Trends of Muslim Academia in Comparative Religions', *Journal of Islamic Thought and Civilization*, 7(1), 53–70, 105.

Hamada, Jalal (2021). *Tarajim a'yan al-usar al-'ilmiyya fi Misr khilal al-qarn al-rabi' 'ashar al-hijri (1301–1400; 1883–1980)*, Amman: Dar al-Fath.

(Ibn) Hisham, Abd al-Malik, and Mustafa al-Saqqa, et al. (eds) (1955). *al-Sira al-nabawiyya li-Ibn Hisham*, Cairo: Mustafa al-Babi al-Halaby.

Høffding, Harald, and B. E. Meyer (eds) (1931). *The Philosophy of Religion*, London: Macmillan.

Hourani, George (1976). *On the Harmony of Religion and Philosophy: A Translation, with Introd. and Notes of Ibn Rushd's Kitab fasl al-maqal, with Its Appendix (Damima) and an Extract from Kitab al-kashf 'an manahij al-adilla*, London: Luzac.

Houtsma, Martijn Theodoor, et al. (eds). *The Encyclopædia of Islam: A Dictionary of the Geography, Ethnography and Biography of the Muhammadan Peoples* (1913–38, 4 vols and Suppl), Leiden: E.J. Brill.

(Ibn) Hujr, Aws, and Muhammad Yusuf Najm (ed.) (1980). *Diwan Aws ibn Hujr*, Beirut: Dar Beirut.

Joy, Morny (ed.) (2011). *After Appropriation: Explorations in Intercultural Philosophy and Religion*, Calgary: University of Calgary Press.

Larousse, Pierre (1928–33). *Larousse du XXème siècle en six volumes*, Paris: Librairie Larousse.

Le Bon, Gustave (1884). *La civilisation des Arabes*, Paris: Firmin-Didot et cie.

Masson-Oursel, Paul (1948). *La philosophie en Orient*, Paris: Presses Universitaires de France.

Morgan, Kenneth (1987). *Islam – the Straight Path: Islam Interpreted by Muslims*, Delhi: Motilal Banarsidass.

Nordeau, Max (1908). *Réponse au Mercure de France*, Paris: Unknown.

Pascal, Blaise, and Gertrude Rawlings (eds) (1900). *Pascal's Pensées or, Thoughts on Religion*, New York: Peter Pauper Press.

Platvoet, Jan, and Arie Molendijk (eds) (1999). *The Pragmatics of Defining Religion: Contexts, Concepts and Contests*, Leiden: Brill.

Reda, Nevin (2010). 'Holistic Approaches to the Qur'an: A Historical Background', *Religion Compass*, 4(8), 495–506.

Reid, Donald (2002). *Cairo University and the Making of Modern Egypt*, Cambridge: Cambridge University Press.

Rousseau, Jean-Jacques, and Louis Flandrin (ed.) (1928). *Discours sur l'origine et le Fondement de l'inégalité parmi les hommes*, Paris: A. Hatier.

Sabatier, Auguste, and T. A. Seed (eds) (1902). *Outlines of a Philosophy of Religion Based on Psychology and History*, London: Hodder & Stoughton.

Schimmel, Annemarie (1971). 'Islam', in G. Widengren and J. Bleeker (eds), *Historia religionum: Handbook for the History of Religions: Volume II. Religions of the Present* (pp. 125–210), Leiden: Brill.

Shinqiti (al-), Mhummad (2017). *Failasuf al-Qur'an al-kareem: Muhammad Abdullah Draz: hayatuhu wa 'atharuhu*, Cairo: Dar al-Mashriq.

(Ibn) Sina, al-Husayn bin Abdullah (1952). *Al-Shifa'*, Cairo: al-Matba'a al-Amiriyyah.

Al-Tirmidhi, Mohammad ibn 'Isa, and Mohammad Shakir (ed.) (1975). *al-Jami' al-sahih wa huwa sunan al-Tirmidhi*, Cairo: Mustafa al-Babi al-Halabi.

Ugurlu, Ali (2019). 'Book Review of Talal Asad's *Secular Translations: Nation-State, Modern Self, and Calculative Reason*', *Arab Studies Quarterly*, 41(2), 197–201.

Voltaire, François-Marie (1829). *Essai sur les moeurs et l'esprit des nations et sur les principaux faits de l'histoire depuis Charlemagne jusqu'à Louis XIII*, Paris: Librairie de Lecointe.

Waardenburg, Jacques (1999a). *Classical Approaches to the Study of Religion: Volume I. Introduction and Anthology: Aims, Methods, and Theories of Research*, Boston: De Gruyter.

Waardenburg, Jacques (1999b). *Muslim Perceptions of Other Religions: A Historical Survey*, New York: Oxford University Press.

Yousif, Ahmad (2011), 'Studying the "Other": Challenges and Prospects of Muslim Scholarship on World Religions', in M. Joy (ed.), *After Appropriation: Explorations in Intercultural Philosophy and Religion* (pp. 77–94), Calgary: University of Calgary Press, 2011.

Al-Zabidi, Muhammad bin Murtadha (1965–2001). *Taj al-'arus min jawahir al-qamus*, Kuwait: al-Majlis al-Watani lil-Thaqafah wa-al-Funun wa-al-Adab (40 vols).

Author's Bibliography

1. Arabic sources

Abd al-Raziq, Mustafa (1944). *Tamhid li-dirasat tarikh al-falsafa al-Islamiyya*, Cairo: Matba'at Issa al-Halaby.

Abd al-Raziq, Mustafa (1945). *al-Din wa al-wahy wa al-Islam*, Cairo: Matba'at Issa al-Halaby.

Al-Aqqad, Abbas (1947). *Allah: Kitab fi nash'at al-'aqidah al-'Ilahiyyah*, Cairo: Dar al-Ma'arif.

Al-Bustani, Butrus (1876). *Kitab da'irat al-ma'arif: wa-huwa qamus 'amm li-kull fann wa-maṭlab (Encyclopédie arabe)*, Beirut: al- Maṭba'a al-adabīya.

Al-Fairuzabadi, Muhammad bin Ya'qub (1033). *al-Qamus al-Muhit*, Cairo: al-Mat'baá al-misriyyah.

Al-Fayyumi, Ahamd bin Muhammad (1922). *Kitab al-missbaḥ al-munir fi gharib al-sharh al-kabir lil-Rafi'i*, Cairo: al-Matba'ah al-Amiriyah.

(Ibn) al-Nadim, Muhammad ibn Ishaq, and Gustav Flügel, et al. (eds) (1872). *Kitab al-fihrist*, Leipzig: F.C.W. Vogel.

Al-Nashshar, Ali (1949). *Nash'at al-Din: al-Nazariyyat al-tatawuriyyah wa al-mu'alliha*, Alexandria: Dar Nashr al-Thaqafah.

Azzam Pasha, Abd al-Rahman (1946). *al-Risalah al-khalidah*, Cairo: Matba'at Lijnat al-Ta'lif wa al-Tarjama wa al-Nashr.

Badawi, Ali (n.d.). *Abhath al-tarikh al-'am lil-qanun*, Cairo: Matba'at Nuri.

Hubb Allah, Mahmud (1948). *al-Hayat al-wijdaniyyah wa al-'aqidah al-diniyyah*, Cairo: Dar Ihya' al-Kutub al-Arabiyyah.

(Ibn) Manzur, Muḥammad ibn Mukarram (1883–91). *Lisan al-'Arab*, Cairo: Matba'at Bulaq.

(Ibn) Rushd (Averroes), and Leon Gautier (eds) (1942). *Traité décisif (Facl al-maqal). Sur l'accord de la religion et de la philosophie suivi de l'appendice (Dhamima), Texte arabe, traduction francaise remaniée avec notes et Introduction*, Algiers: Carbonel.

Izzat Pasha, al-Musheer (1948). *al-Din wa al-'ilm*, Cairo: Matba'at Lijnat al-Ta'lif wa al-Tarjama wa al-Nashr.

James, William, and Mahmud Hubb Allah (eds) (1946). *Iradat al-i'tiqad*, Cairo: Dar Ihya' al-Kutub al-Arabiyyah.

Katip Chelebi, Mustafa bin Abdullah and Muhammad Yaltaqaya, et al. (eds) (1941–3). *Kashf al-zunun 'an 'asami al-kutub wa al-funun*, Istanbul: Wakalat al-Ma'arif.

Wajdi, Mohmmad Farid (1923–5). *Da'irat ma'arif al-qarn al-'ishreen*, Cairo: Matba'at da'irat ma'arif al-qarn al-'ishreen.

2. European sources

Aristotle (n.d.). *Métaphysique*, Paris: Belles Lettres.

Aristotle, and Jean Voilquin (ed.) (1940). *Ethique á Nicomaque*, Paris: Garnier.

Bastide, Roger (1947). *Eléments de Sociologie religieuse*, Paris: Colin.

Barthélemy-Saint-Hilaire, Jules (1865). *Devoirs Mutuels de la Philosophie et de la Religion, dans Mahomet et le Koran*, Paris: Didier.

Bergson, Henri (1932). *Les Deux Sources de la Morale et de la religion*, Paris: Alcan.

Boutroux, Émile (1925). *Morale et religion*, Paris: Flammarion.

Boutroux, Émile (1947). *Science et religion*, Paris: Flammarion.

Burnouf, Émile (1885). *Science des religions*, Paris: Maisonneuve.

Chachoin, Louis (1913). *Evolution des idées religieuses et des religions*, Paris: G. Crès.

Comte, Auguste (1926). *Cours de philosophie positive*, Paris: Garnier.

Descartes, René, and Geneviève Rodis-Lewis, et al. (eds) (1944). *Meditationes de prima philosophia Méditations métaphysiques*, Paris: Librairie philosophique J. Vrin.

Durkheim, Émile (1927). *Les Règles de la méthode sociologique*, Paris: Alcan.

Durkheim, Émile (1937). *Forme Elémentaires de la Vie religieuse*, Paris: Alcan.

Franck, Adolphe (1885). *Dictionnaire des Sciences Philosophiques*, Paris: Hachette.

Gourd, Jean-Jacques (1911). *Philosophie de la religion*, Paris: Alcan.

Guyau, Jean-Marie (1896). *L'irréligion de l'avenir: étude sociologique*, Paris: Alcan.

Hauser, Philippe (1920). *Evolution intellectuelle et religieuse de l'humanité*, Paris: Alcan.

Høffding, Harald (1909). *Philosophie de la religion*, Paris: Alcan.

Hubert, Henri (1904). *Introduction á la traduction française du Manuel d'Histoire des Religions, par Chantepie de la Saussaye*, Paris: Colin.

Jevons, Frank Byron (1896). *An Introduction to the History of Religion*, London: Methuen

Kant, Immanuel (1794). *La Religion dans les Limites de la raison*, Königsberg: Nicolovius.

Kant, Immanuel (1943). *Critique de la raison pratique*, Paris: Presses Universitaires de France.

Lalande, André (1928). *Vocabulaire Technique et Critique de la Philosophie*, Paris: Alcan.

Longuet, André (1921). *L'origine commune des religions*, Paris: Alcan.

Mayer, Michel (1885). *Instructions morales et religieuses*, Paris: A. Durlacher.

Müller, Max (1901). *Lectures on the Origin and Growth of Religion, as Illustrated by the Religions of India*, London: Longmans, Green.

Périssé, Sylvain (1908). *Sciences et Religions à travers les siècles*, Paris: Fischbache.

Pinard De la Boulaye, Henri (1922). *L'étude comparée des religions: essai critique*, Paris: Gabriel Beauchesne.

Platon (1952). *Les Lois*, Paris: Les Belles Lettres.

Reinach, Salomon (1909). *Orpheus: histoire générale des religions*, Paris: Picard.

Réville, Albert (1866). *Prolégomènes de l'histoire des religions*, Paris: Fischbacher.

Sabatier, Auguste (1897). *Esquisse d'une philosophie de la religion*, Paris: Fischbacher.

Saurat, Denis (1933). *Histoire des religions*, Paris: Denoél.

Schleiermacher, Friedrich (1799). *Ueber die Religion: Reden an die Gebildeten unter ihren Verächtern*, Berlin: Johann Friedrich Unger.

Schmidt, Wilhelm (1931). *Origine et évolution de la religion*, Paris: Grasset.

Spencer, Herbert (1863). *First Principles*, London: Williams and Norgate.

Spencer, Herbert (1879). *The Principles of Sociology* (Vol. 1), New York: D. Appleton.

Tylor, Edward Burnett (1871). *Primitive Culture*, London: Murray.

Van der Leeuw, G. (1948). *La Religion dans son essence et ses manifestations*, Paris: Payot.

Index

Abdul-Wahhab, Mohammad 48
Adam, the father of humanity 92, 140
Africa 8, 13, 86
Alexander the Great 4, 5, 6
America 12, 86, 128
Animism 104–12, 145
Aquinas, Saint Thomas 10
Arabia, pre-Islamic 41, 49, 86
Arabic language 1, 26
    conventions of 19–20, 41
    lexicons 17–18
    translations 10
Arabs 10, 11, 17, 21, 128
archaeologists 101
aristocracy 54
Aristotle 4, 6, 77, 131
Aryans 86, 131
Asia 8, 12
atheism 6, 75
atomic fission 58, 70 (*see also* scientific progress)
Augustine, Saint 9, 52
Australia 86, 128, 130, 131, 135 (*see also* tribes)

Barthélemy-Saint-Hilaire, Jules 63
belief (*see also* faith)
    abstract 25
    in eternity 78
    evolution of 89
    in God 84, 85, 86, 92, 104, 110, 112, 113, 116, 117, 118, 120
    in a higher being, truth (etc.) 36, 58, 86, 106, 117, 137
    imposition of 2
    justified 20
    in mysterious forces, entities (etc.) 24, 31, 105, 108, 111
    origins of 5, 87, 92, 101, 103, 112, 113, 129 (*see also* religions, rise of)
    psychology of 90, 113, 141 (*see also* psychology, of believers)
    in a single deity 89–90
    in spiritual beings 22, 30, 93, 108, 112
believer, the 27, 28, 30, 32, 33, 34, 36, 47, 53, 54, 99, 101, 102 (*see also* mentality, of the believer)
Bergson, Henri 64, 116, 117, 118, 119
    The Two Sources of Morality and Religion 116
Brahminic religion *see* Hinduism
Brockelmann, Carl 86
Buddha, the 25, 48
Buddhism 17, 25, 26, 50 (*see also* worship)
Burnouf, Émile-Louis, *The Science of Religions* 23

Catholicism, ecclesiastic laws of 74
causality, the principle of 83
Chachoin, Louis 64
Châtel, Ferdinand François, *The Code of Humanity* 22
China 12
Christ 1 (*see also* Jesus)
Christianity 1, 8, 9, 12, 17, 50, 92
Christians *see* missionaries, Christian
Cicero, Marcus Tullius 8
    On the Laws 22
civilization
    advanced 88
    European 65
    evolution of 82, 89
    material 61, 62, 63, 81, 89
    modern 87
collective consciousness 138–9 (*see also* Religion, social aspects of)
Comte, Auguste 50, 74
    theory of the three stages 65–7
Confucianism 25, 26
Constantine (Roman emperor) 9
Council of Nicaea 9

death, the idea of 107, 112
democracy 54
Descartes, René 77, 126
   Meditations 120, 121, 122
al-Din 17–19, 26, 41 (*see also* Arabic language)
   as native to Arabic 21
   as obligation of obedience 20
   verbal forms 19–20
divine, the
   idea of 108, 112, 118 (*see also* divinity, idea of)
divine revelation 24, 40, 55, 92, 138, 139, 140, 148
divinity 39, 40
   Durkheim's theory of 133
   idea of 25, 27, 118, 132, as viewed by Voltaire 61 (*see also* divine, the)
   nature of 8
   removal of 27, 37
Dominicans *see* missionaries, Christian
dreams, the experience of 110, 111 (*see also* worship, of ancestors)
Durkheim, Émile 25, 36, 58, 85, 98, 100, 101, 102, 111, 112, 127, 128, 129, 130, 131, 132, 133, 134, 135, 136
   The Elementary Forms of the Religious Life 24

Egypt, ancient 1, 2, 3, 128
   influence on Greece 3, 4, 131
empiricism 39, 65, 66, 115, 122
Epictetus 8
Epicureans 6
Epicurus 6
Ethiopians 128
Europe 1, 8, 10, 12, 62, 85, 139
   Christian 48
   European explorations 12–13
   European languages 1
   folktales of 128
   Islamic influence on 9–11
   scientific heritage of 10
   sophistry in eighteenth-century 62
   spread of evolutionism in 85
   theory of revelation in 139
   Western 9, 10, 12

European scholars 10, 15, 85 (*see also* Western scholars)
Europeans 10, 133
evolutionism, critique of 85–90
experiments, scientific 58, 72, 100, 106, 123 (*see also* empiricism)
   experimental methods 71, 72
extrapolation 72

faith (*see also* belief)
   expressions of 47, 49, 50, 86, 135
   intellectual 122–3
   mental 72
   object(s) of 32, 52, 92, 136
   religious 27, 34, 75, 100
   as separate from reason 25
   two forms of, the 80
   in the unseen 28
family unit, the 127, 130, 131 (*see also* tribes)
al-Farabi 44, 46
finality, the principle of 84
Franciscans *see* missionaries, Christian
Frazer, James 85, 132
French revolution, the 61
French school of sociology, the 37, 132

Gaels 128
Greece, ancient 1, 3, 6, 43, 131
   gods of 3, 4, 7
   heroes in 3, 4
   influence on Rome 7–8
   literary and scientific heritage of 7, 9, 10
   Roman conquest of 7
   sacrifice in 3
   writings on religion in 3–4, 5
Greek language 12
Greeks 3, 44, 128
Guyau, Jean-Marie, *The Non-Religion of the Future* 23

Hanifs, the 41, 49 (*see also* Arabia, pre-Islamic)
Hebrew language 10, 12, 21
Hinduism 26, 93
Hisham, Ibn 41
historians 4, 48, 139
historians of religions 25, 26, 87, 102
Høffding, Harald 87, 131

Homer 3, 131
Hubert, Henri 137
human dignity 36, 79, 80, 147
human nature 8, 14, 52, 54, 75

idolatory 24, 86 (*see also* worship, of idols)
   in ancient Egypt 2
Iliad, the *see* Homer
India 4, 12
Indo-European languages 93
interpolation 72
Islam 1, 7, 9, 12, 17, 18, 22, 24, 41, 45, 50
   as historical exception 49
   influence on Europe 10, 11

Jainism 25
James, William 144
Jesus 48 (*see also* Christ)
Jevons, Frank Byron 104
   Introduction to the History of Religion 103
Jina 25
Judaism 17, 92

Ka'ba, the 41
Kant, Immanuel 119, 122, 123, 124, 125, 126
   Critique of Practical Reason 122
   Religion within the Boundaries of Mere Reason 22

Lang, Andrew 86, 132
Laplace, Pierre-Simon 69
Latin (language) 10
Latin authors 7–8
laws
   of economics 135
   moral 39, 40, 114, 116, 119, 123, 124, 125, 126, 142 (*see also* morality)
   of nature 6, 27, 32, 33, 71, 72, 77, 97, 99, 114, 116, 123, 126 (*see also* natural order)
   of property distribution 132
   of reason 34, 64, 65, 84, 124
   religious 39, 40, 80
   scientific 35, 52, 71–2, 90
   social 40, 117, 118, 119, 132
   State 61–2, 78, 79, 80
lay religion 4

LeRoy, Bishop 86
Lisan al-Arab (Arabic lexicon) 18
Littré, Émile 75
Luther, Martin 48

Magainism 92
magic 29, 98, 99
Maimonides 10
Mani 48
Manichaeism 9
Marcus Aurelius 8
Marxism 79
Materialism 6, 30, 35, 43, 65, 68, 70, 126
materialists 31, 32, 35, 57, 65
Mayer, Michel, *Religious and Moral Instructions* 23
Mazdeism 17
Mecca 9
Megasthenes 4
mental leaps 93, 94, 98, 99, 105
mentality
   of the believer 27, 28, 101
   of children 40, 65, 75–6, 111, 130
   religious 94
   of savages, primitives (etc.) 98, 110, 111, 112, 129
   of the Semitic people 85
metaphysics 6, 28, 31, 65
Milliken, Robert A. 80
missionaries, Christian 9, 133
   Catholic (Spanish, Portuguese and French) 12
   Franciscan and Dominican 12
Mohammad, the Prophet 45, 48, 49, 144, 145, 146, 147, 148
monism, scientific 67
monotheism 18, 78, 83, 85
   in ancient Egypt 2
   primordiality of 86
Montgomery, Field Marshal 81
morality
   codes of 133, 134
   moral duty 54, 123, 125–6
   moral laws 116, 119, 123, 124, 125–6
   practical aspects of 40, 42, 46
   principles of 39
   relation with religion 40–2, 55
Moses 48
Müller, Max 25, 94, 104, 105

Comparative Mythology 93
Lectures on the Origin and Growth of Religion 23
myths 4, 12, 24, 62, 87, 90, 93, 132
   mythological point of view, the 94

natural laws 114, 123, 126, 132 (*see also* laws, of nature)
naturalism 104, 105, 143
naturalists 34, 35, 105, 109
natural order, the 29, 34
natural phenomena 40, 65, 103
natural religion, *see* Religion
natural science, *see* science
Neo-Platonism 9
Nordau, Max 68

Oceania 12
Odyssey, the *see* Homer

paganism 7, 8, 17, 48, 85, 86, 91, 110 (*see also* idolatory)
pantheism 7, 67
Pascal, Blaise 115
perfection 51, 78, 90
   the idea of 120–2, 126
   the path to 53, 76
   possibility of 90
Périssé, Sylvain, *The Science of Religion* 23
Pétain, Marshal 81
philology 14, 89, 93
philosophers 24, 31, 50, 54
   Greek 3, 4, 5, 43–4
   Muslim 10, 45, 46
philosophy
   ancient Greek 3–7, 9, 44
   Aristotelean 10
   dry 26, 52, 54
   general 42
   in Islamic history 10
   materialist *see* materialism
   negative 5
   philosophical systems 43
   positive and constructive 5, 6
   as a religion 48
   relation with religion as viewed by Muslims 44–7
   relation with religion as viewed by Westerners 47–8

   as a rhetorical device 5
   schools of 43, 46, 47
   secular 9
   spiritual 2, 31, 34, 43
   compared with religion 43–4
   theoretical and practical 42, 53
Plato 3, 4
   the Academy 5
polytheism 7, 83, 140 (*see also* paganism)
Portuguese, the *see* missionaries, Christian
prayer 28, 31, 34, 96, 97, 101, 104, 109, 116, 133 (*see also* worship)
   meaning of 100
primitive languages 130
primitive people 13, 23, 50, 62, 68, 85, 86, 87, 91, 92, 101, 110, 111, 112, 116, 127, 129, 130, 134, 135 (*see also* tribes)
Prophets 54, 58, 87, 109, 140
Protestantism 12
psyche, the human 30, 61, 67, 96, 114, 120, 141
psychology 13, 30, 52, 71, 78, 113, 120, 146
   of believers 28, 32, 90 (*see also* religiosity)
   infant 66
   psychological barriers 81
   psychological experiences 116
   psychological observations 113, 142
   the psychological state 21, 32, 127
pygmies 86 (*see also* tribes)
Pyrrho 5
Pythagoras 3

al-Qamus al-Muhit (Arabic lexicon) 18
Quatrefages de Bréau, Armand de 86
Qur'an, the 19, 24, 48, 69, 143, 144, 145, 146, 147, 148, 149

reform, religious 48, 49, 90
   in ancient Egypt 2
   in pagan religions 48
   Reformation, the 12
Reinach, Salomon 25, 36, 67
   A General History of Religions 23
Religion
   birth of, the 48, 87, 99, 104, 136, 137, 142

category of 27
concept of 4, 20, 53
conventional meaning of 21
death of 74
Draz's definition of 36, 102 (*see also* al-Din)
early expressions of 13, 85, 86, 87, 105 (*see also* belief, origins of)
essence of 22, 24, 43–4, 134
eternity of 62, 63, 64, 67–8, 73, 74–5, 97, 112
of the first man 13, 85, 91, 92
idea of, the 24, 132, 135
as moral obligation 136
moral approaches to 147
Muslim definition of 24 (*see also* al-Din)
natural 24, 54
nature of 14
as objective fact 21, 36
as obligation 20, 41, 53, 136 (*see also* al-Din)
phenomenon of 13, 61
as philosophy of the masses 48
practical aspects of 47, 53, 54, 114, 135
religious idea, the 21, 37, 39, 51, 93, 104, 117, 140
science of, the 11, 13
social aspects of 54, 81, 135, 137, 139 (*see also* collective consciousness)
as subjective fact 21, 22, 36
Western definitions of 22–4
religions
ambiguous origins of 49
comparative 12
divinely inspired 8
primordiality of 91
Eastern 25, 26
evolution of 13, 89, 120
extant 4, 11, 22, 137
historicity of 49
history of 13, 15, 17, 21, 68, 82, 85, 87
knowledge of other 4, 15
natural 24
revealed 8, 25, 46, 50, 54, 91, 116, 140
primitive 13, 63, 87, 91, 92, 98, 101, 112, 129, 135, 136
proper 24, 25, 136

study of, the 11, 15, 35, 135
unity of 14, 21, 70
religiosity 14, 31, 128, 129, 133
early forms of 61, 86, 89
essence of 104, 115, 130
idea of, the 128
in monotheistic faiths 78
pervasiveness of 62, 63, 67, 80
phenomenon of 14, 62
rise of, the 85, 104, 105, 114, 116, 120, 127 (*see also* belief, origins of)
role in society 79, 80
as the subjective side of religion 21, 36
Renaissance, the 1, 12
Renan, Ernest 68
Réville, Albert, *Prolegomenon to the History of Religions* 23
Romans 7, 10, 128
Rome 1, 7, 8, 10
Rousseau, Jean-Jacques 61
Rushd, Ibn 10
Decisive Treatise on the Harmony of Religion and Philosophy 45

Sabatier, Auguste 104, 114, 115, 116
Outlines of a Philosophy of Religion 113
sacred, the 37, 98, 102, 103
sacred books 140, 142
salvation 22, 26, 104
sanctification 2, 27, 128 (*see also* worship)
in ancient Egypt 2
of higher truth 58
in Hinduism and Buddhism 25
meaning of 37
objects of 112
as rooted in mystery 40, 112
sanctity
meaning of 26, 28
in negative terms 36, 134
in primitive settings 134
of religious laws 39
of society 129, 137
Scepticism 5, 6
sceptics 63, 65
Schleiermacher, Friedrich 27
On Religion: Speeches to Its Cultured Despisers 22
Schmidt, Wilhelm 86
Schroeder, Leopold von 86

science 92, 101, 114, 144
  Arab Muslim 10
  Asian 10
  Aristotelean 10
  classification of 55–6
  compared with religion 51, 55–9, 76
  as a double-edge sword 70, 79
  empirical 39, 67, 91 (*see also* empiricism)
  evolution of 85, 88, 89 (*see also* scientific progress)
  experimental 71, 84, 100, 106
  Greek 10
  human 86, 92, 144
  limits of 35–6, 67, 70–7, 86–7, 92, 101, 114
  natural 11, 49, 58, 71, 72, 73
  physical 66
  practical applications of 61, 70
  translation of scientific texts 10
scientific progress 58, 61, 64, 89, 114
  as intensifying religiosity 70, 74–5, 114
  as widening of the realm of mystery 68–70, 73, 75
scientists 35, 57, 58, 66, 74, 80, 86, 99, 106, 106
Scriptures 12, 140
Semites 85, 86, 131
Semitic languages 12
Sharia, the 46
Sina, Ibn 46
Smith, Robert 131
Sophists, the 5, 6, 62
Socrates 5, 51
sorcery 31, 98
soul, the human 53, 58, 63, 67, 68, 78, 82, 85, 112, 147
  autonomy of 107, 108, 145
  immortality of 54, 110, 124, 125
  meaning of 106–7, 145
souls of the dead 105, 110, 145
Spanish, the *see* missionaries, Christian
Spencer, Herbert 24, 25, 74, 85, 111
  First Principles 22
  Principles of Psychology 105
spiritualists 31, 32
Stoicism 6–8

submission, religious and non-religious 21, 27–35, 37
superstition 24, 63, 85, 87, 88, 90, 91, 111, 112

taboos 36, 117, 129
tolerance, religious,
  in ancient Egypt 2
  in ancient Rome 8
  of authorities 50
tribes
  African 86
  of the Americas 86
  Australian 86, 132, 134
  of Central Australia 130, 131, 135
  primitive 13, 86, 127, 128, 132, 133, 137
  Semitic 86
  of Southeast Australia 131
totemism 127–8, 131–2, 135
Tylor, Edward Burnett 30, 85, 110, 111, 133
  Primitive Culture 22, 105

unity of existence *see* pantheism

Vedas, the 93
vice 6, 37, 108, 124
virtue 37, 52, 53, 55, 80, 119 (*see also* morality)
  Greek theories of 5, 6
  theoretical and practical 39, 46–7
  as viewed by Kant 124–6
Voltaire 61

Wajdi, Mohammad Farid, *Da'irat ma'arif al-qarn al-'ishreen* 68
Western scholars 10, 11, 12, 21, 22, 47, 49 (*see also* European scholars)
Wilson, Woodrow 80
worship 39, 40, 41, 93, 97, 99, 100, 101, 106, 129, 132, 133 (*see also* sanctification)
  act of, the 96, 133
  of ancestors 111–12
  in Buddhism 25–6, 50
  of the dead 105
  of God 41, 95

idea of, the 26, 44
of idols 24, 28
of nature 105
object(s) of 2, 28, 29, 34, 102
ritualized 48

of a single divine being 2, 28, 102s

Zayd ibn Amr ibn Nufayl 41
Zeno of Citium 6

www.ingramcontent.com/pod-product-compliance
Lightning Source LLC
Chambersburg PA
CBHW061834300426
44115CB00013B/2377